CISTERCIAN STUDIES SERIES: NUMBER TWO HUNDRED FORTY-EIGHT

Anthony N. S. Lane

BERNARD OF CLAIRVAUX

THEOLOGIAN OF THE CROSS

CISTERCIAN STUDIES SERIES: NUMBER TWO HUNDRED FORTY-EIGHT

Bernard of Clairvaux
THEOLOGIAN OF THE CROSS

Anthony N. S. Lane

α

Cistercian Publications
www.cistercianpublications.org

LITURGICAL PRESS
Collegeville, Minnesota
www.litpress.org

A Cistercian Publications title published by Liturgical Press

Cistercian Publications
Editorial Offices
Abbey of Gethsemani
3642 Monks Road
Trappist, Kentucky 40051
www.cistercianpublications.org

1   2   3   4   5   6   7   8   9

Library of Congress Cataloging-in-Publication Data

Lane, A. N. S.
  Bernard of Clairvaux, theologian of the cross / by Anthony N.S. Lane.
    p.   cm. — (Cistercian studies series ; no. 248)
  Includes bibliographical references and index.
  ISBN 978-0-87907-248-3 — ISBN 978-0-87907-746-4 (e-book)
    1. Bernard, of Clairvaux, Saint, 1090 or 91–1153.   2. Jesus Christ—Crucifixion—History of doctrines—Middle Ages, 600–1500.   I. Title.

BX4700.B5L33   2013
230'.2092—dc23   2012031161

To Ibrat

CONTENTS

Foreword by John Sommerfeldt   xi

Preface   xiii

List of Abbreviations   xvii

Part I: Preliminaries

1. Bernard on the Cross: A Neglected Theme   3
    A. Histories of the Doctrine   4
    B. Bernard Literature   11

2. The Cross in Earlier Tradition   17
    A. Early Church Fathers   17
    B. Anselm of Canterbury   22
    C. Peter Abelard   27

3. Bernard as Theologian of the Cross   41
    A. Bernard as a Monastic Theologian   41
    B. Bernard on the Cross   48
    C. Bernard's Use of Scripture   53

Part II: Key Passages

4. Key Passages I: Treatises   63
    A. *De laude novae militiae* 10.17–11.29   65
    B. *De diligendo Deo* 3.7–5.15   74

5. Key Passages II: Treatise against Abelard   80
   A. Its Origin   80
   B. The Text   86
   C. Assessment   102

6. Key Passages III: Sermons   106
   A. *Sermo 1 in annuntiatione domini*   107
   B. *Sermo in feria iv hebdomadae sanctae*   114
   C. *Sermo 1 in resurrectione domini*   124

Part III: Teaching on the Cross

7. Redemption and the Cross   135
   A. Christ as the Second Adam   135
   B. Christ Made Merciful through His Passion   138
   C. Salvation Not by the Cross on Its Own   140
   D. How Central Is the Cross?   143
   E. Redemption   146
   F. Reconciliation   148

8. Christ as Teacher / Moral Influence:
   The Usward Aspect   152
   A. The Cross as a Demonstration of Love   152
   B. The Cross Evokes Our Response   154
   C. The Cross as an Example to Follow   156
   D. Opposition to Abelard   158

9. Christ as Victor over Satan and Death   160
   A. Victory over Satan   160
   B. Deception   166
   C. Victory over Death   168
   D. Relation to Other Models   169

10. Christ Died for Our Sins: The Godward Aspect   171
   A. Christ Bore Our Sins   172
   B. The Cross as Sacrifice   174
   C. Christ the Lamb of God   175
   D. The Blood of Christ   177

E. The Wounds of Christ   180
F. Christ Paying the Price   182
G. Christ Bearing Our Punishment   184
H. The Cross as Propitiation for Our Sins   186
I. The Cross as Expiation for Our Sins   188
J. The Cross as Satisfaction for Our Sins   190
K. The Finished Work of Christ   196
L. Conclusion   197

11. Objections to Bernard's Teaching   199
A. Abelard's Objections   200
B. The Necessity for the Cross   203
C. Punishment and Justice, Mercy and Truth   206
D. The Love of the Father   209
E. The Voluntary Love of the Son   212
F. Christ and Adam   214

12. The Application of the Doctrine   218
A. Justification   218
B. Grounds for Hope   220
C. Repentance and Following Christ   222
D. Suffering with Christ   225
E. Pastoral Application   226
F. Preaching the Cross   227
G. The Second Crusade   229
H. The *Amplexus Bernardi*   230

13. Conclusion   233

**Appendix I: Index of Passages on the Cross
with Biblical Citations**   235

Appendix II: Index of Biblical Texts Cited   263

Bibliography   269

FOREWORD

Shortly after I had read the manuscript of this, Professor Lane's, book, I shared the topic with one of my doctoral candidates. His response was understandable: "Bernard's teaching on the Cross? I didn't know he had one." I didn't either until I had read this book. Not only did Bernard develop a doctrine of the cross, but Lane has documented that teaching thoroughly and well.

I was predisposed to appreciate Professor Lane's book because of my previous contact with him. In 1990, the friends of Bernard of Clairvaux celebrated the nonacentenary of Bernard's birth. A mammoth celebratory meeting was held at Western Michigan University, and I was charged with assembling the program. The celebration was a great success. Some ninety-one papers were presented by scholars from all over the world, among them Professor Lane's excellent offering, "Bernard of Clairvaux: A Forerunner of John Calvin?" Of the many authors whose proposals I read with interest, there was only one person whom I did not know: A. N. S. Lane. Nor had I heard of his institution, the London Bible College.

I quote from the abstract appended to the subsequently published paper: "Calvin quoted Bernard many times throughout most of his literary career, on a variety of topics. These included the doctrine of justification." Different from past eras, in today's ecclesial and scholarly climates Bernard can be a meeting ground for Catholic-Protestant dialogue on this subject. The name of Professor Lane's institution is now the London School of Theology, and it and he remain fully committed to a Protestant point of view. But this is not a Protestant book; nor, for that matter, is it a Catholic book. It is a scholarly and detailed description of the theology of one of the most penetrating thinkers in the history of Christian theological endeavor.

Professor Lane's scholarship is impeccable: he has assembled all the relevant sources and examined them with the eye of an always sympathetic yet irrepressibly objective reader.

I heartily commend this work to any serious student of Bernard. It treats a much-neglected topic with the skill of both a serious historian and a gifted theologian.

John R. Sommerfeldt
Professor Emeritus of History
University of Dallas

PREFACE

This book falls into three distinct parts. The first part sets the scene. Chapter 1 surveys past studies of our theme, both in histories of doctrine and in the Bernard literature. This survey shows how little the subject has been studied and the need for a full study. Bernard did not develop his teaching in isolation but was the heir of earlier tradition. Chapter 2 sets out the teaching of the Fathers and of Anselm and Abelard. Chapter 3 explores Bernard's approach as a monastic theologian, his teaching on the Cross, and the way in which he used Scripture.

Bernard's teaching on the Cross is found in many passages scattered throughout his works. Among these are passages where Bernard gives extended treatment to the topic. The second part sets out six of these extended passages, found in three treatises and three sermons. I have made my own translations, and where there are portions of text not relevant to our topic I have often paraphrased them briefly. Some readers may choose to skip this part, which can be done without losing the flow of the argument. The reader would, however, be best advised to read at least chapter 5, which introduces and assesses Bernard's letter-treatise against Abelard, a work of central significance for our topic and to which there is considerable reference in part 3.

The heart of the book lies in the third part, which expounds Bernard's teaching on the Cross. Chapter 7 tackles some introductory topics. Chapter 8 considers the *usward* aspect of Christ's work—its subjective influence upon us. A consideration in chapter 9 of Christ's work as victor over Satan and death includes Bernard's conflict with Abelard on this matter. Chapter 10 sets out Bernard's teaching on the *Godward* aspect of Christ's work—the way in which the Cross puts us right with God—while chapter 11 considers objections to this teaching posed by Abelard and others. Chapter 12 explores a number of ways in which Bernard applies his doctrine of the Cross. Finally, chapter 13 offers a concluding assessment of Bernard's teaching on this topic.

The exposition of Bernard's teaching on the Cross is drawn from 669 passages that to a greater or lesser extent refer to the Cross. These passages are numbered and in the second and third parts are cited as #27, and so forth.[1] Appendix I provides a full index of these passages, listing the biblical texts cited in each passage. Where the reference is to one passage only (or to a single sequence of passages such as #601–6), it is given in the body of the text; where it is to a number of separate passages, it is given in a footnote.

I have worked with the critical edition of Bernard's work published in Rome by Jean Leclercq and others from 1957 to 1977.[2] I am aware of the more recent *Sources Chrétiennes* edition with its useful notes, and have made use of it for chapter 4 especially, but this edition is still far from complete. I have also made good use of two study aids that accompany the Rome edition. The first is the very useful concordance to the complete works.[3] Before that was published I visited the Achelse Kluis three times and made good use of the card index concordance located there. I am very grateful to Fathers Ildefons Majoor, Edmond Mikkers, OCSO, and Vincent Hermans, OCSO, for the help they gave me on those occasions. The second aid is the index to Bernard's biblical allusions,[4] one way to trace a theme in Bernard's writings being to follow the trail of biblical allusions.[5]

In the second part, I have given my own translations of Bernard, with acknowledgement to earlier translations that I have consulted. In the third part, I mostly give my own summary, paraphrase, and

---

[1] They are numbered from #1 to #667, but there are also #261a and #428a. For fuller details, see chap. 3B below.

[2] SBOp 1–8. I have also made use of Jean Leclercq, "*Errata corrigenda* dans l'édition de S. Bernard," RESB 4:409–18. See RESB 4:404 for a word of explanation.

[3] CETEDOC, *Thesaurus Sancti Bernardi Claraevallensis: Index formarum singulorum operum; Concordantia formarum* (Turnhout: Brepols, 1987). See Jean Leclercq, "La concordance de S. Bernard," RESB 4:401–7.

[4] SBOp 9: Guido Hendrix, ed., *Index biblicus in opera omnia S. Bernardi* (Turnhout: Brepols, 1998).

[5] For more on this, see chap. 3C below.

(less often) translation of passages, based on the Latin but taking note of English translations, especially (but not exclusively) those in the Cistercian Fathers Series.

Bernard often makes several different points in one statement—such as his statement that defeating the devil would not be effective without a sacrifice for sin to placate God, which is necessary to reconcile humanity to God (#430). This statement is pertinent to Bernard's teaching on sacrifice, propitiation, reconciliation, and victory over Satan. It is mentioned, therefore, at different points in the book. The resulting repetition is something of a drawback, but it has the advantage of showing how Bernard ties together the different aspects of Christ's work on the Cross.

I would like to express my profound gratitude to Father Jean Leclercq, OSB, to whom (like so many other students of Bernard) I am greatly indebted. When I first began, as a research student, to work on Bernard, someone helpfully arranged for me to meet Father Leclercq at Nashdom Abbey, where he was visiting. We met for the first time after lunch, and when we had settled down after the introductions, he said to my horror, "I suppose as an Englishman you like draughts." My immediate thought was that I had travelled some distance to learn from him about Bernard and instead he wanted to spend the afternoon playing draughts. In fact, he was assuming that I would like a window open to provide some fresh air. The afternoon was immensely helpful and pointed me to the direction to go for my research, and there would have been no difficulty in staying alert even without the benefit of the draught. This was just the first of a number of occasions when he generously gave me of his time and expertise. Second, Father Leclercq also on one occasion most generously gave me a copy of the first three volumes of his *Recueil d'études sur saint Bernard et ses écrits*—together with an order form for the soon to appear fourth volume![6] I was duly grateful and took the hint. Third, he was not cold or aloof. One of my treasured possessions is my copy of his *The Love of Learning and the Desire for God*, in which he mischievously

---

[6] Where I cite from these volumes in the footnotes, the bibliography indicates where the article may have previously appeared.

wrote, "To Tony, Johnnie"! This support and encouragement was also given to countless other budding Bernard scholars, which makes one wonder how he ever had the time to write as much as he did.[7] I once visited him at Clervaux and was taken into his cell. Round the wall was box after box of offprints, one for each year from the 1950s. This minilibrary was composed purely of his own writings.

In what follows I have on occasion taken issue with Leclercq. He was not the sort of person that expected or wished everyone to agree with him all the time, and he was happy to see the rise of others who had their own interpretation of Bernard.[8] It need hardly be said that despite the few critical comments, I have relied heavily on the massive foundation that he laid for modern Bernard scholarship. The footnotes demonstrate this, even without taking into account his contribution to the critical edition on which this study is based.

I am also grateful to him for introducing me to Father Alberic Altermatt, who on two separate occasions when we met gave me some very helpful advice about the present topic.

I first began to work on this topic in 1985, with the benefit of a sabbatical term thanks to a generous grant from the Tyndale Fellowship Theology Project Fund, courtesy of Oliver Barclay. After this initial impetus I became distracted by other writing projects and there was a gap of some twenty years before I was again able to devote serious attention to Bernard.

Finally, this book is dedicated with warm appreciation to my son-in-law, Ibrat Djabbarov.

---

[7] In his *Memoirs: From Grace to Grace* (Petersham, MA: St. Bede's, 2000), 31, he describes his resolve never to be one of those who selfishly concentrate on their own work at the expense of others. "Is helping young researchers at the risk of writing one less article a waste of time?"

[8] For a good illustration of this, see John R. Sommerfeldt, "Bernard of Clairvaux on the Truth Accessible through Faith," in *The Joy of Learning and the Love of God*, ed. E. Rozanne Elder (Kalamazoo, MI, and Spencer, MA: Cistercian Publications, 1995), 239–40.

ABBREVIATIONS

Works of Bernard

1 Nov	*Sermo in dominica I novembris*
4 HM	*Sermo in feria iv hebdomadae sanctae*
5 HM	*Sermo in cena domini*
Abael	*Epistola in erroribus Abaelardi* = *Epistola* 190
Adv	*Sermo in adventu domini*
Adv var	*Sermo varius in adventu domini*
And	*Sermo in natali sancti Andreae*
Ann	*Sermo in annuntiatione domini*
Apo	*Apologia ad Guillelmum abbatem*
Asc	*Sermo in ascensione domini*
Asspt	*Sermo in assumptione BVM*
Bapt	*Epistola de baptismo* = *Epistola* 42
Ben	*Sermo in natali sancti Benedicti*
Ben var	*Sermo varius in natali sancti Benedicti*
Circ	*Sermo in circumcisione domini*
Clem	*Sermo in natali sancti Clementis*
Conv	*Sermo de conversione ad clericos*
Csi	*De consideratione*
Ded	*Sermo in dedicatione ecclesiae*
Dil	*De diligendo Deo*
Div	*Sermo de diversis*
Doni	*Sermo de septem donis Spiritus Sancti*
Ep(p)	*Epistola(e)*
Epi	*Sermo in epiphania domini*

Epi var	*Sermo varius in epiphania domini*
Gra	*De gratia et libero arbitrio*
Hum	*De gradibus humilitatis et superbiae*
Humb	*Sermo in obitu domini Humberti*
Innoc	*Sermo in festivitatibus sancti Stephani, sancti Ioannis et sanctorum Innocentium*
JB	*Sermo in nativitate sancti Ioannis Baptistae*
Mal	*Sermo in transitu sancti Malachiae episcopi*
Mart	*Sermo in festivitate sancti Martini episcopi*
Mich	*Sermo in festo sancti Michaëlis*
Miss	*Homilium super Missus est in laudibus virginis matris*
Mor	*De moribus et officio episcoporum = Epistola 77*
Nat	*Sermo in nativitate domini*
Nat BVM	*Sermo in nativitate BVM*
O Asspt	*Sermo dominica infra octavam assumptionis*
OfVict	*Officium de sancto Victore*
O Pasc	*Sermo in octavo paschae*
OS	*Sermo in festivitate Omnium Sanctorum*
Palm	*Sermo in ramis palmarum*
Par	*Parabola*
Pent	*Sermo in die sancto pentecostes*
P Epi	*Sermo in dominica I post octavam epiphaniae*
Pl	*Sermo in conversione sancti Pauli*
PP	*Sermo in festo sanctorum apostolorum Petri et Pauli*
Pre	*De praecepto et dispensatione*
Pur	*Sermo in purificatione BVM*
QH	*Sermo super psalmum Qui habitat*
Quad	*Sermo in quadragesima*
Res	*Sermo in resurrectione domini*
SC	*Sermo super Cantica Canticorum*
Sent	*Sententia*
Sept	*Sermo in septuagesima*
S Mal	*Sermo de sancto Malachia*
Tpl	*De laude novae militiae = Ad milites templi*

V And	*Sermo in vigilia sancti Andreae*
Vict	*Sermo in natali sancti Victoris*
V Mal	*Vita sancti Malachiae*
V Nat	*Sermo in vigilia nativitatis domini*

Others

AC	*Analecta Cisterciensia*
ASOC	*Analecta Sacri Ordinis Cisterciensis*
CCCM	*Corpus Christianorum, Contunuatio Mediaevalis.* Turnhout, Belgium: Brepols.
CF	Cistercian Fathers Series. Spencer, Washington, DC, Kalamazoo, Collegeville, 1970–.
Cîteaux	*Cîteaux in de Nederlanden* = *Cîteaux: Commentarii Cistercienses*
Coll	*Collectanea Ordinis Cisterciensium Reformatorum* = *Collectanea Cisterciensia*
CS	Cistercian Studies Series. Spencer, Washington, DC, Kalamazoo, Collegeville, 1969–.
CSQ	*Cistercian Studies Quarterly*
DThC	*Dictionnaire de théologie catholique.* Paris (1899) 1903–1950.
PL	J.-P. Migne, *Patrologie cursus completus, series latina.* 221 vols. Paris: 1844–64.
R Ben	*Revue Bénédictine*
RESB	J. Leclercq, *Recueil d'études sur saint Bernard et ses écrits.* 5 vols. Rome: Storia e Letteratura, 1962–92.
RSR	*Revue des sciences religieuses*
RTAM	*Recherches de théologie ancienne et médiévale*
SBOp	*Sancti Bernardi Opera.* 8 vols. J. Leclercq, H. M. Rochais, C. H. Talbot, eds. Rome: Editiones Cistercienses, 1957–77.
SCh	*Sources Chrétiennes* series. Paris: Éditions du Cerf, 1941–.
Vulg	Vulgate translation
ZKG	*Zeitschrift für Kirchengeschichte*

PART I

Preliminaries

1

BERNARD ON THE CROSS:
A NEGLECTED THEME

The eleventh and twelfth centuries figure prominently in historical accounts of the doctrine of the redemptive work of Christ. Discussion invariably focuses on two key thinkers, Anselm and Abelard,[1] but there is a third significant figure from this era, Bernard of Clairvaux. If Bernard is mentioned at all in these accounts, it is usually only for the fact that he helped to secure Abelard's condemnation at the Council of Sens in 1141[2] and subsequently at Rome. But Bernard's doctrine of the Cross was no less developed than that of Anselm or Abelard and, in my view, is considerably richer, fuller, and more satisfactory than either of theirs. If this is so, why is it that we hear so little about Bernard's teaching on this topic? There is a remarkable lacuna in the scholarly literature.[3]

There are two types of work where we might expect an account of Bernard's teaching on the Cross—histories of the doctrine, and works devoted to the teaching of Bernard.

---

[1] Abelard was not a particularly popular or influential writer in the Middle Ages, as can be seen from how relatively infrequently his work was copied. See Nikolaus M. Häring, "Abelard Yesterday and Today," in *Pierre Abélard: Pierre le Vénérable* (Paris: Éditions du Centre National de la Recherche Scientifique, 1975), 341–403.

[2] For more on the dating of the council and of the events leading up to it, see chap. 4, n. 7.

[3] The problem in some quarters is not just a neglect of the topic but a misapprehension of its significance. When I mentioned the topic to one of the great medieval historians of the previous generation, he looked at me with surprise and said, "But, surely, for Bernard the Cross was just a holy relic?"

A. Histories of the Doctrine

Since the nineteenth century, histories of the doctrine of the
work of Christ have tended to focus upon Anselm and Abelard.
Especially influential have been those of Albrecht Ritschl and Adolf
von Harnack, two of the key figures in nineteenth-century Liberal
Theology.[4] An early example of the focus on Anselm and Abelard
comes in Ritschl's account of the doctrine of justification and reconciliation, the first two chapters of which expound the idea of
reconciliation in the Middle Ages. Chapter 1 of Ritschl's study is
devoted to Anselm and Abelard and presents the alternative of either
a purely "juridical" doctrine of satisfaction or a purely "ethical" one,
to the advantage of the latter.[5] So what about Bernard? His dispute
with Abelard over the work of Christ is not even mentioned in the
first chapter, but he is discussed in the third chapter, on the medieval
idea of justification.[6] In other words, Bernard has a contribution to
make to the understanding of subjective piety, but not to the interpretation of the Cross.

An even greater focus on Anselm and Abelard, presenting them as
alternatives, is found in the subsequent German histories of dogma of
the latter part of the nineteenth century.[7] First, and most influential,
was Harnack. He expounds Anselm and Abelard for the doctrine of
the Cross in the earlier Middle Ages, with a brief mention of Peter

---

[4] Harnack lived into the twentieth century, but the tradition of nineteenth-
century theology can be said to extend to the outbreak of the First World War.

[5] Albrecht Ritschl, *Die christliche Lehre von der Rechtfertigung und Versöhnung*, vol.
1 (Bonn: Adolph Marcus, 1870); Albrecht Ritschl, *A Critical History of the Christian Doctrine of Justification and Reconciliation* (Edinburgh: Edmonston and Douglas,
1872). There were later revised editions of the German original.

[6] Ritschl, *Die christliche Lehre*, 98–105; Ritschl, *A Critical History*, 95–101.

[7] These works are discussed in the order in which the first editions appeared,
though in each case it is the latest revised edition that has been used. Hagenbach's
Lehrbuch der Dogmengeschichte was already in its second edition in 1847, well before
Ritschl's work. Hagenbach gives Anselm pride of place, and Abelard appears as just
one of a number of "further developments" of the doctrine, with Bernard noted
as his opponent (Karl R. Hagenbach, *A History of Christian Doctrines*, vol. 2, translation of 5th German edition of 1867 [Edinburgh: T&T Clark, 1880], 275–90).

Lombard and later medieval teaching.[8] He mentions Bernard's teaching on the Cross only briefly in a footnote,[9] although he earlier gives generous coverage to Bernard's piety.[10] Two other important historians of dogma, Friedrich Loofs[11] and Reinhold Seeberg,[12] mention Bernard's opposition to Abelard but otherwise ignore his teaching on the Cross.

Ritschl's influence also made itself felt in Britain, especially through Hastings Rashdall. In his 1925 Bampton Lectures on the idea of the atonement, Rashdall devotes a lecture to the teaching of Augustine, Anselm, and Abelard, again with the purpose of demonstrating the superiority of Abelard. He mentions Bernard in passing as the enraged persecutor of Abelard, and there is an additional note outlining the *Capitula errorum* drawn up by Bernard and sent to the pope.[13]

[8] Adolf Harnack, *Lehrbuch der Dogmengeschichte*, vol. 3, 4th ed. (Tübingen: J. C. B. Mohr [Paul Siebeck], 1910), 388–414; Adolf Harnack, *History of Dogma*, vol. 6 (New York: Russell and Russell, 1958), 54–83. Shortly before Harnack's first edition appeared (1886–90), Joseph Schwane, *Dogmengeschichte der mittleren Zeit (787–1517)* (Freiburg: Herder, 1882), 296–333, also covered the work of Christ in the Middle Ages, focussing on Anselm, Abelard (with the response by Bernard and William of Saint Thierry), Peter Lombard, and Thomas Aquinas especially, with brief mention of a few other figures.

[9] Harnack, *Lehrbuch der Dogmengeschichte*, 3:411–12, n. 1; Harnack, *History of Dogma*, 6:80, n. 1. This is only in response to Seeberg's positive use of him and in order to deny that Bernard taught that Christ bore our penalty.

[10] Harnack, *Lehrbuch der Dogmengeschichte*, 3:342–47; Harnack, *History of Dogma*, 6:10–15.

[11] Friedrich Loofs, *Leitfaden zum Studium der Dogmengeschichte*, 4th ed. (Halle: Max Niemeyer, 1906), 505–15, follows Harnack in his all but exclusive emphasis upon Anselm and Abelard, apart from a brief mention of William of Saint Thierry and Bernard as opponents of the latter. Loofs describes Bernard's mysticism on pages 521–25.

[12] Reinhold Seeberg, *Lehrbuch der Dogmengeschichte*, vol. 3, 2nd/3rd ed. (Leipzig: A. Deichert, 1913), 207–39, avoids the preoccupation with Anselm and Abelard, expounding others such as Hugh of Saint Victor and Peter Lombard, but mentions Bernard only for his opposition to Abelard. Artur M. Landgraf, *Dogmengeschichte der Frühscholastik* 2/2 (Regensburg: F. Pustet, 1954), devotes three chapters to the work of Christ but doesn't consider Bernard as scholastic, though he does refer to him.

[13] Hastings Rashdall, *The Idea of Atonement in Christian Theology* (London: Macmillan, 1919), 357–62 on Abelard, mention of Bernard on 359, *Capitula* on 362–64. For a critique of Rashdall's use of Abelard, see Alister McGrath, "The Moral Theory

Ritschl and the Liberal tradition sought to present Anselm and Abelard as the two alternative exponents of the work of Christ. The argument was that the Cross may be seen either as an objective satisfaction for sins or as a subjective spur to repentance, and that the latter is superior to the former. This approach was modified by Gustaf Aulén, who wrote one of the most influential works on this topic in the twentieth century. In 1930 he gave a course of lectures in Swedish that was published the next year in an abridged English translation under the title *Christus Victor*.[14] Aulén protested against the alternatives offered by the Liberals and argued that there was a third "idea" of the atonement that goes back to the early church and indeed the New Testament. This was what Aulén called the "classic" or "dramatic" idea of Christ as Victor. This idea interprets the atonement as "a Divine conflict and victory" over the evil powers of the world. Unlike the other two approaches, "it represents the work of Atonement or reconciliation as from first to last a work of God Himself."[15]

Aulén performed a valuable service by showing that the objective and subjective models are not all that is on offer, but he unfortunately failed to reject clearly the Liberal assumption that these are *alternative* views. His book is devoted to showing the superiority and antiquity of the "classic idea" over the others, not to showing how each model plays an important role in a rounded doctrine of the work of Christ. In his chapter on the Middle Ages the emphasis lies on Anselm and Abelard; there is no mention of Bernard. Aulén argues that "the classic view of the Atonement was never quite lost in the Middle Ages."[16]

Other authors have given some prominence to Bernard in their historical accounts but have confined themselves entirely, or almost entirely, to his opposition to Abelard.[17] James Orr, for example, in a

---

of the Atonement: An Historical and Theological Critique," *Scottish Journal of Theology* 38 (1985): 205–20.

[14] Gustaf Aulén, *Christus Victor: An Historical Study of the Three Main Types of the Idea of the Atonement*, 2nd ed. (London: SPCK, 1970).

[15] Aulén, *Christus Victor*, 4–5.

[16] Aulén, *Christus Victor*, chap. 5, quotation at 99.

[17] David Smith, *The Atonement in the Light of History and the Modern Spirit* (London: Hodder and Stoughton, 1918), cites Bernard's opposition to Abelard in the

chapter on the atonement, expounds Abelard and Anselm especially, seeing them as representative of the moral and satisfaction theories of the atonement. "To one or other of these generic forms all theories of the atonement may in principle be reduced." He then adds that "Abelard's doctrine was at once resisted by his great opponent Bernard, as alike in itself inadequate, and out of harmony with what had always been the faith of the Church."[18] Others have similarly reduced Bernard to the opponent of Abelard, such as Robert S. Franks,[19] Laurence W. Grensted,[20] Sydney Cave,[21] and Robert Paul.[22] Thus, in all the works so far surveyed one can see the imprint of

---

context of the ransom (70–73), satisfaction (90), and moral influence (94–95) theories, but his own sympathies are with the last of these.

[18] James Orr, *The Progress of Dogma* (London: Hodder and Stoughton, 1901), lecture 7; quotations at 230, exposition of Bernard on 230–31, and a brief mention of him on 229. Orr's acceptance of the premise that ultimately there are two theories between which one must choose doubtless reflects the influence of Ritschl and Harnack, who are regularly cited in the notes to this lecture.

[19] For instance, Robert S. Franks, *A History of the Doctrine of the Work of Christ in Its Ecclesiastical Development*, vol. 1, part 2 (London: Hodder and Stoughton, 1919), chaps. 2–3. Having begun with Anselm and Abelard, he proceeds to expound Bernard, Rupert of Deutz, Hugh of Saint Victor, and Peter Lombard. An initial section, inspired by Ritschl, points to passages in the sermons on the Song of Songs where there is an emphasis on "the patience and love of Christ in His human life and passion" (193–95). Apart from this, Bernard appears only as the opponent of Abelard (195–200).

[20] Laurence W. Grensted, *A Short History of the Doctrine of the Atonement* (Manchester: Manchester University Press; and London: Longmans, Green and Co., 1920), 103–14, gives Bernard some prominence, but his exposition is almost entirely confined to Bernard's *Epistola* 190, against the errors of Abelard.

[21] Sydney Cave, *The Doctrine of the Work of Christ* (London: University of London Press and Hodder and Stoughton, 1937), chap. 5, expounds Augustine, Anselm, Abelard, Bernard, and Thomas. The exposition of Bernard begins with his opposition to Abelard (137–40) and proceeds to the affective piety of Bernard's sermons on the Song of Songs (140–43). Cave's concern is not to set out Bernard's doctrine of the Cross but rather to respond to the critique found in Ritschl's chapter on "The Mediaeval Idea of Justification."

[22] Robert S. Paul, *The Atonement and the Sacraments* (London: Hodder and Stoughton, 1961), 65–90, expounds the Middle Ages, focussing on the three *As*— Anselm, Abelard, and Aquinas. Bernard is mentioned briefly as the opponent of Abelard (80, 84).

Ritschl—whether in the exclusive focus upon Anselm and Abelard or in seeing their two theories as alternatives. The only significant addition to this is the account of Bernard's opposition to Abelard.

The person who has given the most serious attention to Bernard in a historical account of the doctrine of redemption is Jean Rivière, writing at the beginning of the last century. He devoted a chapter each to Anselm and Abelard, giving full consideration to how their teaching was received by their contemporaries,[23] as well as chapters on later medieval developments and on the question of the devil's rights.[24] Rivière expounded Bernard's opposition to Abelard and also devoted some space to Bernard's other teaching on redemption.[25] His aim was to correct the imbalance of previous historical accounts:

> Historians never fail to observe that St. Bernard defended against Abælard the rights of the devil, but they seem to confine Bernard's work to this, forgetful of the fact that he, amongst other things, and at even greater length, explained and defended the traditional doctrine of expiation.[26]

Some years later Rivière built on this work with a series of journal articles on the dogma of redemption at the beginning of the Middle Ages, which were then brought together into a book. He devoted an entire article to the role of Bernard[27] in which, as in his earlier work,

---

[23] Jean Rivière, *The Doctrine of the Atonement: A Historical Essay*, vol. 2 (London: Kegan Paul, Trench, Trübner and Co., 1909), chaps. 18–19. French original: *Le dogme de la rédemption: Essai d'étude historique* (Paris: Lecoffre, 1905), his doctoral dissertation from the Catholic University of Toulouse.

[24] Rivière, *Doctrine of the Atonement*, chaps. 20, 24.

[25] Rivière, *Doctrine of the Atonement*, 64–68, followed by 68–71, 215–23, is confined to the conflict with Abelard, with the addition of two citations from Bernard's sermons (219).

[26] Rivière, *Doctrine of the Atonement*, 64.

[27] Jean Rivière, "Le dogme de la rédemption au début du moyen âge III—rôle de saint Bernard," RSR 13 (1933): 186–208, which reappears with very minor additions in *Le dogme de la rédemption au début du moyen âge* (Paris: J. Vrin, 1934), 199–221. Here, unlike the earlier book, he engages heavily with contemporary scholars, especially H. Gallerand and M. Turmel. A subsequent article, "Le conflit des 'filles de dieu' dans la théologie médiévale," RSR 13 (1933): 553–90, which

he focused almost entirely on the conflict with Abelard, though again with the introduction of some material from Bernard's other works.[28] Rivière (unlike most of the others reviewed here) showed evidence of familiarity with Bernard's teaching on the Cross outside of his treatise against Abelard—but his exposition nonetheless remains fundamentally an account of that controversy supplemented by other material from Bernard.[29]

The legacy of the scholarship that we have surveyed is that, even today, many accounts of the doctrine of the work of Christ in the early Middle Ages look no further than Anselm and Abelard, as if these were representative of the era. Two recent examples illustrate this. A book by Joel Green and Mark Baker on the atonement contains a chapter surveying historical models of the atonement in which Anselm and Abelard loom large and no other medievals are mentioned.[30] A more careful study is found in a recent essay by Gwenfair Walters on the atonement in medieval theology, but this also focuses on Anselm and Abelard, presenting their two theories as alternatives. She mentions Bernard, but only as the opponent of Abelard.[31] The malign influence of Ritschl and Harnack has cast a shadow over most subsequent scholarship, both in the exclusive focus

---

reappears with additions in *Le dogme de la rédemption au début du moyen âge*, 309–49, contains some further material on Bernard.

[28] Rivière, "Le dogme de la rédemption," 199, 201, 204, 206; Rivière, *Le dogme de la rédemption au début du moyen âge*, 212, 214, 217, 219. There is also a separate discussion of Bernard's use of Ps 85:10 in his first sermon on the annunciation ("Le conflit des 'filles de dieu,'" 563–68; *Le dogme de la rédemption au début du moyen âge*, 319–24).

[29] Rivière wrote the article on "Rédemption" in DThC 13:1912–2004. This contains a short section on the medievals (1942–51) that again mentions Bernard in the context of Abelard. J. Rivière, *Le dogme de la rédemption: Études, critiques et documents* (Louvain: Bureaux de la Revue [d'Histoire Ecclésiastique], 1931), contains chapters on a number of historical figures, not including Bernard.

[30] Joel B. Green and Mark D. Baker, *Recovering the Scandal of the Cross: Atonement in New Testament and Contemporary Contexts* (Downers Grove: IVP, 2000), 116–52.

[31] Gwenfair M. Walters, "The Atonement in Medieval Theology," in *The Glory of the Atonement: Biblical, Historical and Practical Perspectives*, eds. C. E. Hill and F. A. James (Downers Grove: IVP, 2004), 239–62.

on Anselm and Abelard and in the representation of their doctrines of the work of Christ as alternatives.[32]

In addition to the literature so far surveyed, there is, of course, a substantial body of specialist literature on Bernard's conflict with Abelard, and this will be examined in due course.[33] Here also Bernard's teaching on the Cross is widely neglected. Few of the many works on the conflict actually examine Bernard's and Abelard's teaching on the work of Christ, despite the fact that over half of Bernard's letter-treatise against Abelard is devoted to that topic.[34] As Michael Clanchy notes, redemption is "the subject to which St Bernard devoted his most vituperative language in the prosecution of Abelard."[35] Reinhold Seeberg, in an article on Abelard and Bernard, correctly states that for Bernard the heart of Abelard's errors lies in his teaching on redemption.[36] Despite this, much of the scholarship has ignored it.

When it comes to the history of the doctrine of the work of Christ, David's Knowles's more general comments are certainly true: "Modern historians of medieval thought and theology often go near to forgetting St. Bernard. . . . He might never have existed, save as a persecutor of those who sought new ways."[37]

---

[32] Unfortunately, fascicle 3:2b of the multivolume *Handbuch der Dogmengeschichte* (Freiburg: Herder, 1951ff.) has yet to appear, its topic being medieval soteriology.

[33] See chap. 5C below.

[34] Some of them completely ignore the issue of the work of Christ—e.g., Jean Jolivet, "Sur quelques critiques de la théologie d'Abélard," *Archives d'histoire doctrinale et littéraire du moyen âge* 38 (1963): 7–51. Thomas J. Renna, "Bernard vs. Abelard: An Ecclesiological Conflict," in *Simplicity and Ordinariness*, ed. John R. Sommerfeldt, CS 61 (Kalamazoo, MI: Cistercian Publications, 1980), 94–138, explores the differences between the two but makes no mention of the work of Christ.

[35] Michael T. Clanchy, *Abelard: A Medieval Life* (Oxford: Blackwell, 1997), 283.

[36] Reinhold Seeberg, "Die Versöhnungslehre des Abälard und die Bekämpfung derselben durch den heiligen Bernhard," *Mittheilungen und Nachrichten für die evangelische Kirche in Rußland* 44 (1888): 121–53, at 143.

[37] David Knowles, "The Middle Ages 604–1350," in *A History of Christian Doctrine*, ed. Hubert Cunliffe-Jones (Edinburgh: T&T Clark, 1978), 253.

B. Bernard Literature

Bernard's doctrine of the Cross has not been served well by histories of doctrine. But at least his teaching has been expounded in the specialist Bernard literature. Or has it? There is a vast body of literature on Bernard. Separate volumes list works of and about Bernard published to 1890, from 1891 to 1957, and from 1957 to 1970, and since then there have been regular surveys in journals.[38] I have trawled the literature exhaustively and exhaustingly and found very little on this topic. Scholarship has focussed strongly on Bernard and the four *m*'s: Bernard the mystic; Bernard the monk; Bernard the meddler (in politics); Bernard and Mary. The Cross has attracted very little attention until the last decade or so when there have been some brief studies that touch on the topic, a welcome development.

There are two questions to be considered. First, to what extent have the major expositions of Bernard's theology drawn attention to his teaching on the Cross? Second, how many studies are there that have been devoted to his teaching on the Cross in particular?

In answer to the first question, there is very little material on our topic. Abbé Vacandard made a vital contribution to Bernard studies in the late nineteenth century with his two-volume life of Saint Bernard, on the basis of which he wrote the article on Bernard in the *Dictionnaire de Théologie Catholique*.[39] The article contains two columns on

---

[38] The major bibliographies are Leopold Janauschek, *Bibliographia Bernardina qua sancti Bernardi primi abbatis Claravallensis operum cum omnium tum singulorum editiones ac versiones vitas et tractatus de eo scriptos* (Vienna: Alfred Hölder, 1891); Jean de la Croix Bouton, *Bibliographie bernardine 1891–1957* (Paris: P. Lethielleux, 1958); Eugène Manning, *Bibliographie bernardine (1957–1970)*, Documentation cistercienne 6 (Rochefort, 1972); Guido Hendrix, *Conspectus bibliographicus sancti Bernardi ultimi patrum 1989–1993*, RTAM Supplementa 2, 2nd ed. (Leuven: Peeters, 1995). Apart from these, I have consulted the annual bibliographies in the Cistercian journals (especially Coll) and *Medioevo Latino*. As well as looking for works specifically on the topic, I have examined all the major works on Bernard that might be expected to include something on this theme. No doubt there is some material somewhere that has escaped my notice, but the general picture of neglect of this theme will not be affected.

[39] Elphège Vacandard, *Vie de saint Bernard, abbé de Clairvaux* (Paris: Victor Lecoffre, 1895); "Bernard (saint), abbé de Clairvaux," DThC 2:746–85.

redemption, but this is confined to Bernard's treatise against Abelard.[40] In the second volume of his biography Vacandard first notes that the doctrine of salvation by Christ, including his death for us, formed part of Bernard's regular teaching prior to the controversy with Abelard. He then expounds this teaching briefly, with an emphasis on the Cross as a lesson in humility and love, before discussing Bernard's teaching against Abelard.[41] Vacandard's brief account consists chiefly of extended quotations and is short on analysis. Studies subsequent to Vacandard have tended to focus on the incarnation rather than the Cross. Discussion of the latter is usually completely, or almost completely, confined to the dispute with Abelard. The neglect of the Cross can even be seen in the greatest Bernard scholar of the twentieth century, Jean Leclercq. In a summary of Bernard's theology he scarcely mentions the Cross. He expounds salvation as imitation of Christ in a passage that would have pleased Abelard.[42] Even Homer nods.[43]

There are a few noteworthy exceptions to this pattern of neglect. Unexpectedly, Robert Linhardt's work on Bernard's mysticism, from the 1920s, gives some attention to the Cross, though underestimating its importance for Bernard.[44] Gillian Evans, in her *The Mind of St. Bernard of Clairvaux*, recognises that, prior to the encounter with Abelard, Bernard offers "a treatment of Incarnation and Redemption more comprehensive, if less fully worked out, than that of Anselm in the *Cur Deus Homo*." She expounds this observation from the treatise for

---

[40] DThC 2:764–67.

[41] Vacandard, *Vie*, 2:71–74, citing nine passages from five different works, but only four of these passages refer to the Cross. There is a brief mention of the Cross in 1:479–80, where two passages from SC are quoted. The teaching against Abelard is in 2:131–33.

[42] Jean Leclercq, "General Introduction to the Works of Saint Bernard (III)," CSQ 40 (2005): 378–92, especially 385–87. Earlier, though, he had argued that what the Cross evokes for Bernard is not primarily the sufferings of Jesus but the fruit of this suffering, the redemption that he brought ("La dévotion médiévale envers le crucifié," *La maison dieu* 75 [1963]: 124–32, especially 129).

[43] Horace, *Ars poetica*, 358–59.

[44] Robert Linhardt, *Die Mystik des hl. Bernhard von Clairvaux* (Munich: Natur und Kultur, 1923), 105–15, 195–98. We will note below places where the importance of the Cross is underestimated.

the Templars, from the letter on the errors of Abelard, and from other writings, relating Bernard's teaching to that of Anselm and Abelard.[45]

While in books on Bernard there is very little mention of the Cross outside of the controversy with Abelard, more material can be found in some articles, especially in recent years. A handful of brief popular studies[46] and a much fuller article[47] do little more than quote extracts from Bernard's works on various particular themes. Jean Leclercq, in an article on medieval devotion to the Crucified One, devotes a short section to Bernard.[48] A study by Alberich Altermatt of Bernard's Christology as seen in the liturgical sermons contains a section devoted to the passion and death of Jesus Christ.[49] There is a body of other literature on Bernard's Christology, most of which contains very little reference to the Cross.[50] This is unfortunate since, as Köpf states,

[45] Gillian R. Evans, *The Mind of St. Bernard of Clairvaux* (Oxford: OUP, 1983), 152–62, not all of which is devoted to the death of Christ. See also p. 143. Pp. 152–62 substantially incorporate her "*Cur Deus Homo:* St. Bernard's Theology of the Redemption; A Contribution to the Contemporary Debate," *Studia Theologica* 36 (1982): 27–36, with minor verbal changes.

[46] Basilius Hänsler, "Christi Blut und die Irrlehre bzw. das Schisma nach dem hl. Bernhard," *Cistercienser Chronik* 35 (1923): 133–36; Basilius Hänsler, "Christi Blut und das Heilige Land, sowie Christi Blut und die Ordensleute nach dem hl. Bernhard," *Cistercienser Chronik* 37 (1925): 59–61; Basilius Hänsler, "Vom Blut Christi in St. Bernhards Kapitelreden," *Cistercienser Chronik* 40 (1928): 110–14; Kurt Knotzinger, "Kreuzweg nach St. Bernhard von Clairvaux," *Cistercienser Chronik* 74 (1967): 105–10; M. José Olmedo, "Devoción de san Bernardo a la pasión," *Cistercium* 26 (1953): 41–44.

[47] Robert Thomas, "La dévotion à Notre-Seigneur et à sa passion dans l'ordre de Cîteaux," in *Autour de la spiritualité cistercienne*, Pain de Cîteaux 16 (N.p.: Chambarand, 1962), 117–206, contains considerable material specifically on Bernard and the passion. Of the fourteen chapters, six are specifically on the passion (133–64), and almost half of the passages there cited are from Bernard.

[48] Leclercq, "La dévotion médiévale envers le crucifié," 119–32 (126–29 on Bernard).

[49] Alberich Altermatt, "Christus pro nobis: Die Christologie Bernhards von Clairvaux in den 'Sermonum per annum,'" AC 33 (1977): 116–29.

[50] Such as the series of articles by Amatus van den Bosch in Cîteaux 8 (1957): 245–51; 9 (1958): 5–17, 85–105; 10 (1959): 85–92, 165–77, 245–67; 12 (1961): 105–19, 193–210; and in Coll 21 (1959): 185–205; 22 (1960): 11–20, 341–55; 23 (1961): 42–57.

Bernard's image of Christ is to a large extent determined by Christ's passion and Cross, which call us to contemplation and imitation.[51] The most substantial work on our theme comes from Johannes Gottschick, whose studies on the medieval doctrine of reconciliation include more material on Bernard than on any other figure. The author's commendable aim is to correct the excessive preoccupation of recent scholarship with Anselm.[52] Ulrich Köpf has studied Bernard's theology of the Cross in the light of his exegesis, especially as found in his sermons on the Song of Songs. Köpf argues that Bernard, no less than Abelard, points to modernity with his subjective understanding of the Cross and by dwelling on Christ's sufferings and the experience of the believer.[53] There are also four other brief studies, all from the 1990s,[54] by Joël Regnard,[55] Dennis Billy,[56] Oluf Schönbeck,[57] and Sister Brigitte.[58]

[51] "Sein Christusbild ist in hohem Maße durch Leiden und Kreuz bestimmt, aber auch durch die Betonung der Bedeutung des Heilswerks Christi für uns . . . die uns zur Betrachtung und Nachfolge einlädt." Ulrich Köpf, "Kreuz IV: Mittelalter," in *Theologische Realenzyklopädie*, vol. 9 (Berlin and New York: Walter de Gruyter, 1990), 753.

[52] Johannes Gottschick, "Studien zur Versöhnungslehre des Mittelalters," ZKG 22 (1901): 378–438, of which 384–403 and 409–17 are devoted to Bernard.

[53] Ulrich Köpf, "Schriftauslegung als Ort der Kreuzestheologie Bernhards von Clairvaux," in *Bernhard von Clairvaux und der Beginn der Moderne*, ed. Dieter R. Bauer and Gotthard Fuchs (Innsbruck and Vienna: Tyrolia, 1996), 194–213. For more on Bernard's teaching, see Ulrich Köpf, "Die Passion Christi in der lateinischen religiösen und theologischen Literatur des Spätmittelalters," in *Die Passion Christi in Literatur und Kunst des Spätmittelalters*, ed. Walter Haug and Burghart Wachinger (Tübingen: Max Niemeyer, 1993), 25, 27–31.

[54] I have not managed to trace Otto Langer, "Passio und compassio: Zur Bedeutung der Passionsmystik bei Bernhard von Clairvaux," in *Die dunkle Nacht der Sinne*, ed. G. Fuchs (Dusseldorf: n.p., 1989), 41–62. The summary in Hendrix, *Conspectus Bibliographicus*, 104, suggests that the overlap with the present work will not be great.

[55] Joël Regnard, "In nous sauve non seulement par sa mort mais aussi par sa vie: La rédemption chez saint Bernard," Coll 58 (1996): 141–48, points to the fact that, for Bernard, redemption is by the life of Christ as well as by his death.

[56] Dennis J. Billy, "Redemption and the Order of Love in Bernard of Clairvaux's *Sermon 20 on 'The Canticle of Canticles*,'" *Downside Review* 112 (1994): 88–102.

[57] Oluf Schönbeck, "Saint Bernard, Peter Damian, and the Wounds of Christ," CSQ 30 (1995): 275–84, argues that Bernard's interpretation lies in the tradition of Peter Damian.

[58] Sr. Brigitte, "Jésus et Jésus crucifié chez saint Bernard," Coll 57 (1995): 219–37, considers Bernard's citations of 1 Cor 2:2.

In 1989 Daniel Akin wrote on Bernard's teaching on the work of Christ in a chapter of his doctoral thesis.[59] Akin argues that Bernard had a holistic view of the work of Christ and used a full range of metaphors and models,[60] and he illustrates his argument by quoting extensively from the abbot's own writings. Bernard held together the objective (Anselmian) and subjective (Abelardian) aspects of the work of Christ.[61] To Akin's credit, his detailed study of Bernard's teaching on the Cross brings out as very few studies have done the comprehensive nature of Bernard's teaching. There are, however, some weaknesses in his study. Chief among these is Akin's complete dependence upon English, both for the primary and for the secondary literature.[62] This does not affect the big picture of his thesis, which is sound, but it does affect some of the details.[63] The present study, by contrast, is based on the full range of Bernard's Latin writings (rather than a wide range of English translations) and aims to take account of *every* passage where the Cross is mentioned.[64] Finally, in 2008 the

---

[59] Daniel L. Akin, "Bernard of Clairvaux: Evangelical of the Twelfth Century (A Critical Analysis of His Soteriology)" (PhD thesis, University of Texas at Arlington, 1989), chap. 3. A shorter version of this appeared in his "Bernard of Clairvaux and the Atonement," in *The Church at the Dawn of the 21st Century: Essays in Honor of W. A. Criswell*, ed. P. Patterson, J. Pretlove, and L. Pantoja (Dallas: Criswell Publications, 1989), 103–28. This omits almost a quarter of the PhD thesis chapter. I am grateful to Dr. Akin for sending me a scanned copy of the published chapter. The fourth chapter of the thesis is likewise presented in abridged form in his "Bernard of Clairvaux: Evangelical of the 12th Century (An Analysis of His Soteriology)," *Criswell Theological Review* 4 (1990): 327–50.

[60] Akin, "Bernard," 81, 82–83, 88, 89, 90, 102 / 103, 105, 110; the first set of figures relate to the (fuller) thesis, the second to the (more accessible) published version.

[61] Akin, "Bernard," 88–89, 97–98, 129 / 105, 109, 123.

[62] One annoying feature is that he cites a number of the sermons from the unscholarly selection of extracts presented in *Saint Bernard on the Christian Year* (London: Mowbray, 1954) and simply gives the page reference in that edition, which gives no indication of the actual source to those without access to that edition.

[63] To give just one example, Tpl 10.17 is cited for the idea of expiation, but while the word appears in the translation, it is not found in the original (Akin, "Bernard," 105–6 / 112). See chap. 4, n. 15, below. Akin's explicit aim is to relate Bernard's teaching to contemporary Evangelicalism (Akin, "Bernard," 1–18 [introduction], 101, 103, 105, 132 / 110, 111, 111–12, 124–25).

[64] For a full list of these passages, see appendix 1.

present author published an article entitled, like this book, "Bernard of Clairvaux: Theologian of the Cross."[65] That article presents briefly the main conclusions of the present work.

At the Mainz colloquium for the eight hundredth anniversary of Bernard's death, Artur Landgraf commented that so much had already been written on Bernard's theology that it is scarcely possible any longer to say much new that is of interest to any but specialist researchers.[66] The intervening half century calls his judgement into question, which most certainly does not apply to Bernard's teaching on the Cross. This is definitely not a topic on which so much has been written, and still today it is not one where there is nothing new to be said that is of interest to any but specialist researchers.

[65] Anthony N. S. Lane, "Bernard of Clairvaux: Theologian of the Cross," in *The Atonement Debate*, ed. D. Tidball, D. Hilborn, and J. Thacker (Grand Rapids, MI: Zondervan, 2008), 249–66.

[66] Artur M. Landgraf, "Der heilige Bernhard in seinem Verhältnis zur Theologie des zwölften Jahrhunderts," in *Bernhard von Clairvaux: Mönch und Mystiker*, Joseph Lortz, ed. (Wiesbaden: Franz Steiner, 1955), 45.

2

THE CROSS
IN EARLIER TRADITION

A. Early Church Fathers

As we have seen, in the nineteenth century two accounts of the work of Christ were offered—the objective model that he died for our sins and the subjective model that he died to evoke a response on our part. The two key thinkers associated with these models are, respectively, Anselm with his *Cur Deus homo* and Abelard with his Excursus on Romans 3:19-26. Both *Cur Deus homo* and the Excursus will be expounded shortly. In 1930 Gustaf Aulén added a third model—the classic idea of Christus Victor.[1] Underlying most of the scholarship when Aulén wrote was the fallacious assumption that these models were alternatives, that it was necessary to choose one at the expense of the others. But the New Testament writers and the Fathers alike made use of all three of these models and never suggested that one was right and the others wrong. Today the great majority of scholars accept that these models are complementary perspectives on redemption, not alternatives between which we must choose.

The meaning of the objective and subjective models is relatively uncontroversial. The objective model refers to Christ's work of reconciliation in putting us right with God, in dealing with the obstacles

---

[1] See chap. 1A above.

blocking our fellowship with God that have been created by sin. This model can be expressed by the use of a great variety of imagery, such as sacrifice, paying a price, expiation, and satisfaction. The subjective model refers to the effects upon us of the work of Christ. These effects are produced by his teaching, by the example that he set, and by the way in which he brings us revelation of God and, especially, of God's love for us. Where the Cross is concerned, the subjective model especially involves the idea that the Cross demonstrates God's love, leading to a reciprocal response of love on our part. The Cross also provides a pattern, an example, for us to follow. These two models can be described, respectively, as the *Godward* aspect of the work of Christ and its *usward* aspect.[2]

While the line of demarcation around the first two models is clear, the same cannot be said for the classic model, which has three main components: Christ as the Second Adam, who recapitulates the human race; Christ as Victor over Satan; and Christ as bringing victory over death. There is no consensus in the literature as to how these components should be grouped. Some follow Aulén in grouping them together as a single model. Others divide what Aulén called the classic model into two different models, though without any consensus as to how to make the division.[3] The problem is that there is no obvious reason why Christ as Victor over Satan belongs to the same model as Christ as the Second Adam—except inasmuch as *everything* that Christ achieved flows from his position as the Second Adam. On the other hand, Christ's victory over death is very clearly related both to his work of recapitulation (the resurrection in particular) and to his victory over Satan.

For Bernard of Clairvaux, the objective and subjective models, the *Godward* and *usward* aspects, are clearly distinct and have their

---

[2] In expounding Bernard, we will use the term "aspect" rather than "model." This has the advantage that it conveys the idea of different aspects of one reality, with less temptation to think of two aspects as being mutually exclusive. Aspect is also, appropriately for Bernard, a less formal and systematic term.

[3] E.g., Henry E. W. Turner, *The Patristic Doctrine of Redemption* (London: Mowbray, 1952), has separate chapters entitled "Christ the Victor and the Doctrine of Recapitulation" and "Christ the Giver of Incorruption and Deification."

own chapters in this book.[4] The various components of the classic model are arranged according to how Bernard handles them. He gives scant attention to the component of Christ as Second Adam, though the Adam-Christ contrast is important for Bernard's defence of the *Godward* aspect of the Cross. Accordingly, "Christ as Second Adam" will be covered in the first of the chapters on Bernard's teaching on the Cross, while "Christ and Adam" will be covered under his response to objections.[5] On the other hand, because Bernard repeatedly links victory over Satan with victory over death, I will treat both of these components in the chapter on Christ as Victor over Satan and death.[6]

For the early Church Fathers the work of Christ was a relatively uncontroversial topic, and most of their teaching on it was occasional. The nearest to a treatise on the topic, Athanasius's *De incarnatione*, was primarily an apologetic work, not a systematic treatment. Gregory of Nyssa, however, while expounding Christ's victory over Satan, used three ideas that were to prove controversial and that have great relevance for our topic. He spoke of Satan's *rights* over us since he had legally acquired us:

> Those who give up their liberty for money become the slaves of their purchasers. By their selling themselves, neither they nor anyone else can reclaim their freedom, even when those who reduce themselves to this wretched state are nobly born. And should anyone, out of concern for one so sold, exercise force against the purchaser, he would seem unjust in dictatorially freeing one legally acquired. On the other hand, no law stands in the way of his buying back the man's freedom, if he wants to. In the same way, when once we had voluntarily sold ourselves, he who undertook out of goodness to restore our freedom had to contrive a just and

---

[4] Chapters 10–11 and chapter 8, respectively. The different models can be helpfully distinguished; they cannot, however, be divided into watertight compartments. They relate to one another, and the exposition of Bernard in Part III will seek to show how they are interconnected in his thought.

[5] Chaps. 7A and 11F below.

[6] Chap. 9 below.

not a dictatorial method to do so. And some such method is this: to give the master the chance to take whatever he wants to as the price of the slave.[7]

In order to free us, God had to pay a ransom *to* Satan. Christ as the sinless one did not deserve to die, and his death in our stead appeared an attractive proposition for Satan. The snag for Satan, however, was that since Christ was God, Satan was unable to hold him and so Christ rose from the dead. But would Satan not have realised that this would happen? No, because he was unaware of Christ's deity. Just as a greedy fish gulps down the bait without seeing the hook concealed underneath, so Satan bit on the bait of Christ's sinless humanity and was caught on the hook of his deity.[8]

Gregory then faces the charge that God was employing deceitful methods by tricking Satan in this way. Gregory does not deny the charge: "For in a way it was a fraud and deception for God, when he placed himself in the power of the enemy who was our master, not to show his naked deity, but to conceal it in our nature, and so escape recognition." God may have deceived Satan, but his action was both just and loving. "Justice is evident in the rendering of due recompense, by which the deceiver was in turn deceived." The action was loving because it effected our salvation.[9] It was even beneficial for Satan since Gregory believed that even Satan would finally be saved.[10]

Three ideas here were controversial: the idea that Satan had *rights* over us; that Christ's death was a ransom offered *to Satan*; that God *deceived* Satan. Gregory's fellow Cappadocian, Gregory of Nazianzus, firmly rejected the idea of the payment of a ransom to Satan:

---

[7] Gregory of Nyssa, *Oratio catechetica magna* 22, in *Christology of the Later Fathers*, ed. Edward R. Hardy with Cyril C. Richardson, Library of Christian Classics, vol. 3 (London: SCM, 1954), 299.

[8] Gregory of Nyssa, *Oratio catechetica magna* 23–24. Gregory also portrays Satan's seduction of Adam and Eve in the same terms, the fishhook of evil being baited with a semblance of good (21).

[9] *Oratio catechetica magna* 26; Hardy–Richardson, 302–3.

[10] *Oratio catechetica magna* 26, 35.

For whom, and with what object, was the blood shed for us, the great and famous blood of God, our high-priest and sacrifice, outpoured? Admittedly we were held in captivity by the Devil, having been sold under sin and having abdicated our happiness in exchange for wickedness. But if the ransom belongs exclusively to him who holds the prisoner, I ask to whom it was paid, and why. If to the Devil, how shameful that that robber should receive not only a ransom from God, but a ransom consisting of God Himself, and that so extravagant a price should be paid to his tyranny before he could justly spare us![11]

Augustine famously added to Nyssa's fishhook analogy his own mousetrap analogy in which Christ's blood was the bait. "To pay our price, he set the mousetrap of his Cross; as bait he placed there his own blood."[12] But his account of this is different from Gregory's. As a result of sin, humanity was in the power of the devil, because God justly permitted this. God chose to defeat the devil by means of justice rather than power so as to set a good example to humanity. By slaying Christ, the innocent one, the devil overstepped his power, and so it is right that those whom he held as debtors should be set free. At the same time, Augustine repeatedly stated that just as by committing sin humanity placed itself in the devil's power, so humanity is rescued from the devil's power by the remission of sins. By killing Christ, the devil both overstepped his power and brought about the remission of sins. At the same time, Christ defeated the devil by power when he rose again from the dead.[13] If the devil was deceived, it was by his own pride.[14] Augustine's account seriously qualifies that of Gregory of Nyssa. Satan's power over us is justly

---

[11] Gregory of Nazianzus, *Oration* 45.22, as cited by John N. D. Kelly, *Early Christian Doctrines*, 5th ed. (London: Adam and Charles Black, 1977), 383. For other objectors, see Turner, *Patristic Doctrine of Redemption*, 58–60.

[12] Augustine, Sermon 130.2 (*The Works of Saint Augustine, Part III: Sermons*, vol. 4, ed. John E. Rotelle [Brooklyn: New City Press, 1992], 311) and frequently elsewhere in his sermons.

[13] Augustine, *De trinitate* 13.12.16–15.19.

[14] Augustine, *De trinitate* 4.13.17.

permitted rather than a strict right, and no ransom is paid to Satan. Although the latter did not realise the consequences of his action, there is no talk of deception.

It was not until the eleventh and twelfth centuries that the question of how Christ defeated Satan next received critical examination. The principle figures were Anselm and Abelard. Both criticised the view that Satan had any rights over us or that a ransom needed to be paid to him. Anselm is famous for teaching that the Cross was necessary as a satisfaction to restore God's lost honour. We will need to consider whether or not Bernard knew Anselm's teaching. Abelard is famous for allegedly reducing the significance of the Cross to its subjective effect upon us, and we will need to assess the accuracy of that charge. Bernard certainly had some knowledge of Abelard's teaching, but the question is how well he knew it and how fairly he represented it.

B. Anselm of Canterbury

The most famous work by Anselm, the Italian archbishop of Canterbury (ca. 1033–09), is *Cur Deus homo* (*Why God Became Man*),[15] in which he considers the significance of the Cross for humans' relationship to the devil and to God. *Cur Deus homo* is written in the form of a dialogue between Anselm and Boso (one of his monks at Bec). Later in his *Meditation on Human Redemption* Anselm summarises the argument of the *Cur Deus homo* and spells out its subjective effects on us.

In the *Cur Deus homo* Anselm sets out to answer questions raised by unbelievers. In particular, there were those who argued that it was dishonouring God to suggest that he might have become a human being and suffered a shameful death. "Unbelievers, deriding us for

---

[15] Quotations are from Anselm of Canterbury, *The Major Works* (Oxford: OUP, 1998). On *Cur Deus homo*, see Gillian R. Evans, *Anselm and Talking about God* (Oxford: OUP, 1978), chap. 7; Gillian R. Evans, *Anselm* (London: Continuum, 2005, reprint of 1989), chap. 7; David S. Hogg, *Anselm of Canterbury: The Beauty of Theology* (Aldershot, Hants, and Burlington, VT: Ashgate, 2004), chap. 6; Jasper Hopkins, *A Companion to the Study of St. Anselm* (Minneapolis: University of Minnesota Press, 1972), 187–98; John McIntyre, *St. Anselm and His Critics: A Re-Interpretation of the* Cur Deus Homo (Edinburgh and London: Oliver and Boyd, 1954).

our simplicity, object that we are inflicting injury and insult on God when we assert that he descended into a woman's womb; was born of a woman; grew up nurtured on milk and human food and—to say nothing of other things which do not seem suitable for God—was subject to weariness, hunger, thirst, scourging, crucifixion between thieves, and death" (1.3; *Major Works*, 268).

Anselm's response is that the incarnation was very fitting because it was for our salvation. It was fitting that the devil, who caused our fall through a tree, should be defeated by a man's death upon a tree (1.3). Boso replies that in order to establish these points Anselm has to show that the Cross was necessary, that there was "a cogent reason which proves that God ought to have, or could have, humbled himself for the purposes which we proclaim" (1.4; *Major Works*, 269). Otherwise it appears to be a superfluous gesture. Anselm argues that it had to be the Creator himself who rescued us (1.4–5), but this argument leads to further questions: "Now, in what captivity, or in what prison or in whose power were you held, from which God could not set you free without ransoming you by so many exertions and, in the end, by his own blood?" (1.6; *Major Works*, 270). In particular, if God is all-powerful, could he not simply release us by a word? Since it is God who punishes us, could he not simply choose not to do so? "In whose power is hell, or the devil, in whose power is the kingdom of heaven, if not the power of him who created all things?" Why should he resort to such drastic means when they were not necessary? Why should an omnipotent God need to come down from heaven to defeat the devil? (1.6; *Major Works*, 271).

By raising these questions, Anselm is led to consider the devil's power over us. The traditional view, as expounded by Gregory of Nyssa, for example, was that our sin gave the devil rights over us, that he was our lawful owner. Because of this, God needed to free us by justice, not simply by power. The devil made the mistake of killing Christ, who was both innocent and God, and thus justly lost his power over sinners.[16] Anselm rejects this theory. It might be true

---

[16] The traditional view sometimes included the idea that God deceived or hoodwinked the devil. Anselm rejects this in his "Meditation on Human Redemption,"

if neither we nor the devil belonged to God, but in fact we do. Justice gives God the right to punish the devil for having seduced us. Equally, God is entitled to seize us back from the devil because the devil's possession of us is unjust. It is just that we are tormented by the devil, since that is the punishment that we deserve, but that does not mean that the devil is acting justly or that he has rights over us. We deserve punishment and he is an appropriate source of it, but on his part he is acting out of malice, not out of love of justice. He acts with God's permission, not by God's command. Our punishment is justly deserved, but that does not mean that it is justly inflicted by the devil. "There was nothing in the devil, therefore, which made God obliged not to use his mighty power against him for the purpose of liberating mankind" (1.7; *Major Works*, 274).

In other words, if we seek the necessary reason for the Word's becoming flesh and dying on the Cross, we will not find it in the devil's alleged power over us. Anselm argues instead that the purpose of Christ's redemption was to repair the relationship between God and humanity. Sin dishonours God and so God cannot just forgive. There needs to be satisfaction or compensation for his lost honour (1.11). He needs to uphold justice and law and cannot simply leave sin unpunished. Therefore, we must either offer satisfaction for our sins or pay for them by being punished (1.12–13). Anselm argues that the latter option is not possible, since God needs humanity to replace the fallen angels, so satisfaction needs to be offered for our sins (1.16–19). It is important to realise *why* such satisfaction is necessary. Anselm's argument is not that it was necessary in order for us to be saved, true though that is. That would be insufficient—he needs to go further and show why it would not be more fitting for God to abandon us to hell. Anselm does so by arguing that it was necessary *for God*, that there was no other option open to God. God faced this necessity not because he was weak but only because of previous decisions that he had made in full awareness of the consequences.

---

in *The Prayers and Meditations of Anselm*, ed. Benedicta Ward (Harmondsworth: Penguin, 1973), 231.

It is necessary, therefore, for humanity to offer satisfaction to God. The problem is that we cannot do this by offering God perfect obedience, since that is no more than we already owe him;[17] also, Anselm proves by an ingenious argument that the satisfaction to be offered must be greater than the universe (1.20–21). Of ourselves we are incapable of providing this satisfaction, so God is left with a dilemma: humanity owes God a debt that we have no ability to pay, and divine justice means that God cannot simply overlook it. At the same time, we must be saved lest God fail in his design (1.25).

In the second book of *Cur Deus homo* Anselm shows how God resolves the dilemma. The debt that is owed is greater than the whole universe, so only God *can* pay it. It is human beings who have sinned, so only a human being *ought* to pay it (2.6). The Saviour needs, therefore, to be both divine and human—hence the incarnation (2.7). Jesus lives a life of perfect obedience, but that is what he owes to the Father as a human being. As the sinless one, however, he does not need to die (2.10). His voluntary acceptance of an undeserved death on the Cross was a work of supererogation, doing more than was required of him. As such, it deserves a reward. But Christ, as God, already has everything, so the merit earned by Christ's voluntary death is offered to God as a satisfaction for the sins of humanity (2.18–19).

Anselm's account is often unfairly criticised as if his aim were to offer a complete doctrine of the work of Christ. It was not. His aim was to show why it was that the Word needed to become incarnate and to die on the Cross.[18] What Anselm teaches on the work of Christ is subject to that limited aim; that is why there are important themes that are neglected, such as the significance of the resurrection or of our union with Christ. The work of Christ is substitutionary to the extent that Christ, as human, does something in the place of the rest of us. This is not, however, *penal* substitution, because the

---

[17] This is contrary to 2.18, where Anselm says that celibacy is a work of supererogation that merits a reward.

[18] "As in most of his writings, Anselm set out in the *Cur Deus homo* to answer a specific question. He did not attempt a treatise covering the whole conspectus of issues about Christology and redemption" (Evans, *Anselm*, 82).

problem being addressed is the need to satisfy God's honour rather than his justice.[19] Borrowing ideas from the penitential system that also resonated in a feudal society,[20] Anselm saw the purpose of the Cross as the restoration of God's honour.

So according to the *Cur Deus homo*, the Cross was not needed to free humanity from the devil but was needed to repay the debt of satisfaction that humanity owed to God. There are occasional references to Christ's role as an example for us to follow,[21] but not to the Cross as a demonstration of love that provokes a response on our part. The latter comes out strongly, however, in Anselm's *Meditation on Human Redemption*: "Christian soul, brought to life again out of the heaviness of death, redeemed and set free from wretched servitude by the blood of God, rouse yourself and remember that you are risen, realize that you have been redeemed and set free. . . . Taste the goodness of your Redeemer, be on fire with love for your Saviour."[22]

There is another contrast between the *Meditation* and the *Cur Deus homo*. In the latter, Anselm argues that the incarnation and the Cross were not merely necessary for us but that there was no other possible alternative for God. That is, given basic truths like the character of God and the fact of creation and sin, God had no choice but to send Christ to die on the Cross. The emphasis is different in the *Meditation on Human Redemption*: "God was not obliged to save mankind in this way, but human nature needed to make amends to God like this. God had no need to suffer so laboriously, but

---

[19] He does, however, argue that God needs to uphold justice and law and cannot simply leave sin unpunished (1.12–13).

[20] "The most obvious and immediate source of the idea [of satisfaction] would appear to be the penitential system of the church, which was developing just at this time" (Jaroslav Pelikan, *The Growth of Medieval Theology [600–1300]* [Chicago: University of Chicago Press, 1978], 143). Tertullian and Cyprian introduced the idea that Christians need to offer God satisfaction for sins committed after baptism. Hilary applied the concept of satisfaction to the Cross (Jaroslav Pelikan, *The Emergence of the Catholic Tradition [100–600]* [Chicago: University of Chicago Press, 1971], 147–48). For a warning against overemphasising the influence of contemporary society upon Anselm, see Hogg, *Anselm of Canterbury*, 163–65.

[21] The role of Christ as an example is mentioned in *Cur Deus homo* 2.11, 18–19.

[22] Ward, ed., *Prayers and Meditations*, 230.

man needed to be reconciled thus."[23] In *Cur Deus homo* Anselm is concerned to show unbelievers that God was acting reasonably in undergoing the incarnation and the Cross; in his *Meditation* he is concerned to impress on believers the grace of God in intervening for their salvation. These two concerns pull in contrary directions.

C. Peter Abelard

The other key thinker is, of course, the mercurial Peter Abelard, whose life was brilliant and erratic. Most accounts of Abelard's teaching on the work of Christ focus entirely on the few pages that he wrote in the Excursus on Romans 3:19-26 in his *Commentary on Romans*.[24] As Thomas Williams notes, this Excursus "has been the target of both scholarly study and theological polemic ever since Bernard of Clairvaux's energetic propaganda war against Abelard."[25] The Excursus is certainly highly significant for our topic because Bernard responds to it in detail in his Letter 190 to Pope Innocent.[26] In order to set Bernard's letter in its context, the text of Abelard's Excursus is included here, laid out in a way that clarifies Abelard's questions and the answers that he gives.[27] I have divided the Excursus into sections 1–8 and will use these numbers to refer to it. Thus, "Excursus 2.2" refers to the question "From whom has he redeemed us?" Those passages quoted by Bernard are italicised, showing that Bernard engages with almost all of Abelard's questions.

[23] Ward, ed., *Prayers and Meditations*, 232.

[24] CCCM 11:113–18. According to CCCM 11:27–37, the final redaction of this commentary was written between the completion of the full third redaction of the *Theologia "scholarium"* and 1137, which according to CCCM 12:387–92 means in or shortly before 1137.

[25] Thomas Williams, "Sin, Grace and Redemption," *The Cambridge Companion to Abelard*, ed. Jeffery E. Brower and Kevin Guilfoy (Cambridge: CUP, 2004), 259.

[26] On this letter, see chap. 5 below.

[27] This is my own translation with some reference to the translation in *A Scholastic Miscellany: Anselm to Ockham*, ed. Eugene R. Fairweather, Library of Christian Classics, vol. 10 (London: SCM, 1956), 280–84. The text is complete, except for a few connecting phrases. My own editorial explanations are added in square brackets, and the numbering of points is mine.

Abelard, Excursus on Romans 3:19-26[28]

[1] A very great question:[29]

> What is that redemption of ours through the death of Christ? In what way does the apostle state that we are justified by his blood [Rom 3:25]—we wicked servants who have committed the very deed for which the innocent Lord was slain and who therefore seem instead to be worthy of greater punishment?

[2] We must first investigate:

1. By what necessity did God assume human nature in order to redeem us by dying in the flesh?
2. From whom has he redeemed us—that is, who was holding us captive, whether justly or by force?
3. According to what justice has he liberated us from the power of that person?
4. What was the price that he paid which that person was willing to accept [in exchange for] releasing us?

[3] It is said

1. that God has redeemed us from the power of the devil;
2. that it was the devil who rightly [*iure*] possessed total power over humanity as a result of the transgression of the first man, who became subject to the devil by voluntarily obeying him;

---

[28] After completing this translation, I came across H. Lawrence Bond, "Another Look at Abelard's Commentary on Romans 3:26" (http://www.vanderbilt. edu/AnS/religious_studies/SBL2004/larrybond.pdf), which offers a detailed analysis of the Excursus. This has led to some minor changes in my translation. The weakness of the article is that it considers the Excursus in almost total isolation from the rest of Abelard's Romans commentary. I am grateful to Richard Sturch for help with a couple of translation issues.

[29] Robert S. Franks, *A History of the Doctrine of the Work of Christ in Its Ecclesiastical Development*, vol. 1 (London: Hodder and Stoughton, [1919]), 186, draws attention to the parallels between this Excursus and Augustine, *De trinitate* 13.10.13–15.19. In 13.11.15 Augustine asks what is meant by "justified by his blood."

3. that the devil would forever possess this power unless a deliverer came.

But

[4. Does Satan have *dominion?*]

1. *Since Christ liberated the elect alone, in what way did the devil hold possession of them more than he now does, whether in this age or in the future?*[30]

2. *Is it possible that the devil also tormented the poor man resting in Abraham's bosom like the rich man who was lost,* granted that he may have tortured him less?

3. *And did he even have dominion over Abraham himself and the other elect?*[31]

4. In what way did that malign torturer have dominion over [Lazarus], who according to the record was carried by the angels into Abraham's lap, and who indeed "is now being comforted but you are being tormented," as Abraham himself bears witness [Luke 16:25]?

5. Furthermore, [Abraham] states that "a great chasm has been fixed" between the elect and the reprobate so that there is no way for the latter to cross over to the former [Luke 16:26]. Still less may the devil, who is more wicked than all others, acquire any dominion, let alone a permanent place, in that place where no unrighteous person has access.

[5. What *rights* does Satan have?][32]

1. Indeed, what right [*ius*] to possess the human race could the devil possibly have unless perhaps he had received them for purposes of torture, either because the Lord permitted this or even because he handed them over?

2. Indeed, if any slave wanted to desert his lord and place himself under the power of another, would he

---

[30] Quoted in Abael 7.18.
[31] Quoted in Abael 7.18.
[32] These points are similar to those made by Anselm in *Cur Deus homo* 1.7.

be permitted to act in such a way that his lord could
not, if he wished, justly [*iure*] seek the slave out and
bring him back?

3. Who indeed doubts that, if a slave of any master se-
    duces his fellow slave and leads him astray, causing him
    to stray from obedience to his own master, the master
    will decide that the seducer is much more guilty than
    the seduced?

4. How unjust it would be that he who led the other
    astray should as a result gain any privilege or power
    over him; and even if he had previously had any right
    over the one he had led astray, would he not by the
    wickedness of his seduction deserve to lose that right?
    As it is written, "Privilege deserves to be lost when
    someone abuses the power entrusted to him."[33] If one
    slave was about to be placed in command of another
    and to receive power over him, it would be most
    improper for the more wicked one to be in charge,
    who had absolutely no grounds for such a privilege.
    It would be much more reasonable for the one who
    was led astray to possess a full claim for reparation over
    the one who had injured him by leading him astray.

5. Furthermore, the devil has not been able to bestow
    upon humanity the immortality that he promised as
    a reward for transgression, which might have given
    him some sort of right to retain humanity.

[6. Conclusion]

1. *And so from these reasonings it seems proved that the devil
    by leading humanity astray acquired no right over him,
    except perhaps (as stated) to the extent that the Lord per-
    mitted it by handing man over for punishment to [the devil]
    to be his jailer or torturer.*[34] For humanity's only sin was
    against his own Lord, whose obedience it had forsaken.

---

[33] *Decretum Gratiani* cap. 63, causa 11.
[34] Paraphrased by William of Saint Thierry, who is quoted in Abael 5.11.

If, therefore, the Lord so wished, [he could] remit the sin, as happened with the Virgin Mary and as Christ also did for many others even before his passion—as is stated of Mary Magdalene [Luke 8:2], and as it is written that he said to the paralytic, "Be of good heart, son; your sins are remitted" [Matt 9:2].

2. If, I say, the Lord was willing to forgive human transgressors apart from his passion and to say to their torturer, "I do not want you to punish them anymore," what just complaint would the torturer have? For, as we have shown, he had received no right to torture other than permission from the Lord. So, if the Lord should cease this permission, the torturer would be left with no right, and, indeed, should he complain or murmur against the Lord, it would be appropriate for the Lord immediately to reply, "Is your eye wicked because I am good?" [Matt 20:15]. The Lord was not unjust toward the devil when, from the sinful mass [of humanity], he took sinless flesh and humanity devoid of all sin.[35] Indeed, it was through the grace of the Lord sustaining him and not by his own merits that he obtained, as man, his sinless conception and birth and remained without sin.

3. If he wanted to remit sins to others by the same grace, could he not have freed them from the punishment? Clearly, after the sins that caused the punishment have been forgiven, there appears to remain no ground for punishing them further. Could not he, who showed such grace to humanity as to combine him with himself into one person,[36] also incur the lesser cost of remitting his sins?

---

[35] The "Lord" who took sinless flesh was the Word who took human nature in the incarnation. In the following sentence the Lord whose grace sustains Christ is presumably the Father, unless Abelard is making a Nestorian distinction between the man Jesus and the divine Word.

[36] Presumably a reference to the Word's taking human nature in the incarnation.

[7. So what need is there for the Cross?][37]

1. *Since the divine compassion could have liberated humanity from sin simply by giving the order, what was the necessity, reason, or need for the Son of God, having taken flesh, to endure so many and so great things: fasting, taunts, scourging, spitting, and finally shameful and most cruel death on the Cross, together with criminals [iniquis]?*[38]

2. *How does the apostle say that we are justified or reconciled to God by the death of his Son when God should have been the more angry at humanity as they offended so much more by crucifying his Son than by contravening his first command by tasting a single piece of fruit?*[39] For the more sins were multiplied by people, the more justly should God have been angered by humanity.

3. *And if that sin of Adam was so great that it could be expiated only by the death of Christ, what expiation will there be for the very act of murdering Christ*[40] and for the evil deeds (so many and so great) committed against him or his people?

4. *Is it possible that the death of his innocent Son was so pleasing to God the Father that by it he was reconciled to us (who brought it about by sinning) and that it was on account of this that the innocent Lord was murdered?*

5. *Would he not have been able much more easily to pardon sin if this greatest sin had not taken place?*[41] Would he not have been able to do such a good thing for humanity if evil deeds had not been multiplied?

---

[37] The first of these questions can well be seen as a concluding question on the need for redemption from Satan, rounding off the conclusion on that topic. At the same time, its position and its subject matter link it with the subsequent questions about the rationale for the Cross. For some questions similar to these, see Abelard, *Theologia "scholarium" III* 119–20 (CCCM 13:549).

[38] Quoted in Abael 8.19.

[39] Quoted in Abael 8.21.

[40] Quoted in Abael 8.21. Anselm answers this question in *Cur Deus homo* 2.14–15.

[41] Quoted in Abael 8.21.

6. How have we been made more righteous through the death of the Son of God than we were before [this great sin]? To the extent that we should be freed from punishment?

7. And to whom was the price of blood paid to redeem us unless to him in whose power we were—that is, to him who handed us over to his torturer, that is, to God (as we have said)? For ransoms are organised and received not by the torturers but by the lords of those held captive.

8. Again, in what sense did he give these captives up "for a price" if he was himself the one that demanded or fixed the price for their release?

9. *To whom does it not seem cruel and unfair that someone should demand the blood of an innocent one as payment for something or that it should be in any way pleasing to him that an innocent one is killed—let alone that God should consider the death of his Son so pleasing as by it to be reconciled to the whole world?*[42]

These and similar points seem to us to pose a not insignificant question about our redemption or justification through the death of our Lord Jesus Christ.

[8. Abelard's Solution][43]

1. Now it seems to us that this is how we have been justified by the blood of Christ and reconciled to God: his Son took our nature upon himself and persevered in it to death, instructing us by both word and example.

---

[42] Quoted in Abael 8.22.

[43] Franks, *A History of the Doctrine of the Work of Christ*, vol. 1, 188, states that Abelard's solution is a fuller development of the ideas of Augustine's *De catechizandis rudibus* 4.7. This is true to the extent that Augustine there speaks of the role of the incarnation as a demonstration of God's love evoking our loving response. There is no suggestion in Augustine, however, that the work of Christ can be *reduced* to this. The word "love" appears twelve times in this solution, translating three different Latin words: *amor, caritas,* and *dilectio* (or *diligo*). There is no obvious difference in meaning of the three words in this passage.

Through this unique act of grace displayed to us he
has bound us to himself yet more by love, so that our
hearts might be inflamed by the great kindness of
divine grace, and true love should no longer dread
enduring anything for him. Indeed, we do not doubt
that it was by anticipating this same gift by faith that
the ancient Fathers were inflamed to the highest love
for God, just as people are in this time of grace. For it
is written: "Those that went before and those that followed cried out, 'Hosanna to the Son of David,'" and
so forth [Mark 11:9]. Those who live after the passion
of Christ are actually more righteous than those who
lived before; that is, they love God more, because a gift
that is fulfilled inflames people more to love than one
that is merely anticipated.

2. *Our redemption consists in the utmost love* [dilectio]
   [aroused] *in us by Christ's passion,*[44] which not only liberates us from bondage to sin but also gains for us the
   true liberty of sons of God, so that we fulfil everything
   not out of fear but rather out of love for him who has
   displayed so much grace toward us that no greater can
   be found. He himself attests this: "No one has greater
   love than to lay down his life for his friends" [John
   15:13]. Indeed, he says elsewhere of this love, "I came to
   cast fire upon the earth, and what do I want except for
   it to burn?" [Luke 12:49]. He thus testifies that he came
   to extend this true liberty of love among humanity.

3. The apostle pays careful attention to this in the following words: "Because the love of God has been
   poured out into our hearts through the Holy Spirit,
   who has been given to us. For to what end did Christ
   . . ." [Rom 5:5-6]. And again, "God shows his love
   for us in that when we still . . ." [Rom 5:8]. We shall
   expound these statements more fully in their place
   [in the commentary]. For the present, however, may

---

[44] Quoted in Abael 9.24.

this suffice as a brief statement of how we view the manner of our redemption, in keeping with brevity of exposition. Consideration of any remaining inadequacies we will defer for our treatise *Tropologies*.[45]

* * *

On the basis of this passage alone, one would conclude that Abelard reduces the significance of the Cross to its subjective effect on us. He can be and has been interpreted that way. Some have done so in order to demonstrate his heterodoxy, the best-known example being Bernard.[46] Others have come up with the same interpretation for the opposite reason, in order to claim Abelard for a purely exemplarist doctrine of the work of Christ. Hastings Rashdall famously commented that here, "for the first time—or rather for the first time since the days of the earliest and most philosophical Greek fathers—the doctrine of the atonement was stated in a way which had nothing unintelligible, arbitrary, illogical, or immoral about it; in a way which appeals to the most unsophisticated intellect, to the most unsophisticated conscience, and to the simplest piety."[47]

Is that correct? Is the Excursus Abelard's final word on the topic? Or does it need to be supplemented by what he teaches elsewhere?[48] Looking to earlier works is unsafe since he might have changed his mind. It is reasonable, though, to interpret the Excursus in the light of the remainder of his Romans commentary.[49] Here we find further

---

[45] We have no work from Abelard by that title, either because it was not written or because it has been lost.

[46] Abael 7.17, 8.22–9.25. See chap. 5 below.

[47] Hastings Rashdall, *The Idea of Atonement in Christian Theology* (London: Macmillan, 1919), 360. For a critique of Rashdall's interpretation of Abelard, see Alister McGrath, "The Moral Theory of the Atonement: An Historical and Theological Critique," *Scottish Journal of Theology* 38 (1985): 205–20.

[48] A question sharply posed by Rolf Peppermüller, *Abaelards Auslegung des Römerbriefes* (Münster: Aschendorff, 1972), 97.

[49] Many of the passages discussed below are found in Laurence W. Grensted, *A Short History of the Doctrine of the Atonement* (Manchester: Manchester University Press; and London: Longmans, Green and Co., 1920), 103–10; and Jean Rivière, *Le dogme de la rédemption au début du moyen âge* (Paris: J.Vrin, 1934), 113–23.

evidence for the view that he reduces the significance of the Cross simply to its subjective effect on us. On Romans 5:6 he asks, "I was right to say that love is poured out in our hearts, for what reason was there for Christ to die other than clearly to enlarge the love of God in us?"[50] Again, Abelard comments, Paul says that Christ "died for no other reason than that true freedom of love might be increased in us, through that highest love which he exhibited to us."[51] Abelard's exposition of Romans 5:6-9 concludes with the comment that we will be saved through Christ, "who died once for us, who often intercedes for us, and who constantly instructs us."[52]

On the other hand, Thomas Williams points in a recent study to evidence from the Romans commentary indicating that Abelard "does acknowledge an 'objective transaction' in the death of Christ."[53] Williams starts by claiming that Christ's death on the Cross is a demonstration of love only if there was some need for it, only if it accomplishes something objectively.[54] This argument may be true,

---

[50] CCCM 11:155. This and the next two passages are cited by Peppermüller, *Abaelards Auslegung des Römerbriefes*, 98–99.

[51] CCCM 11:155.

[52] CCCM 11:156.

[53] Williams, "Sin, Grace and Redemption," 260. The phrase "objective transaction" is taken from Richard Swinburne. Williams's chapter considers the two charges against Abelard of exemplarism and Pelagianism. The latter charge will be considered below in chap. 5C. Williams builds on the earlier discussion of Philip L. Quinn, "Abelard on Atonement: 'Nothing Unintelligible, Arbitrary, Illogical, or Immoral about It,'" in *Reasoned Faith: Essays in Philosophical Theology in Honor of Norman Kretzmann*, ed. Eleanore Stump (Ithaca, NY, and London: Cornell University Press, 1993), 281–95.

[54] Williams, "Sin, Grace and Redemption," 262. The same point is made by James Denney in a famous illustration: "If I were sitting on the end of the pier, on a summer day, enjoying the sunshine and the air, and someone came along and jumped into the water and got drowned 'to prove his love for me,' I should find it quite unintelligible. I might be much in need of love, but an act in no rational relation to any of my necessities could not prove it. But if I had fallen over the pier and were drowning, and someone sprang into the water, and . . . saved me from death, then I should say, 'Greater love hath no man than this.' I should say it intelligibly, because there would be an intelligible relation between the sacrifice which love made and the necessity from which it redeemed." James Denney, *The Death of Christ* (London: Tyndale Press, 1951), 103.

but if so, it establishes that Abelard *ought* to have seen an objective side to the work of Christ, not that he actually did so. To be fair, Williams claims only that this "should make us expect Abelard to acknowledge some objective benefit that accrues to us in virtue of the passion of Christ."[55] In fact, Abelard states that Christ delivers us from bondage to sin. We cannot buy ourselves back, and it required innocent blood to be given for us.[56] Williams claims that "one could hardly ask for a clearer affirmation of an 'objective transaction,'"[57] but it could be argued that this language is but a metaphorical description of how Christ's death arouses love in us that overcomes the power of sin, a process described in the Excursus. Such a reading of Abelard is not implausible given that he opposed the idea that a ransom is paid to Satan and questioned the coherence of the idea that such a payment be made to God.[58] Williams's argument is more solid where he points to passages in the remainder of the Romans commentary that refer to Christ bearing our punishment in our place, and to these we now turn.

In commenting on Romans 4:25, Abelard states that there are two ways in which it was "for our trespasses" that Christ was handed over: first, it was because of *our* sins that Christ died, and it was we who committed the sin whose punishment he bore; second, by dying he removed our sins—that is, by the price of his death he removed the punishment for our sins—and introduced us into Paradise.[59] Here we have the language of penal substitution, and it is hard to see how these statements could be reduced to the subjective effects of the Cross. Commenting on Romans 5:19, Abelard states that when we say that sins are forgiven, we mean that punishment of sin is remitted;

[55] Williams, "Sin, Grace and Redemption," 262.

[56] *Romans Commentary* 7.14 (CCCM 11:205); Williams, "Sin, Grace and Redemption," 262–63.

[57] Williams, "Sin, Grace and Redemption," 263.

[58] These issues are discussed in Williams, "Sin, Grace and Redemption," 263–65.

[59] *Romans Commentary* 4.25 (CCCM 11:153); Williams, "Sin, Grace and Redemption," 266. Abelard does, however, immediately proceed to talk about how the Cross inspires love in us: "Et per exhibitionem tantae gratiae, quia ut ipse ait maiorem dilectionem nemo habet, animos nostros a uoluntate peccandi retraheret et in summam sui dilectionem incenderet."

when we say that Christ bore our sins, we mean that he endured the punishment of our sins.[60] Finally, on Romans 8:3 Abelard explains the way in which Christ destroyed sin in the flesh. He bore in the flesh the punishment for our sin and took away from us that punishment.[61] Williams concedes that Abelard's concept of penal substitution is "admittedly sketchy" and questions how it coheres with the rest of his teaching,[62] but he has established that Abelard did not eliminate all objective significance from the death of Christ.[63]

Most scholars concur with Williams in holding that, despite the Excursus, Abelard continued to ascribe objective value to the death of Christ in his Romans commentary.[64] A century ago Rivière ar-

---

[60] *Romans Commentary* 5.19 (CCCM 11:164); Williams, "Sin, Grace and Redemption," 265–66.

[61] *Romans Commentary* 8.3 (CCCM 11:211); Williams, "Sin, Grace and Redemption," 266.

[62] Williams, "Sin, Grace and Redemption," 266–67. J. Patout Burns, "The Concept of Satisfaction in Medieval Redemption Theory," *Theological Studies* 36 (1975): 289–91, 303–4, also attributes the doctrine of penal substitution to Abelard.

[63] In another passage that attributes objective value to the work of Christ, Abelard refers to Christ's merits as making up what is lacking in ours, for our salvation. *Romans Commentary* 5.19 (CCCM 11:163): "Homo itaque factus, lege ipsa dilectionis proximi constringitur ut eos, qui sub lege erant nec per legem poterant saluari, redimeret, et quod in nostris non erat meritis ex suis suppleret. Et sicut sanctitate singularis exstitit, singularis fieret utilitate in aliorum etiam salute. Alioquin quid magnum sanctitas eius promereretur si suae tantum saluationi, non alienae sufficeret?" (This is cited by Franks, *A History of the Doctrine of the Work of Christ*, vol. 1, 191. Richard E. Weingart, *The Logic of Divine Love* [Oxford: OUP, 1970], 139–44, examines this passage at length. John Marenbon, *The Philosophy of Peter Abelard* [Cambridge: CUP, 1997], 322, questions the objectivity of Weingart's exposition of Abelard.)

[64] This conclusion is reached by Peppermüller, *Abaelards Auslegung des Römerbriefes*, 103–4, even though his account (96–104) strongly emphasises the subjective side. Weingart argues that the exemplary quality of the Cross is consequent upon its redemptive character (*Logic of Divine Love*, 125–26).

Weingart's account is not wholly satisfactory. He emphasises that it is we who need to be reconciled to God, not vice versa (66, 88–89, 92–93). There is much on those elements of traditional views that Abelard would not accept (82, 84–93, 135), but at the same time he denies that Abelard reduces the work of Christ to its subjective effects (125–26, 131–39, 145–46, 202–3). There was no extrinsic

gued that the passages just considered from the commentary are merely orthodox fragments in a system that really has no room for them.[65] In response to this claim, David Luscombe stated that passages where Abelard speaks of Christ bearing the penalty of our sins and benefiting the dead are not "merely the casual survivals of traditional language." They are evidence that while Abelard "one-sidedly developed the exemplarist thesis, he had not thereby deliberately rejected all other elements of the broader picture."[66]

It is hard to tie together all that Abelard says on the work of Christ.[67] It is probably safest to conclude that he was not wholly consistent, that in the Excursus he appears to wish to reduce Christ's work to its subjective effect but that he did not confine it to that even within the Romans commentary. This ambivalence can be seen in his commentary on Romans 8:3-4. Having explained "he condemned sin" in objective terms of Christ bearing our punishment, Abelard then proceeds to state that this means "to destroy all accusation and guilt through love, increased in us by this greatest benefit."[68] Again, on Romans 4:11 Abelard speaks of us being bought from the devil, whose slave we were, the price being the blood of Christ[69]—which

---

necessity imposed on God for the Cross, but there is "a necessity inherent in the divine nature, for God's essence is love and love must manifest itself in activity" (92–93). It is never quite clear, though, what this necessity is or what the Cross actually achieves, other than its subjective effects. This lack of clarity is not helped by Weingart's aversion to the distinction between the objective and subjective sides of Christ's work (131–32).

[65] Rivière, *Le dogme de la rédemption*, 113–28, at 126.

[66] David E. Luscombe, *The School of Peter Abelard* (Cambridge: CUP, 1969), 138.

[67] Peppermüller, *Abaelards Auslegung des Römerbriefes*, 118–21, sees this not as a conflict between Abelard's new ideas and remnants of traditional teaching but as the outworking of two different ideas: the justification and reconciliation of the individual through Christ's example; liberation from the corporate guilt of original sin through the Cross and through baptism. Against this it should be noted that Christ bore the punishments (plural) of our sins (plural): "poenas peccatorum nostrorum sustinuisse" (*Romans Commentary* 5.19 [CCCM 11:164]).

[68] *Romans Commentary* 8.4 (CCCM 11:211). Peppermüller, *Abaelards Auslegung des Römerbriefes*, 102, points out that the immediately preceding passage (on 8.2) is also in harmony with the Excursus, although less explicit.

[69] *Romans Commentary* 4.11 (CCCM 11:140).

appears flatly to contradict the argument of the Excursus. In the Excursus we see Abelard's desire to interpret the work of Christ in solely subjective terms, but he was unable to do that consistently throughout the commentary, where, as we have seen, there are passages that clearly give an objective significance to the Cross. Perhaps one could say that Abelard's heart inclined him to limit the work of Christ to its subjective effects (as seen in the Excursus) but that his head did not allow him to pursue this aim consistently (as evidenced by passages in the remainder of the commentary). In the end he made the subjective effects of Christ's work *primary*,[70] but without altogether eliminating the objective effects.

[70] This is how Grensted puts it (*Short History of the Doctrine of the Atonement*, 105), and Quinn concurs with this judgement ("Abelard on Atonement," 291).

3

BERNARD
AS THEOLOGIAN OF THE CROSS

A. Bernard as a Monastic Theologian

There was a time when the words "theology" and "theologian" were reserved for scholastic theology and its practitioners. Those using these terms in this way could appeal to Bernard's own usage. He uses these words only of Abelard, and not in a complimentary fashion.[1] More recent scholarship has, however, reassessed Bernard's relation to theology. Étienne Gilson's *The Mystical Theology of Saint Bernard*, based on a series of lectures that Gilson gave in Wales in 1933, was the pioneering work of this reassessment.[2] Gilson's conclusion was that "St. Bernard was in no wise a metaphysician, but he must remain in our eyes a theologian whose speculative vigour and power of synthesis puts him among the greatest."[3] Jean Leclercq,

---

[1] See chap. 5, nn. 32–33. The word "theology" had, however, long been used in the monastic tradition (Jean Leclercq, "Études sur le vocabulaire monastique du moyen âge," *Studia Anselmiana* 48 [1961]: 70–79, 157–59; Jean Leclercq, "Naming the Theologies of the Early Twelfth Century," *Mediaeval Studies* 53 [1991]: 330).

[2] Étienne Gilson, *The Mystical Theology of Saint Bernard* (London: Sheed and Ward, 1940). The lectures were given in English (p. vii), but the book first appeared in French in 1934. Part of the significance of Gilson's work is that he was a specialist in medieval philosophy, writing books on Augustine, Thomas Aquinas, Bonaventure, and Duns Scotus.

[3] Gilson, *Mystical Theology*, viii. Earlier, in 1911, Martin Grabmann had referred to Bernard's deep theological thought (cited by Ulrich Köpf, "Monastische und scholastische Theologie," *Bernhard von Clairvaux*, 105–6).

acknowledging his debt to Gilson, further developed this revised assessment of Bernard.[4] Prior to scholasticism and continuing alongside it, argues Leclercq, there was a tradition of "monastic theology,"[5] of which Bernard was a leading exponent.[6] While Bernard himself did not like the word "theology," his secretary, Geoffrey of Auxerre, later referred to Bernard as "that great theologian," referring in particular to his *Sermones in Cantica*.[7] Bernard was the last great representative of the earlier medieval tradition of monastic theology, and Mabillon gave him the title "the last of the Fathers."[8] Bernard has also famously been called the "mellifluous doctor," and Pope Pius VIII proclaimed him a Doctor of the Church in 1830.[9]

Leclercq identifies the sources, object, and method of monastic theology. While scholastics made use of pre-Christian philosophy, monastic theologians were suspicious of it and confined themselves almost entirely to Christian sources. While monastic theology concentrated on central Christian doctrines and their practical outworking, scholasticism encouraged an abstract and speculative theology. Likewise, while scholastic theology progressed by the use of speculation and disputation, by logic and analysis, monastic theology drew inspiration

[4] Jean Leclercq, "Le saint Bernard de Gilson: Une théologie de la vie monastique," *Doctor communis* 38 (1985): 227–33.

[5] Very influential in disseminating the contrast between monastic and scholastic theology was Jean Leclercq, *L'amour des lettres et le désir de Dieu* (Paris: Éditions du Cerf, 1957); *The Love of Learning and the Desire for God: A Study of Monastic Culture*, trans. Catharine Misrahi (New York: Fordham University Press, 1961).

[6] See Jean Leclercq, "S. Bernard et la théologie monastique du XIIᵉ siècle," in *Saint Bernard théologien*, ASOC 9, no. 3-4 (July–December 1953): 7–23.

[7] "Magnus ille theologus" in the prologue of book 2 of his commentary on the Song of Songs (Jean Leclercq, "Les écrits de Geoffroy d'Auxerre," RESB 1:36).

[8] Mabillon described Bernard as "ultimus inter Patres, sed primis certe non impar" (PL 182:26), a phrase used in the encyclical *Doctor Mellifluus* of Pope Pius XII. See Olivier Rousseau, "S. Bernard, 'Le dernier des pères,'" in *Saint Bernard théologien*, 300–308; and Thomas Merton, *The Last of the Fathers* (London: Hollis and Carter, 1954).

[9] Jean Leclercq, "Saint Bernard docteur," RESB 2:387–90; Jean Leclercq, "Études sur saint Bernard et le texte de ses écrits," ASOC 9 (1953): 184–91. The ideas of Bernard as "doctor" and "mellifluous" both go back to the twelfth century, but they were rarely combined before the fifteenth century.

from Scripture, liturgical prayer, and the practices of the contemplative life. These two approaches to theology are both necessary and legitimate, and they are to be seen as complementary to one another.[10]

Bernard's account of the different motivations for seeking knowledge well illustrates the monastic approach. To seek knowledge for its own sake is shameful curiosity; to seek it for the sake of one's reputation is shameful vanity; to seek it for financial gain or for honours is shameful profiteering; to seek it for one's own benefit is prudence; to seek it in order to serve others is love.[11]

Later Leclercq extended the distinction between types of theology from twofold to threefold: the contemplative theology of the cloister, the pastoral theology of the cathedral school, and the speculative theology of the intellectuals. He recognised that these were not watertight groupings and that reality was more complex than this.[12] Ulrich Köpf, surveying the changing perception of Bernard in recent scholarship, like Leclercq, expressed reservations about the distinction between monastic and scholastic theology while still finding it valuable and indispensable.[13] It is helpful and legitimate to characterise Bernard as a monastic theologian, so long as we don't regard these distinctions as rigid.

Bernard's relation to the schools is complex.[14] It is true that he was unhappy with some of the directions being taken by contemporary theologians and that he opposed both Abelard and Gilbert

---

[10] Leclercq, "S. Bernard et la théologie monastique du XIIᵉ siècle," 22–23.

[11] SC 36.3, reversing the order of the last two. See Sent 1.19, 3.57, 3.108 for shorter versions.

[12] Jean Leclercq, "The Renewal of Theology," *Renaissance and Renewal in the Twelfth Century*, ed. Robert L. Benson and Giles Constable (Cambridge, MA: Harvard University Press, 1982), 70–84. For an account of his evolving view, see Jean Leclercq, "Naming the Theologies of the Early Twelfth Century," *Mediaeval Studies* 53 (1991): 327–31.

[13] Köpf, "Monastische und scholastische Theologie," 96–135.

[14] Matthew A. Doyle, *Bernard of Clairvaux and the Schools* (Spoleto: Fondazione Centro Italiano di Studi sull'alto Medioevo, 2005); Jacques Verger, "Le cloître et les écoles," *Bernard de Clairvaux: Histoire, mentalités, spiritualité*, SCh 380 (Paris: Éditions du Cerf, 1992), 459–73; Jacques Verger, "Saint Bernard et les scolastiques," *Vies et légendes de saint Bernard de Clairvaux* (Cîteaux: Commentarii Cistercienses, 1993), 201–10.

of Poitiers, but that is only one side of his relation to the schools.
Again, his *On Conversion, a Sermon to Clerics* sought to lure budding
scholars away from the schools to the cloister,[15] and according to the
Vita prima Bernardi, this sermon netted three souls.[16] On the other
hand, Bernard famously supported Peter Lombard's academic career,
despite the fact that he had been a disciple of Abelard.[17] Also, Leclercq
rightly argues that Bernard's *De gratia et libero arbitrio* has some of the
features of scholastic theology—although, unlike much scholastic
theology, Bernard presents his teaching in a positive manner, not in
opposition to the views of others.[18] This latter treatise of Bernard
in particular was widely cited by later medieval scholastic theologians, mostly Franciscans rather than Dominicans.[19] There are other
places in his works where Bernard employed dialectical methods in
theological debate.[20]

A key issue for scholastic theology was the relation between faith
and reason.[21] On this issue there are clear contrasts among Anselm,
Abelard, and Bernard and their respective teaching about the Cross.
Anselm is a credible candidate for the title of "founder of scholasticism," depending on how one defines the term. He maintained the
traditional Augustinian programme of "faith seeking understanding."

---

[15] Conv; SBOp 4:69–116; especially Conv 13–15 and 20–15.

[16] *Vita prima Bernardi* 4.2.10 (PL 185:327).

[17] Ep 410. For other examples, see John R. Sommerfeldt, "Bernard of Clairvaux
and Scholasticism," *Papers of the Michigan Academy of Science, Art and Letters* 48
(1963): 266–70.

[18] Leclercq, "S. Bernard et la théologie monastique du XIIᵉ siècle," 17–18.

[19] Jean Châtillon, "L'influence de S. Bernard sur la pensée scolastique au XIIᵉ et
au XIIIᵉ siècle," *Saint Bernard théologien*, 268–88. See also Artur M. Landgraf, "Der
heilige Bernhard in seinem Verhältnis zur Theologie des zwölften Jahrhunderts,"
Bernhard von Clairvaux: Mönch und Mystiker, ed. Joseph Lortz (Wiesbaden: Franz
Steiner, 1955), 57–58.

[20] See Sommerfeldt, "Bernard of Clairvaux and Scholasticism," 270–77. Other examples include Conv 5 and Bapt. "Es wäre aber verkehrt zu meinen, daß Bernhard
sich gegen die dialektische Methode as solche ausgesprochen hätte" (Landgraf, "Der
heilige Bernhard in seinem Verhältnis zur Theologie des zwölften Jahrhunderts," 46).

[21] "The effort to harmonize reason and faith was the motive force of medieval
Christian thought" (Gordon Leff, *Medieval Thought: St Augustine to Ockham* [Har-
mondsworth: Penguin, 1958], 19).

He used the same phrase as the title for his *Proslogion*, and in his *Cur Deus homo* he applied the method to the question of redemption, arguing that the incarnation and the Cross are reasonable because no other option was open to God.

A generation later the new scholastic approach to theology pioneered by Anselm had established itself, and Bernard found himself drawn into controversy with Abelard, its greatest contemporary exponent. Abelard, by contrast with Anselm, stated in the prologue to his *Sic et non* that "by doubting we come to enquiry, and by enquiry we perceive the truth."[22] In his famous Excursus, Abelard applied this method to the Cross and questioned aspects of the traditional teaching. The approach of Bernard the mystical writer was very different. Johannes Schuck in 1926 argued that in his *Sermones in Cantica* Bernard worked from the principle of *credo ut experiar* ("I believe in order to experience"), by contrast with Augustine and Anselm's *credo ut intelligam* ("I believe in order to understand"): if we believe, then one day we will reap the harvest of experience.[23] But while his *Sermones in Cantica* portray faith as the way to experience, in his response to Abelard Bernard's approach is closer to Anselm's "faith seeking understanding." Throughout his works Bernard seven times quotes Isaiah 7:9 (LXX), "Unless you will believe, you will not understand," once being in opposition to Abelard.[24]

---

[22] *Medieval Literary Theory and Criticism c. 1100–c. 1375: The Commentary Tradition*, ed. Alastair J. Minnis and Alexander B. Scott, rev. ed. (Oxford: OUP, 1991), 99; Peter Abailard, *Sic et non: A Critical Edition*, vol. 1, ed. Blanche B. Boyer and Richard McKeon (Chicago and London: University of Chicago Press, 1976), 103.

[23] SC 84.7. See Kilian McDonnell, "Spirit and Experience in Bernard of Clairvaux," *Theological Studies* 58 (1997): 3–18, with quotation of Schuck at 4. McDonnell emphasises that "however highly he esteems experience, clearly, in spite of appearances to the contrary, Bernard's ultimate norm is not experience but faith and the Scriptures" (9). Elsewhere after citing Isa 7:9 (LXX), "Unless you will believe you will not understand," Bernard states that "if you will not long for [God], you will not love perfectly" (Ep 18.2). See also Erich Kleineidam, "Wissen, Wissenschaft, Theologie bei Bernhard von Clairvaux," *Bernhard von Clairvaux: Mönch und Mystiker*, ed. Joseph Lortz (Wiesbaden: Franz Steiner, 1955), 155.

[24] SC 28.5, 38.2, 48.6; Sent 1.12; Epp 18.2, 107.10, 338.1, the last of these being against Abelard. Burch rather implausibly presents Abelard as the last of the

The contrast between Bernard and Abelard can be seen from Bernard's letter-treatise *On the Errors of Peter Abelard* in the first paragraph that he devotes to the issue of redemption (5.11). If Abelard's approach is to question tradition, Bernard's is to accept it; where Abelard employs rational investigation, Bernard advocates humble acceptance of mystery. Earlier scholarship often portrayed this as an absolute contrast, Abelard the rationalist versus Bernard the anti-intellectual. But these are caricatures, neither of which is true. It would be wrong to suggest that Bernard left no room for rational investigation and Abelard none for faith, as if Bernard were unable to question tradition and Abelard had no time for it.[25]

This is not to say that there were no differences. The difference between Bernard and Abelard lies not so much in the latter's propensity to ask questions as in the manner in which he answers them. Abelard's Excursus is famous, not to say infamous, for the questions that he posed concerning the work of Christ. Bernard was himself quite capable of using the method of questioning, and he had already done so with the issue of redemption in chapter 11 of his *In Praise of the New Knighthood*. The list below includes only genuine questions, not rhetorical questions such as "How will the death of Christ profit someone who lives evilly or the life of Christ someone who dies

---

Fathers, who applied the Augustinian and Anselmian principle of faith seeking understanding, and Bernard as the innovator who was the first of the scholastics (Bernard of Clairvaux, *The Steps of Humility*, ed. George B. Burch [Notre Dame: University of Notre Dame Press, 1963], 268–74). He is rightly chided for this by Amatus Van den Bosch, "L'intelligence de la foi chez saint Bernard," Cîteaux 8 (1957): 92–99.

[25] See Jean Jolivet, *Arts du langage et théologie chez Abélard*, 2nd ed. (Paris: J. Vrin, 1982), 348; Wendelin Knoch, "Der Streit zwischen Bernhard von Clairvaux und Petrus Abaelard—ein exemplarisches Ringen um verantworteten Glauben," *Freiburger Zeitschrift für Philosophie und Theologie* 38 (1991): 299–315; John R. Sommerfeldt, "Abelard and Bernard of Clairvaux," *Papers of the Michigan Academy of Science, Art and Letters* 46 (1961): 493–501. Elizabeth Gössmann, "Dialektische und rhetorische Implikationen der Auseinandersetzung zwischen Abaelard und Bernhard von Clairvaux um die Gotteserkenntnis," *Sprache und Erkenntnis im Mittelalter*, vol. 2, ed. Jan P. Beckmann and others (Berlin and New York: Walter de Gruyter, 1981), 890–902, surveys the change in the scholarly assessment of Abelard, especially since 1932.

culpably?" (18). Some of the questions, like the first three, simply introduce a point, while others are more obviously responding to objections, being introduced by words like *inquis*, *ais*, or *sed*. The critical edition puts some of these questions in quotation marks, and this is replicated below.

- How do we know that Christ can remit sins? (21)
- How do we know that he is God? (21)
- But how can we be confident that he has removed death? (22)
- How could he die if he was God? (22)
- But how can the death of this man be effective for another? (22)
- "What sort of justice," you say, "is this, the innocent dying for the ungodly?" (23)
- "Even if the righteous is not unjustly able to make satisfaction for the sinner, how can one do this for many? It would appear sufficient for justice for one person by dying to restore life to one person." (23)
- But maybe one can restore righteousness to many, but not life? (23)
- "But," you say, "it is deservedly that we are all involved in Adam's offence because we sinned in him, we were in him when he sinned, and we are born from his flesh through the concupiscence of the flesh." (24)[26]
- "But carnal concupiscence," you say, "is evidence of the transmission of the heritage of the flesh and the sin that we feel in the flesh manifestly proves that we are descended, according to the flesh, from the flesh of a sinner." (24)[27]
- If, then, the law of the Spirit of life in Christ Jesus has delivered us from the law of sin and death, why do we still die rather than being immediately clothed with immortality? (28)

---

[26] This is not actually a question, but there is the implied objection that we have no such intimate connection with Christ.

[27] Again there is the implied objection that there is no such evidence for our spiritual heritage.

At times this method of questioning is not so far removed from Abelard's in the Excursus. The difference lies mainly in the spirit in which it is done and the nature of the answers given. It is with some justice that John Sommerfeldt argues that Bernard was concerned with Abelard's errors, not his method, though that is not the whole story.[28]

B. Bernard on the Cross

As we have seen, most historical theological accounts of the doctrine of the Cross in the eleventh and twelfth centuries focus heavily on Anselm and Abelard; and in many such accounts the only reference to Bernard is to the fact that he helped to secure Abelard's condemnation at the Council of Sens in 1141 and subsequently at Rome.[29] But Bernard's doctrine of the Cross was no less developed than that of Anselm or Abelard and, in my view, is considerably richer, fuller, and more satisfactory than either of theirs.

Bernard's teaching on the Cross is rich, but it is less systematic than that of Anselm. There is no Bernardine treatise devoted to the topic. Instead, there are references to the doctrine of the Cross scattered throughout all Bernard's works, with some sections of sustained exposition. It is tempting to state that his teaching is less systematic than that of Abelard, too, but that is not really true. Abelard's famous Excursus is relatively brief (under two thousand words in the translation given in chapter 2). Bernard's response in his *Epistle* 190, on *The Errors of Peter Abelard*, is longer and no less systematic,[30] answering Abelard's points one by one. The reason why Abelard rather than Bernard figures so prominently in the history of this doctrine is that

---

[28] John R. Sommerfeldt, *Bernard of Clairvaux on the Life of the Mind* (New York and Mahwah, NJ: Newman Press, 2004), 120–38. He allows, though, that Bernard was badly informed about Abelard's view of the relation between faith and reason. Abelard did not, for example, claim a more secret revelation.

[29] See chap. 1A. For the date of the council, see chap. 4, n. 7.

[30] This is so in part because Abelard himself was not particularly systematic. See Marcia Colish, "Systematic Theology and Theological Renewal in the Twelfth Century," *Journal of Medieval and Renaissance Studies* 18 (1988): 146–47.

Liberal Theology since the nineteenth century has found Abelard's Excursus very congenial. Most histories of the doctrine ignore Bernard, confining themselves to his opposition to Abelard rather than considering his teaching in its own right.[31]

Bernard refers repeatedly to the Cross. As stated in the preface, I have identified 669 passages where he does so. These passages are numbered and in the second and third parts of this book are cited as #27, and so forth.[32] Appendix I provides a full index of these passages. What is meant by "passage" here? First, it refers to sections. Thus, a sustained discussion in *De diligendo deo* 3.7–9 counts as three passages.[33] Second, where a discussion of the Cross continues over several sections, even sections that may not explicitly mention the Cross count as passages. For example, in Nat 3.4–6, though only section 4 explicitly mentions the Cross (the passion), the theme of the passion is carried through in sections 5 and 6, where Bernard discusses the relation between the disease and the medicine. Similarly, Nat 5.1–5 is a sustained account of the passion, even though the Cross is not mentioned in every section.

Finally, while the overwhelming majority of passages refer indisputably to the Cross, in some cases it is a matter of judgement whether a passage refers to the Cross. Here there is a measure of objectivity in that the same criteria have been used throughout. For example, references to Christ defeating Satan (e.g., using Matt 12:29 = Luke 11:21-22) are taken to refer to the Cross.[34] Although I have searched through all of Bernard's writings, it is likely that there are passages that I have missed. At a late stage in the proceedings I found two new passages; these have been numbered 261a and 428a in

---

[31] See chap. 1 above.

[32] Where the reference is to one passage only (or to a single sequence of passages such as ##601–6), it is given in the body of the text; where it is to a number of separate passages, it is given in a footnote.

[33] This means that with the *Sentences* and *Parables* a "passage" can be as much as five or six pages of Latin text, as in #520, #530, #546, and #553. This inconsistency in length is the price of consistency in the criterion used.

[34] There are places where Bernard uses these verses without referring to Christ's defeat of Satan, and these are not counted—e.g., Pent 3.1; Conv 14.27.

order to avoid having to renumber over four hundred passages. Any passages that have been overlooked will not be major passages, and whatever they say is extremely unlikely to make any difference at all to the picture that has emerged from the 669 passages considered.

Many of these passages contain no more than a passing reference to the Cross, a larger number make one or more significant points about it, and a smaller number contain sustained exposition of the theme. It is obviously these last that will most interest us, and the following three chapters contain translations, with comments, of the sustained exposition of the Cross found in six important works. It would be wrong, though, to focus exclusively on such passages. The importance of the Cross for Bernard is seen precisely by the way in which he mentions it so often. It is also seen in the richness of the vocabulary that he uses. He speaks repeatedly of Christ's death as a sacrifice offered as a satisfaction bringing reconciliation and redemption. Through it, death and the devil were defeated and we have been set free. Christ bore our punishment on the Cross and paid our debt by his blood. He purged our sins and made peace between earth and heaven. And so on. It is only occasionally that Bernard expounds these themes at greater length, but the frequency of their mention shows how fundamental and important for his theology they were. The longer explanations simply fill in the content that is intended by the briefer references.

Significant is not just the number of references to the Cross but their distribution. Amatus Van den Bosch claims that Bernard's Mariology and Christology are found almost exclusively in his sermons.[35] This is certainly not true of his teaching on the Cross.[36] Our 669 passages are distributed across the whole spectrum of his corpus. The sermons have the narrowest of overall majorities, with 337 out of 669 passages, but the *Sermones in Cantica* and the letters each have 115, while the sentences and parables (counted together) and the treatises

---

[35] Van den Bosch, "L'intelligence de la foi chez saint Bernard," 85.

[36] Gillian R. Evans, *The Mind of St. Bernard of Clairvaux* (Oxford: OUP, 1983), 162, states that Bernard presented his teaching on redemption in his preaching rather than write a treatise on it. While the sermons do predominate, there are two substantial expositions in treatises: Tpl and Abael. See chaps. 4 and 5 below.

each have 51.[37] If we count the three letter-treatises (including that against Abelard)[38] as treatises rather than letters, the figure rises to 78 for the treatises and drops to 88 for the letters. A fairer way would be to count the references per volume of the critical edition, which takes into account the fact that there are three volumes of sermons for only one of treatises.[39] The volumes of sermons score highest, with 91, 164, and 81 passages each.[40] The two volumes of *Sermones in Cantica* together contain 115, as do the two volumes of letters, but whereas the passages are evenly divided in the former volumes, with the volumes of letters the totals are 45 and 70. Finally, the treatises volume has 53,[41] and the sentences and parables volume has 51. While the distribution is not completely even, there is no doubt that Bernard's teaching is spread across the whole spectrum of his corpus and that no genre of writing is excluded. In short, the Cross is not a topic that Bernard addressed on selected occasions only.

Bernard refers repeatedly to the Cross. But to what extent does he have a *theology* of the Cross?[42] Jean Rivière states that the early Fathers "merely spoke of [redemption] incidentally" and left us with "a multitude of fragmentary views and texts concerning details of the doctrine," but failed to provide a real synopsis of the doctrine. Expiatory sacrifice and penal substitution lay at the heart of their teaching, but they never sought "its inmost reason or ultimate cause." The idea of sacrifice is "posited but not explained or justified" in the Fathers' writings.[43] Rivière argues that for the early Fathers, the repairing of sin by a proportionate satisfaction is the central truth

---

[37] See appendix I for the data. I have ignored the two passages in OfVict because this work does not fit into any of these categories.

[38] The three are Mor, Bapt, and Abael.

[39] For this purpose SBOp 6/1 and 6/2 are counted as two separate volumes.

[40] The astute reader might note that 91 + 164 + 81 = 336, while 337 passages come from the sermons. The discrepancy arises from the fact that the 337th passage (#667) comes from a sermon that is not found in SBOp.

[41] This time counting the two passages from OfVict.

[42] In other words, to what extent is his teaching on the Cross theologically coherent? Comparison to later "theologies of the Cross" is not intended.

[43] Jean Rivière, *The Doctrine of the Atonement: A Historical Essay*, vol. 1 (London: Kegan Paul, Trench, Trübner and Co., 1909), 320–22.

from which all others flow. The Fathers, however, presented many different ideas about the work of Christ but "never succeeded in finding a simple idea, which, by throwing light on the others, might give them both force and oneness." According to Rivière, Anselm's theory of satisfaction was the "one simple idea [that] sufficed to combine all the scattered details in one harmonious synthesis."[44]

Where does Bernard stand here? He certainly provides us with "a multitude of fragmentary views and texts concerning details of the doctrine" and many "scattered details." Equally certainly, he does not provide "one simple idea [that] sufficed to combine all the scattered details in one harmonious synthesis." Rivière wrote in the period between the nineteenth century's reduction of the doctrine to a choice between objective and subjective models, and Aulén's reduction of it to the classic idea or model. Today there is, rightly, more suspicion about claims to have reduced the doctrine to "one simple idea." That Bernard did not do this is to his credit. But does Bernard provide us with "a real synopsis of the doctrine" or simply leave us with a kaleidoscope of "fragmentary views and texts concerning details of the doctrine"?[45] Like the Fathers, he certainly wrote about redemption "incidentally," but he also a number of times gave a sustained exposition of the doctrine. He was also forced to confront questions of coherence as a result of the penetrating questions posed by Abelard. To what extent did he succeed? Rivière argues that in his response to Abelard, Bernard "poses as a defender of the faith, but not as a theologian." Rivière concedes that in *De laude novae militiae* Bernard does seek some explanation of the mystery of redemption, but adds that despite this search Bernard was nowhere "inclined to study seriously the doctrine of the Atonement." His aim was to expound the doctrine and repeat the teaching of the Fathers, with little concern to explain it.[46] In his later work Rivière reaches a similar conclusion. In Bernard's letter-treatise we find all

[44] Jean Rivière, *The Doctrine of the Atonement: A Historical Essay*, vol. 2 (London: Kegan Paul, Trench, Trübner and Co., 1909), 251–54.

[45] Rivière, *Doctrine of the Atonement*, vol. 1, 321.

[46] Rivière, *Doctrine of the Atonement*, vol. 2, 67–71.

the elements of a dogma of redemption, but they are summarised with great vigour rather than theologically analysed.[47]

Leclercq's assessment is rather different. Writing of Bernard's teaching as a whole (though it could equally be said of his teaching on the Cross in particular), he states, "It is now clear that in Saint Bernard we find a theology, a structured, elaborate, and sometimes subtle body of teaching. His work also includes speculative theology: he had a proven capacity for vigorous and precise thought on the Christian mysteries. But his teaching is not scholastic in the sense that it is not systematic. It is, rather, synthetic; everything is closely linked together."[48]

Gillian Evans reaches a similar conclusion. Bernard's teaching on the incarnation and redemption is "more comprehensive, if less fully worked out, than that of Anselm." It is only to a limited extent original, but "it makes a considerable contribution in its attempt to reconcile views which seemed to many contemporaries contradictory, or, at best, alternatives."[49] She concludes that Bernard's "teaching on Incarnation and Redemption, piecemeal though it is, is both consistent and comprehensive."[50]

When expounding Bernard's teaching on the Cross, we shall need to evaluate these rival claims.

C. Bernard's Use of Scripture

There is another way into Bernard's theology. Bernard's writings are permeated by biblical citations and allusions. Jean Leclercq quotes with approval the comment of Pierre Dumontier that Bernard spoke "Biblical" in the way that one speaks French, though he thought it more accurate to say that he *wrote* Biblical.[51] The works of Bernard

[47] Jean Rivière, "Le dogme de la rédemption au début du moyen âge III—rôle de saint Bernard," RSR 13 (1933): 203.

[48] Jean Leclercq, "General Introduction to the Works of Saint Bernard (III)," CSQ 40 (2005): 365.

[49] Evans, *Mind of St. Bernard of Clairvaux*, 153.

[50] Evans, *Mind of St. Bernard of Clairvaux*, 162.

[51] Jean Leclercq, "De quelques procédés du style biblique de S. Bernard," RESB 3:249. Dumontier's comment, from his *Saint Bernard et la Bible* (Paris: Desclée de

are a tapestry of which the thread is biblical. The whole is a work of art in which warp and weft are knotted harmoniously together.[52] The editors of the *Sancti Bernardi Opera* edition have done an excellent work of listing the citations and allusions, and for many of Bernard's works they average at something like one reference for every two lines. There are a total of some thirty-one thousand references in the eight volumes.[53] The biblical passages cited include half of the verses of the New Testament and one in every six and a half verses (15.5 percent) of the Old Testament.[54] These are impressive totals and compare well with most other theologians.[55] In fact,

---

Brouwer, 1953), 157, is oft quoted. Jean Leclercq and Jean Figuet, "La Bible dans les homélies de S. Bernard sur 'Missus est,'" RESB 3:229–37, refer to Bernard's biblical vocabulary, as does Christine Mohrmann, "Observations sur la langue et le style de saint Bernard," SBOp 2:xiv–xvii. Leclercq also argues that Bernard *thought* biblically: "Le cheminement biblique de la pensée de S. Bernard," RESB 4:11–33. Concerning the *Sentences* in particular, Leclercq goes on to say that Bernard *sees* biblically: "Introduction to the *Sentences* of Bernard of Clairvaux," CSQ 46 (2011): 286–88. For Bernard's heavy reliance upon Scripture, see *Vita prima Bernardi* 1.4.24 (PL 185:241), cited by Dumontier, *Saint Bernard et la Bible*, 117, 129. For Bernard's use of Scripture in expounding the Cross, see Ulrich Köpf, "Schriftauslegung als Ort der Kreuzestheologie Bernhards von Clairvaux," *Bernhard von Clairvaux*, 199–208.

[52] Henri Rochais and Jean Figuet, "Le jeu biblique de Bernard," Coll 47 (1985): 119.

[53] Jean Figuet, "La Bible de Bernard: Données et ouvertures," SCh 380:237. On the way in which Bernard used Scripture, see Natalie B. Van Kirk, "Finding One's Way through the Maze of Language: Rhetorical Usages That Add Meaning in Saint Bernard's Style(s)," CSQ 42 (2007): 11–35.

[54] Figuet, "La Bible de Bernard," SCh 380:238–39, contains very helpful tables setting out the statistics for each portion of Scripture, with analysis on 240–45. Bernard's sources vary from the Vulgate to the Old Latin translation, to the liturgy, to patristic sources (245–52). His knowledge of Scripture does not simply come from his own private reading of it (Jean Leclercq, "S. Bernard et la tradition biblique d'après les Sermons sur les Cantiques," RESB 1:317–18). For an attempt to trace patristic sources in these sermons, see Jean Leclercq, "Aux sources des sermons sur les Cantiques," RESB 1:275–98.

[55] The index to Karl Barth's *Church Dogmatics* gives 16,918 separate references, but these will be references given by Barth himself, not allusions detected by an editor. Barth refers to 46 percent of Old Testament verses and 75 percent of New Testament verses, an impressive total, though some will simply be citations of long passages (Christina A. Baxter, "Barth—a Truly Biblical Theologian?" *Tyndale Bulle-*

Bernard's allusions to Scripture and use of biblical language extend well beyond even this large number.[56] "Convinced not only of the truth of the Bible but also of its beauty, its value for salvation, and its efficacy for moral conversion, Bernard used it as much as possible, in all kinds of ways, according to the full range of its meaning, and with complete freedom."[57]

Leclercq analyses a sample passage and concludes that Bernard has produced a mosaic of biblical fragments, skilfully arranged.[58] He also refers to his "anthological method."[59] Bernard does not simply juxtapose biblical passages but composes them into a symphony, playing on the music of the words.[60] As Leclercq puts it elsewhere, "some pages are nothing short of biblical mosaics in which not only the words but also the style, grammar, rhythm, and even silences are inspired by the Latin Bible."[61] Sometimes this is just a play on words, a *jeu biblique*, where the words have a meaning quite different from their original context.[62] In one instance Bernard echoes a

---

tin 38 [1987]: 3–6). It must be remembered that Barth's *Dogmatics* amount to some six million words, almost three times the length of Thomas's *Summa Theologiae*, and that Barth is handling Scripture very differently from Bernard.

[56] Rochais and Figuet, "Le jeu biblique de Bernard," 121–26, argue this, giving many examples.

[57] Rochais and Figuet, "Le jeu biblique de Bernard," 119 (my translation).

[58] RESB 3:256, after an analysis of Miss 1.1 (3:249–56).

[59] RESB 3:249. See also Leclercq and Figuet, RESB 3:237–41. The term "procédé anthologique" is borrowed from René Laurentin's work on Luke 1–2.

[60] Jean Leclercq, "La Bible dans les homélies de S. Bernard sur 'Missus est,'" RESB 3:257. The musical theme recurs in the conclusion of Jean Leclercq, "Sur le caractère littéraire des sermons de S. Bernard," RESB 3:209–10, where Bernard is compared to Mozart. Both were noted for "la qualité dans la simplicité."

[61] Leclercq, "General Introduction to the Works of Saint Bernard (III)," 368. For more on Bernard's handling of Scripture, see Leclercq, "S. Bernard et la tradition biblique d'après les Sermons sur les Cantiques," 298–319.

[62] See Leclercq and Figuet, RESB 3:241–45. Bernard himself admits to indulging in word play (*litteralis lusus*) and defends his use of the word "play" (SC 61.2). On Bernard's word plays in general, see Jean Figuet, "Des jeux de mots de saint Bernard . . . à saint Bernard," Coll 52 (1990): 66–83. He estimates that there is on average one word play per page of SBOp (74). For a literary study of his word plays, see Dorette Sabersky-Bascho, *Studien zur Paronomasie bei Bernhard von Clairvaux* (Freiburg [CH]: Universitätsverlag, 1979).

passage from Job (10:22), "Ubi . . . nullus ordo sed sempiternus horror inhabitat," by stating, "Ubi nullus dolor sed sempiternus honor inhabitat."[63] Here Bernard has adapted Job's words to say something totally different. It is not that Bernard is (wrongly) claiming the support of Job for what he is saying, but simply that "Biblical" is the language that he uses to express himself. There is a difference between mere verbal allusion, where Bernard uses biblical language to express an idea, and citations or quotations, where Bernard is to some extent appealing to a passage for support, not just borrowing its turn of phrase. Where in quoting he changes the wording of a passage, this need not reflect a variant reading or a faulty memory—at times he deliberately alters the wording for his own purposes.[64]

Conveniently for our purposes, Bernard has the habit of repeatedly using the same passage to make the same point. Thus, for example, he repeatedly describes Christ on the Cross as repaying what he had not stolen, each time using Psalm 69:4: "I am forced to restore what I did not steal." One way to trace a theme in Bernard's writings, then, is to follow the trail of biblical allusions.[65] The range of passages cited (and the frequency of citation) gives some idea of the breadth of Bernard's teaching. There are extensive references to the passion narratives. Isaiah 53 and key passages in Paul are also heavily cited.[66] There follows a list of the Bible verses (or groups of verses when they regularly come together) that Bernard applies to the Cross eight or more times in our 669 passages. This list also includes some

[63] Epi var 7, cited in Rochais and Figuet, "Le jeu biblique de Bernard," 125.

[64] For examples of this, see John D. Anderson, "Paul in Book 5 of the *De consideratione* of Bernard of Clairvaux," CSQ 42 (2007): 142–44. More examples will be found in part 3 below.

[65] SBOp 9 is an index to them: Guido Hendrix, ed., *Index Biblicus in Opera Omnia S. Bernardi* (Turnhout: Brepols, 1998).

[66] On Bernard's appropriation of Isa 53, see Donato Bono, "Il *Servo Sofferente (Is 53)* nelle opere di san Bernardo," *Rivista cistercense* 28 (2011): 49–86. On Bernard's appropriation of Paul, see Gertrud Frischmuth, *Die paulinische Konzeption in der Frömmigkeit Bernhards von Clairvaux* (Gütersloh: C. Bertelsmann, 1933), which contains only a few pages relating to the Cross (52–53, 324–25). Leclercq, "S. Bernard et la tradition biblique d'après les Sermons sur les Cantiques," 299–300, states that Bernard's piety could be called "Pauline," referring to the title of Frischmuth's work.

citations that were missed by the critical edition.[67] Parallel passages in the gospels are grouped together, and the total number of *different* passages where they are cited is given.[68]

The most popular texts[69] are two from Paul: Galatians 6:14 (twenty-three times) and Philippians 2:8 (twenty-two times). These are followed by Matthew 12:29 = Luke 11:21-22 (twenty times) and Isaiah 53:7-9 (nineteen times).[70] Close behind come John 15:13 (nineteen times) and 19:34 (eighteen times) and Luke 23:39-43 (eighteen times). The range of biblical citations—including both narrative and doctrinal texts pointing to the love behind the Cross, to its objective achievement, and to its exemplary role—indicates well the breadth of Bernard's teaching on the Cross.

---

[67] Which are given in italics in appendixes I and II.

[68] Thus Matt 12:29 is cited thirteen times and Luke 11:21-22 fifteen times, and these twenty-eight citations are spread over twenty different passages of Bernard.

[69] Not that volume of citations *necessarily* proves anything. See the warning of Figuet, "La Bible de Bernard: Données et ouvertures," SCh 380:264–65.

[70] If we also count the times that Isa 53:7-9 is cited via New Testament texts, the total rises to thirty times, but the results would be different if we treated these as three separate verses.

Bible Citation	Number of occurrences in the 669 passages	Number of different passages where parallel citations occur
Psalm 85:10–11	11	
Isaiah 53:2–3	15	
Isaiah 53:4–6	15	
Isaiah 53:7–9	19	
Isaiah 53:12	13	
Matthew 12:29	13 ⎫	20
= Luke 11:21–22	15 ⎬	
Matthew 16:24	11[71]	
Matthew 26:39, 42	8 ⎫	16
= Mark 14:36	4 ⎬	
= Luke 22:42, 44	9 ⎭	
Matthew 27:35	3 ⎫	10
= John 19:23–24	9 ⎬	
Matthew 27:38–44	12 ⎫	12
= Mark 15:29, 32	1 ⎬	
Luke 23:34	10	
Luke 23:39–43	18	
John 1:29	13	
John 6:53–55	10	
John 11:49–53	9	
John 12:32	12	
John 15:13	19	
John 19:30	10	
John 19:34	18	

[71] SBOp 5:83 claims Luke 9:23 as the source for the main text of #309 and Matt 16:24 as the source for the variant text. The former citation is brief and could easily come from Matthew or Luke. Since Bernard never elsewhere cites Luke 9:23, there is no reason to see it as the source here.

Bible Citation	Number of occurrences in the 669 passages	Number of different passages where parallel citations occur
Acts 8:32–33	13	
Romans 4:25	9	
Romans 5:6–8	15	
Romans 5:10	12	
Romans 5:15–19	8	
Romans 6:5	9	
Romans 6:9–10	8	
Romans 8:17	10	
Romans 8:32	10	
1 Corinthians 1:30	10	
1 Corinthians 2:2	15	
1 Corinthians 2:8	14	
2 Corinthians 5:14–15	11	
2 Corinthians 5:16	10	
Galatians 5:24	8	
Galatians 6:14	23	
Philippians 2:8	22	
Philippians 3:18	11	
Colossians 1:20	11	
Colossians 2:14	12	
Hebrews 2:17–18	9	
1 Peter 1:18–19	12	
1 Peter 2:22–23	17	
1 John 5:6–8	15	
Revelation 7:14	9	
Revelation 14:4	8	

PART II

Key Passages

4

KEY PASSAGES I:
TREATISES

Bernard's teaching on the Cross is scattered throughout hundreds of passages of varying length. Given the fact that this teaching is so varied, there is considerable scope for the interpreter to mould it into the shape that he desires by the careful selection and arrangement of citations. Naturally, that is not the aim of the present study, but it is hard to avoid all unconscious bias. In order to correct any false impressions that might be given, the three chapters of part 2 review six key passages where Bernard gives extended treatment to the topic. In all of these passages, some material is omitted because it is of no relevance to the work of Christ; some material is paraphrased because it is of indirect relevance; material specifically on the Cross is translated literally.[1] I have made my own translation rather than used existing ones because the latter are often too imprecise in their account of the redemptive work of Christ. Also, if one used translations by three different people of three different passages, there would be no consistency in the way in which key terms were translated. This review of the six passages will have the double benefit of introducing many of the themes that will

---

[1] Scriptural references are given for quotations rather than allusions—the latter will be found in appendix I. In distinguishing between these, I have been guided by material that is in upper case in SBOp, but without always following the judgement of SBOp.

be considered in part 3 and also of showing how Bernard holds these themes together. Readers are free if they wish to skip these chapters and proceed directly to the exposition of Bernard in part 3, but these six passages will feature significantly in that exposition, and familiarity with them will enable the reader better to follow that exposition. Also, it would be advisable to read at least chapter 5, which introduces and assesses Bernard's letter-treatise against Abelard, a work of central significance for our topic and to which there is considerable reference in part 3.

Three of the six key passages are from Bernard's treatises, including his letter-treatise against Abelard, which we will consider in the next chapter. All were written by 1141 at the very latest. According to *Sancti Bernardi Opera*,[2] *De diligendo Deo* was written between 1126 and 1141, the dates when Aimeric became chancellor of the Roman church and when he died. The more recent *Sources Chrétiennes* edition dates Dil more precisely between 1132 and 1135.[3] Both editions agree in placing the *De laude novae militiae* between 1128/29 (the confirmation of the institution of the Templars at the Council of Troyes) and 1136 (the death of the founder).[4] David Carlson argues that Tpl must have been written before October 1131, the date by which Bernard must have become aware of the church's ban on participation in tournaments, which he fails to mention in the treatise.[5] Against an early date is the consideration that time must be allowed for the Templars to have achieved some measure of fame.[6] Bernard's *Epistola in erroribus Abaelardi* can probably be dated to 1140.[7] There is

---

[2] SBOp 3:111.

[3] SCh 393:23–27.

[4] SBOp 3:207; SCh 367:21. See Jean Leclercq, "Un document sur les débuts des Templiers," RESB 2:87–99.

[5] David Carlson, "The Practical Theology of Saint Bernard and the Date of the *De laude novae militia*," in *Erudition at God's Service*, ed. John R. Sommerfeldt, CS 98 (Kalamazoo, MI: Cistercian Publications, 1987), 142–45.

[6] SCh 367:21.

[7] There has been a long-running controversy over the date of the events leading to Abelard's condemnation at the Council of Sens. For a full account of previous debate and reasons why opposition to Abelard ran from William of Saint Thierry's letter to Bernard sent during Lent in 1140 to the Council of Sens in 1141, see

no certainty about the order of the first two works, but it is slightly more likely that *De laude novae militiae* is earlier, so we will consider this work first.

While there are indications of the dates of some of Bernard's treatises, there is almost no evidence for the dates of most of Bernard's liturgical sermons.[8] Fortunately, one of the few exceptions is the third sermon on the annunciation, which can be dated to 1150.[9] One of our key sermons is the first of that series, and we can reasonably assume that, at least in its present form, it dates from not long before the third sermon and certainly long after 1141, the latest date for any of our treatises. In fact, all of the dates that can be put on any of the liturgical sermons are after 1140, with the exception of 1139 for the sermons on Psalm 91, and this date relates to the first redaction of these sermons rather than to their final form.[10] We will, accordingly, start in this and the following chapter with the three passages from the treatises, followed in chapter 6 by the three passages from the sermons. We will consider the sermons in their liturgical order since there is no way of knowing their chronological order.

A. *De laude novae militiae* 10.17–11.29[11]

At the beginning of *In Praise of the New Knighthood* (Tpl 1.1; #142), Bernard exhorts the Templars to go forth and repel the enemies of the Cross of Christ. This passing reference to the Cross points forward to what was to become one of the major themes of the treatise. The majority of the work is structured around sites in the Holy Land, and it is in connection with various of these that

---

Constant J. Mews, "The Council of Sens (1141): Abelard, Bernard and the Fear of Social Upheaval," *Speculum* 77 (2002): 342–82, which sets the debate in the context of social conflict.

[8] Jean Leclercq and Henri Rochais, "La tradition des sermons liturgiques de S. Bernard," RESB 2:206–7.

[9] Leclercq and Rochais, "La tradition des sermons liturgiques de S. Bernard," 206.

[10] Leclercq and Rochais, "La tradition des sermons liturgiques de S. Bernard," 206.

[11] The translation/paraphrase is my own, with some reference to the translation in CF 19. This on occasions takes liberties with the text, and with key passages I have sought to keep closer to Bernard's Latin. The text is also found in SCh 367.

Bernard expounds his theology of the Cross, but not (strangely) in the context of the first and relatively long discussion of the temple of Jerusalem (Tpl 5.9–11).

Tpl 6.12 (#143). Bethlehem is significant for Bernard as the place where Christ was born—but even more for its name, which means "house of bread." With what sort of nourishment should preachers feed the people of God? After we have come to realise that the flesh does not profit (John 6:64), we can say like Paul that we no longer know Christ after the flesh (2 Cor 5:16). Children need milk and animals eat hay, but the mature are ready for solid food. While the perfect are able to handle spiritual truths and no longer need the flesh, it is necessary to present only Christ, and him crucified, to those that are still children or beasts of the herd (1 Cor 2:2). This Origenist belittling of the humanity of the incarnate Christ might suggest that the Cross is not very important in Bernard's soteriology, but that is not what we find in the remainder of the treatise.[12]

Tpl 7.13 (#144). Nazareth, like Bethlehem, is interpreted according to its meaning: "flower."[13] This interpretation leads Bernard to talk about smell and also to penetrate beneath outward appearances, that is, the flesh. The Jews failed to recognise the Word beneath the flesh, the divinity within the humanity, or the spiritual meaning beneath the letter of the written Word. They did not realise that Christ came not to commit sin but to take it away (1 Pet 2:22, 24[14]). So the spiritually blind bound him, scourged him, and buffeted him without realising that he would rise from the dead. Had they realised that, they would not have crucified the Lord of glory (1 Cor 2:8).

Tpl 10.17 (#145). The brief discussions of the Mount of Olives, the Valley of Josaphat, and the River Jordan (Tpl 8.14–9.16) contain

---

[12] As is noted by R. J. Zwi Werblowsky in his introduction in *Bernard of Clairvaux, Treatises III*, CF 19 (Kalamazoo, MI: Cistercian Publications, 1977), 122. On the influence of Origen, see chap. 7D below.

[13] For Bernard's etymology of "Nazareth," see Jean Leclercq, "De quelques procédés du style biblique de S. Bernard," RESB 3:257–62.

[14] Bernard is surely alluding to 1 Pet 2:22, 24, not 2 Cor 5:20 as in SBOp 3:226 and not John 1:29, because of the contrast between not committing and taking away.

no reference to the Cross. It is, not surprisingly, when Bernard moves on to Calvary (*locus Calvariae*) that references to the Cross begin in earnest. Christ is compared to Elisha, who was mocked with the words "Go up, baldy" (*ascende calve*; 2 Kgs 2:23):

> So also Christ, our baldy [*calvus noster*], ascended to the Cross, was exposed to the world for the sake of the world with unveiled face and uncovered brow, making a purgation for sins. He was not ashamed of the ignominy of a cruel and shameful death[15] and did not tremble at the punishment in order to snatch us away from eternal disgrace and restore us to glory. Indeed, what did he have to be ashamed of who washed us from our sins—not as water that is itself dirtied but as a ray of sunshine that remains pure while it dries up dirt? He is the Wisdom of God whose purity reaches everywhere.

Tpl 11.18 (#146). By far the longest chapter of the treatise concerns the Holy Sepulchre, and it is here that Bernard devotes most attention to the Cross.[16] He begins by explaining why we are moved more by recollecting Christ's death than his life:

> Among the holy and desirable sites the sepulchre holds the primacy in a certain way, and I do not know of any devotion experienced where he dwelt when alive greater than that experienced where he lay dead; and the recollection of his death more greatly moves to piety than does the recollection of his life. I suppose that the latter is considered harsher, the former sweeter, and that to human weakness the calm of his sleep is more pleasing than the hardship of his way of life, the security of his death than the uprightness of his life. Christ's life is a pattern for mine, but his death redeems me from death. The one brings instruction for life, the other the destruction of death. His life is harsher [because it brings demands]; his death is sweeter [because it brings comfort]. But both are necessary. How will the death of Christ profit

---

[15] CF 19:153 gratuitously adds "in order to expiate our sins."

[16] This chapter has rightly been called "un véritable petit traité théologique" (SCh 367:42–46, at 42).

someone who lives evilly or the life of Christ someone
who dies culpably? Shall the death of Christ liberate from
eternal death those who now sin mortally, or was the life
of Christ able to liberate the holy fathers who died before
he came? As it is written, "Who is there that will live and
not see death, who will pluck his soul from the hand of the
underworld" [Ps 89:48]? We need both to live religiously
and to die with peace of mind, and he has taught us by his
life how to live and by his death how to die with peace of
mind. He died as one about to rise again and so brings the
hope of resurrection to the dying. He also brings a third
benefit[17] without which the other two have no worth, since
he also forgives sins. What use could uprightness and length
of life be, where true and supreme happiness is concerned,
to someone who is bound by sin, even if only original sin?
Sin of course preceded death, because if man had indeed
avoided sin, he would never have tasted death.

Tpl 11.19. The next paragraph does not deal directly with the
Cross but is nonetheless important for us because it explains why
the Cross was necessary. Sin leads to death, as God had justly warned
in Genesis 2:17. This is not an arbitrarily imposed sentence:

God is the life of the soul, as the soul is the life of the body.
By sinning voluntarily the soul willingly loses life; unwillingly she also loses the power to give life [to the body].
Of her own accord she spurned life because she did not
want to live; she does not have the power to give life to
whomever and wherever she wants. The soul did not want
to be ruled by God; she is unable to rule the body. If she
does not obey her superior, why should she rule over her
inferior? The Creator finds his creature in rebellion against
him; the soul finds her attendant in rebellion against her. The
human creature is found to be a transgressor against divine

---

[17] As is rightly noted in SCh 367:42, the identification of a "third" benefit is odd
since the prime benefit of the death of Christ in this chapter is to bring forgiveness of sins.

law; he also finds another law in his members, in opposition to the law of his mind and enslaving him to the law of sin. Again, sin separates us from God, as it is written [Isa 59:2]; so death also separates us from our bodies. Nothing but sin can separate the soul from God, and nothing but death can separate the body from the soul. What is excessively harsh in what she has suffered in retribution, since she is only suffering from her subordinate that [rebellion] which she presumed against her own maker? Surely nothing could be more fitting than that death leads to death— spiritual death to corporal, culpable death to penal [*poenalem*], voluntary death to necessary.

Tpl 11.20 (#147).

Since, therefore, humanity has been condemned to this twin death, according to each nature—the one spiritual and voluntary, the other bodily and necessary—the God-man mercifully and powerfully cancelled both by his one death, which was bodily and voluntary. By that one death of his he condemned [*damnavit*] our double death. This is fitting, for one of our two deaths was reckoned to be the reward for our fault [*culpae meritum*] and the other to be the debt of punishment [*poenae debitum*]. Christ submitted to the punishment, though innocent of the fault. He died of his own accord, only in the body, and merited life and righteousness for us. If he had not suffered bodily, he would not have paid the debt; if he had not died voluntarily, his death would have had no merit. Death is merited by sin and is a debt owed because of sin, as we said. So in remitting sin and dying for sinners, Christ nullified the merit and paid the debt.

Tpl 11.21. This paragraph does not mention the Cross but answers the question of how we know that Christ can forgive sins.[18] He is able to do this because he is God, as is shown by his miracles. It is against God alone that we have sinned, and so he it must be who

---

[18] On the Boso-like questioning from this point, see chap. 3A above.

forgives—which he is able to do because he is omnipotent. I can forgive offences against me, if I wish, so God can do the same.[19]

Tpl 11.22 (#148).

And who can doubt that he is willing [to forgive]? Do you suppose that he who assumed our flesh and submitted to our death will refuse us his righteousness? As he was voluntarily incarnate, voluntarily suffered, was voluntarily crucified, will he keep back righteousness alone from us? That he is able is evident from his deity; that he wills it was made known by his humanity. But again, how can we be sure that he has removed death? Because he who did not deserve [*non meruit*] death endured it. How can the debt that he has already paid for us be required again of us? He bore the punishment of our sin [*peccati meritum*] and gave us his righteousness by paying the debt of death and restoring life. Life will return when death is dead, just as righteousness returns when sin is removed. Death has been put to flight by death in Christ, and Christ's righteousness is imputed [*imputatur*] to us. But how could he die if he was God? Because he was also human. But how can the death of this man be effective for another? Because he was righteous. For surely because he was human he could die; because he was righteous he should not die for nothing. One sinner cannot pay the debt of another by dying, because each must die for himself. But because he did not need to die for himself, surely his death for another cannot be in vain? The more undeservingly he dies who had not merited death, the more justly will those live for whom he dies.

Tpl 11.23 (#149).

"But what sort of justice [*iustitia*] is this," you say, "the innocent dying for the ungodly?" This is mercy, not justice. If

---

[19] Taken out of context, this statement could be taken to mean that God can simply forgive sins freely without the need for the debt of death to be paid. That is not the point that Bernard is making here, and to take this passage that way would be to make nonsense of the rest of chap. 11.

it had been justice, he would have died under obligation [*ex debito*], not freely. If under obligation, he would indeed have died, but he for whom he died would not live. But although it is not justice, it is not contrary to justice—otherwise God could not at the same time be both righteous [*iustus*] and merciful.[20] "But even if the righteous is not unjustly able to make satisfaction [*satisfacere*] for the sinner, how can one do this for many? It would appear sufficient for justice for one person by dying to restore life to one person." The apostle responds to this: "As the transgression of one brought condemnation to all, so the righteous deed of one brought justification of life to all. As through the disobedience of the one man many were made sinners, so through the obedience of one man were many made righteous" [Rom 5:18-19]. But maybe one can restore righteousness to many, but not life? "Through one man," he says, "came death, and through one man life. As in Adam all die, so in Christ all shall be made alive" [1 Cor 15:21-22]. What then? When one sins, all are held to be guilty; shall the innocence of the one be counted only for the one who is innocent? The sin of the one produced death for all; shall the righteousness of the one restore life to one only? Is God's justice more able to condemn than to restore? Is Adam more powerful for evil than Christ for good? Will Adam's sin be imputed [*imputabitur*] to me and Christ's righteousness not pertain to me? Has the disobedience of the former ruined me, while the obedience of the latter will be of no benefit to me?

Tpl 11.24. Bernard then pauses to meet two objections. First, it is deservedly (*merito*) that we are all involved in Adam's offence because we sinned in him; we were in him when he sinned, and we are born from his flesh through the concupiscence of the flesh—an

---

[20] In Latin, justice and righteousness are the same word, *iustitia*, but it is impossible to keep to one or the other in English without being very stilted in places. The result is that here and elsewhere the same Latin root word is translated differently within the same sentence, but we must not lose sight of the fact that there is no distinction in the original.

Augustinian interpretation of Romans 5:12 especially. The implied objection is that we have no such intimate connection with Christ. Bernard denies this objection, appealing to the fact that God chose us in Christ before the ordering of the world (Eph 1:4). So we were in Christ according to the spirit long before we were in Adam according to the flesh.

Second, carnal concupiscence is evidence of the transmission of the heritage of the flesh, and the sin that we experience in the flesh manifestly proves that we are descended, according to the flesh, from the flesh of a sinner. That is true, but Bernard reminds us that the elect also experience a spiritual heritage, the working of the Holy Spirit in their hearts. Thus, this paragraph reaffirms that the work of Christ is no less effective than the sin of Adam.

Tpl 11.25 (#150). Bernard reiterates and reinforces the point that Christ's work is no less effective than Adam's sin:

> If we all die in Adam, why will we not all far more powerfully be made alive in Christ? Indeed, "there is a difference between the misdeed and the gift. For the judgement arising from the one misdeed led to condemnation, but grace led from many misdeeds to justification" [Rom 5:15-16]. Christ was able both to remit sins since he is God and to die since he is human. By dying he was able to pay the debt of death because he was righteous, and one was able to provide righteousness and life for all, just as sin and death spread from one to all.

Tpl 11.26 (#151). Bernard begins this paragraph by declaring the purpose of Christ's life and the value of his teaching, his mighty works, and his example for us. All that remained was for Christ to add the grace of the forgiveness of sins, and the work of our salvation was completed:

> We need not fear that the power to forgive sins is lacking to God nor that the will to do so is lacking to one who suffered so much for sinners—if, that is, we have a proper concern (as we ought) to imitate his example and revere his

miracles, not disbelieving his teaching or [being] ungrateful for his sufferings.

Tpl 11.27 (#152).

Everything concerning Christ is good for us; everything is salvific and necessary—his weakness as well as his majesty. Though by the power of his deity he removed the yoke of sin by a command, by the weakness of his flesh he shattered the rights of death by dying. [Paul repeatedly teaches the efficacy of God's weakness and foolishness. Christ suffered voluntarily rather than necessarily.] So his death frees us from death, his life from error, and his grace from sin. His death completed the victory through his righteousness, because the righteous one, having paid back what he had not stolen [Ps 69:4], justly recovered what he had lost. As for his life, it fulfilled through wisdom what pertains to wisdom, which becomes an example and mirror of life and instruction for us. Again, his grace forgave sins by that omnipotent power that (as we said) does everything whatsoever he wants. Christ's death is the death of my death because he died that I might live. How can someone for whom Life died not live? How will anyone stray with Wisdom as a guide? How will anyone be held guilty whom Justice [*Iustitia*] has acquitted? He declared himself to be the life in the Gospel, saying "I am the life" [John 14:6]. The apostle bears witness to the other two, saying, "who has been made for us righteousness [*iustitia*] and wisdom by God the Father" [1 Cor 1:30].

Tpl 11.28. In this paragraph Bernard considers why if Christ has delivered us from the law of sin and death (Rom 8:2) we still have to die and sin remains.[21] Bernard answers essentially with the New Testament tension of "already but not yet." Also, God loves both mercy and truth (Ps 84:11 [LXX]), so it is necessary both that we

---

[21] This question is also asked in #404.

should die (because of Gen 2:17; 3:19)[22] and that we should rise again (because of his mercy).

Tpl 11.29 (#153). In the final paragraph Bernard reminds us that this discussion relates to the Holy Sepulchre and discusses the reactions of the pilgrim on seeing it. We should remember that we are buried with Christ through baptism into death (Rom 6:4-5). Bernard goes on to discuss the remaining two locations more briefly. Bethpage symbolizes confession and priesthood. Dealing with sin requires both repentance in the heart and outward confession with the lips (Tpl 12.30). Finally, Bethany is the house of obedience. Christ valued obedience so highly that he preferred it to his own life, being obedient to the Father to death (Phil 2:8; Tpl 13.31; #154).

Summary of Bernard's teaching in Tpl 10.17–11.29

The predominant theme in this exposition of the work of Christ is that he has paid our debt (*debitum*), bearing the penalty or punishment (*poena*) of death that was our due because of God's truthfulness (to the promise of Gen 2:17) and his justice.[23] Bernard also develops the contrast between Adam and Christ, showing our solidarity with both, themes that he developed further in his letter-treatise against Abelard.

B. *De diligendo Deo* 3.7–5.15 [24]

On Loving God, unlike *In Praise of the New Knighthood*, does not have a special focus on the Cross, but this is nonetheless a theme that recurs frequently in the earlier chapters.

---

[22] To which one might respond, "How can the debt that he has already paid for us be required again of us?" (11.22).

[23] Jean Leclercq, "The Joy of Dying according to St Bernard," CSQ 25 (1990): 165–66, states that "the word which occurs at once [in Tpl 11], and will recur frequently, is 'security.'" In fact, *securitas* and cognates appear only three times, all in the first paragraph. *Debitum* appears nine times; *poena* and cognates appear three times.

[24] The translation/paraphrase is my own, with some reference to the translation in CF 13. The text is also found in SCh 393. Patrick W. H. Eastman, "The Christology in Bernard's *De Diligendo Deo*," CSQ 23 (1988): 119–27, summarises the argument of the treatise, with some reference to Christ's passion.

The Cross appears in the very first paragraph (Dil 1.1; #128): "God deserves [*meruit*] much from us as he gave himself for us who were undeserving [*immeritis*]. What better could he give than himself?" The prime reason for loving God is that he loved us first (1 John 4:10). We should love him in return, especially when we consider who it is that loves, whom he loves, and how much. God loved us freely while we were still his enemies (Rom 5:10). He loved us to the extent of giving his only Son (John 3:16), of not sparing him but delivering him over for us (Rom 8:32). As the Son himself put it, there is no greater love than giving up one's life for one's friends (John 15:13). So the righteous one deserved to be loved by the ungodly, the highest by the lowest, the omnipotent by the weak. There is no explicit reference to the Cross here, but the use of John 15:13 and the full text of Romans 5:9–10 makes it clear that Bernard is thinking of the death of Christ, not just the incarnation.

After the first paragraph, Bernard considers the gifts of creation, especially free choice (*liberum arbitrium*), knowledge, and virtue. These are not sufficient for our salvation, because it is impossible by the power of our own free choice to turn to God's will rather than our own (Dil 2.2–6).

Dil 3.7 (#129). The faithful recognize their total need of Jesus, and him crucified. They are ashamed at their failure to love him more but realize that the more they have been loved, the easier it is to love.[25] "The church sees the Father's only Son bearing his Cross, the Lord of majesty struck and spat at, the author of life and glory pierced with nails, struck by a spear, drenched with taunts, and laying down his life for his friends. When she sees this, the sword of love transfixes her soul the more." A citation of Song of Songs 2:5 then leads to a discussion of fruits, identified as the pomegranates of Song 6:10 whose colour is that of Christ's blood. The bride sees death dead and

---

[25] Taken on its own, this section could imply a Pelagian view whereby God draws us simply by the external example of his love, but Bernard elsewhere (especially Gra) clearly has a fully Augustinian doctrine of grace. See Aage Rydstrøm-Poulsen, *The Gracious God: Gratia in Augustine and the Twelfth Century* (Copenhagen: Akademisk, 2002), 307–42.

the author of death defeated. Captivity is led captive so that at the name of Jesus every knee may bow. The bride then sees the curse of Genesis 3:18 reversed. "To the fruits of the passion, which she has taken from the tree of the Cross, she wishes to add some of the flowers of the resurrection, whose fragrance may especially entice the bridegroom to revisit her more frequently."

Dil 3.8 (#130). This paragraph begins with discussion of Song of Songs 1:16, where the bride refers to the lovers' couch as flowery. The bridegroom seeks the company of those whose minds diligently meditate on the grace of his passion and the glory of his resurrection. The tokens of the passion are like last year's fruit, the time spent under the authority of sin and death, while the emblems of the resurrection are like this year's flowers, growing under grace and producing fruit for the End. Christ's flesh was sown in death and blossoms in resurrection.

Dil 3.9 (#131). Bernard continues with the allegory of the flowers and fruit and what it is that encourages the bridegroom to visit the bride:

> We need therefore, if we want to have Christ as a frequent guest, to keep our hearts protected by faithful testimonies, both to the mercy of the one that died and to the power of the one that rose again—as David said, "Two things I have heard, that power belongs to God and that mercy belongs to you, O Lord" [Ps 62:11-12]. Accordingly, the testimonies of both are exceedingly trustworthy, since Christ died for our offences, rose again for our justification, ascended for our protection, sent the Spirit for our consolation, and at some time will return for our perfection. He demonstrated his mercy in death, his power in resurrection, and both in the remainder.

The allegory continues in the following paragraph (Dil 3.10), but without any mention of the Cross.

Dil 4.11 (#132). Bernard then turns to the theme of remembrance, which brings him eventually to the daily remembrance of the passion in the Eucharist. "'Whoever eats my flesh and drinks my blood has eternal life' [John 6:54]. That is, whoever meditates on my death and mortifies his earthly members, according to my example, has eternal life.[26] In other words, if you suffer with me, you will reign with me." Many are offended at this, being vexed to hear the message of the Cross and judging the memory of the passion burdensome. We must remember Christ's words of judgement on sinners and of blessing for the righteous. His yoke is pleasant compared to the anguish of the lost, and his burden is light. "Miserable slaves of Mammon, you cannot at the same time glory in the Cross of our Lord Jesus Christ and hope in financial wealth, nor pursue gold and prove how sweet the Lord is. As you did not feel him to be sweet in your memory, you will doubtless feel him to be bitter when he is present."

Dil 4.12 (#133). "The faithful soul, by contrast, sighs eagerly for his presence, rests sweetly in the memory of him, and glories in the disgrace of the Cross, until it is fit to see the glory of God in his revealed face." There follows further allegory, in which the left hand of Song 2:6 is identified as the recollection of that supreme love because of which he laid down his life for his friends.

Dil 4.13 (#134). This paragraph focuses on the Bride's response to the Bridegroom's great mercies. She should be so swept away and moved by them that she despises whatever cannot be desired without despising them. God's love is prevenient. The Father so loved the world that he gave his only Son (John 3:16); the Son surrendered his soul in death (Isa 53:12); the Holy Spirit teaches all things and reminds of Jesus' teaching (John 14:26).

Dil 5.14 (#135). The foregoing shows why God is deserving of our love. Those who are not aware of these things will love less, though they may be aware of their debt to God as Creator. But we believe not just in the God of creation and providence but also in

---

[26] Taken on its own, this statement could suggest that Bernard saw the Eucharist purely as a memorial, which is of course not true. For his teaching, see René-Jean Hesbert, "Saint Bernard et l'eucharistie," in *Mélanges saint Bernard* (Dijon: Association des amis de saint Bernard, 1954), 156–76.

God as the most abundant redeemer, as is stated in Psalm 130:7: "With him is abundant redemption." Christ "once for all entered the holy place, having achieved eternal redemption" (Heb 9:12). Scripture has much to say about our future hope.

Dil 5.15 (#136).

> What can I render to the Lord for all this? Reason urges the infidel, as does natural justice, to surrender his whole self to him from whom he has received his whole self and whom he should love with his whole self. Faith surely shows him all the more loveable to me, he whom I understand to be more esteemed than I, as I hold him to have lavished on me not just myself but also himself. In fact, the time of faith had not yet arrived, God had not yet become known in the flesh, died on the Cross, come forth from the grave, or returned to the Father—he had not yet, I say, commended his great love to us, concerning which we have already spoken much—when man was already commanded to love the Lord his God with all his heart, his soul, and his strength, that is, with all that he is, that he knows, that he is able.

Bernard continues to expound the debt of gratitude that we owe for our creation:

> Moreover, how much increase in benefit do we suppose there was when God saved humanity and beasts, as he multiplied his mercy? I speak of we who changed our glory into the likeness of grazing cattle and by sinning are compared to foolish beasts. If I owe my entire self having been made, what can I add for having been remade, and remade in this way? For I was not so easily remade as I was made, since it is written not only about me but about all that was made, "He spoke and they were made" [Ps 148:5]. He who made me by speaking only once in remaking me spoke much, performed miracles, endured hardships—and not only hardships but shameful treatment. What shall I render to the Lord for all that he has rendered to me? In his first work he gave me myself; in the second he gave himself. Given therefore

and restored, I owe myself for myself and I owe myself twice over. What can I render God for himself? Even if I could repay myself a thousand times, what am I to God?

After this extended treatment of the Cross there is only one further reference to it in *Loving God*, again about God giving himself. God has nothing better to give us than himself. He gave himself as merit for us, he keeps himself as our reward, he appoints himself as refreshment for holy souls, and he gives himself as the redemption of captive souls (Dil 7.22; #137).

Summary of Bernard's Teaching in Dil 3.7–5.15

The Cross is not a central theme of *Loving God*, yet in an extended section of allegory that focuses on the love of God it is a recurring theme. The doctrine of the work of Christ is not developed in its own right but is integrated into Bernard's mystical teaching.

5

KEY PASSAGES II:
TREATISE AGAINST ABELARD

A. Its Origin

Bernard's *Epistle* 190 to Pope Innocent, *On the Errors of Peter Abelard*, is his best-known writing on the work of Christ. Indeed, for many who have written on that subject it is his *only* known writing on the topic. The previous chapter and the next one demonstrate that it is far from unique, though it remains very important and will play a significant role in the exposition of Bernard found in part 3.[1]

Bernard's letter-treatise was prompted by William of Saint Thierry, who wrote to Bernard during Lent of (probably) 1140,[2] warning him about Abelard's heresies (*Epistola* 326).[3] This letter lists thirteen

---

[1] For an account of the controversy, see Michael T. Clanchy, *Abelard: A Medieval Life* (Oxford: Blackwell, 1997), 282–87, 306–25. Clanchy makes the point that Bernard's letters as we now have them "may be no more than drafts," there is "no proof that they ever reached their recipients, though the inference is that they did," and that "even the letters as dispatched did not necessarily express Bernard's own words," since the abbot used amanuenses (317). All of these points are doubtless true in general, but given the special circumstances of this particular letter-treatise, it is unlikely that any of them apply in this case.

[2] For the date, see chap. 4, n. 7.

[3] Ep 326 (PL 182:531–33). Text and discussion also in Jean Leclercq, "Les lettres de Guillaume de Saint-Thierry à saint Bernard," RESB 4:349–57. On William's role,

offensive "points of indictment [*capitula*] gathered from his writings" of which just one, the seventh, relates to the work of Christ: "That it was not in order to liberate us from the yoke of the devil that Christ took flesh and suffered."[4] This letter served as a preface to William's more substantial *Disputatio adversus Petrum Abaelardum ad Gaufridum Carnotensem et Bernardum*.[5] This treatise, unlike the letter, devotes a substantial chapter to the work of Christ, comprising almost a quarter of the whole.[6] William drew upon a number of Abelard's works and also upon the *Liber sententiarum*,[7] now lost, which claimed to present Abelard's teaching, but which Abelard denied having written.[8] Constant Mews is not altogether convinced by the denial, arguing that it "may have been compiled by an amanuensis either from dictation or from Abelard's lecture notes [or from both]." It is not in the same category as works from "the school of Peter Abelard."[9]

Bernard's aim in his letter-treatise is to expose and refute Abelard's heresies. In many passages he addresses Abelard in the second person,

---

see Jean-Marie Déchanet, *William of St. Thierry: The Man and His Work* (Spencer, MA: Cistercian Publications, 1972), 53–63; Piero Zerbi, "Guillaume de Saint-Thierry et son differend avec Abélard," in *Saint-Thierry: Une abbaye du VIᵉ au XXᵉ siècle*, ed. Michel Bur (Saint-Thierry: Association des Amis de l'Abbaye de Saint-Thierry, 1979), 395–412; "William of Saint Thierry and His Dispute with Abelard," trans. Jerry Carfantan, in *William, Abbot of St. Thierry*, CS 94 (Kalamazoo, MI: Cistercian Publications, 1987), 181–203.

[4] "Quod Christus non ideo assumpsit carnem et passus est, ut nos a iugo diaboli liberaret" (PL 182:532).

[5] CCCM 89a:17–59.

[6] Chap. 7 (CCCM 89a:42–51). This is also unlike a work with a similar title sometimes alleged to be by William (M.-B. Carra de Vaux Saint-Cyr, "Disputatio catholicorum patrum adversus dogmata Petri Abaelardi," *Revue des sciences philoso-phiques et théologiques* 47 [1963]: 205–20).

[7] E.g., *Disputatio* 10 (CCCM 89a:57).

[8] Charles S. F. Burnett, "Peter Abelard, *Confessio fidei 'universis'*: A Critical Edition of Abelard's Reply to Accusations of Heresy," *Medieval Studies* 48 (1986): 138. On this and other responses of Abelard to Bernard, see Jacques Verger, "Saint Bernard vu par Abélard et quelques autres maîtres des écoles urbaines," in *Histoire de Clairvaux* (Bar-sur-Aube: Némont, 1991), 161–65.

[9] Constant J. Mews, "The *Sententiae* of Peter Abelard," RTAM 53 (1986): 130–32, 168–84, quotations at 173–74.

which probably indicates that this material was intended for use against Abelard in a face-to-face accusation at the Council of Sens.[10] Associated with the letter is a list of nineteen *capitula*, or brief statements, of the errors of Abelard's heresy.[11] It is uncertain whether these belong with the letter, but they clearly belong to the same debate and were used by Bernard.[12] In addition to these nineteen and William's list of thirteen *capitula*, there is also an independent, anonymous list of fourteen entitled *Capitula haeresum Petri Abaelardi*.[13] To complicate matters further, the manuscript tradition has more than one version of Bernard's letter-treatise, some not including the *capitula*.[14] Constant Mews proposes a seven-stage process leading to the definitive version of the letter-treatise. According to this, Bernard wrote his work in response to William; the *Capitula haeresum Petri Abaelardi XIV* were drawn up (by Thomas of Morigny, Mews suggests); these were further adapted (with input from William and Bernard) to become

[10] Clanchy, *Abelard*, 311.

[11] Abael, capit. #616. On these *capitula*, see Leopold Grill, "Die neunzehn 'Capitula' Bernhards von Clairvaux gegen Abälard," *Historisches Jahrbuch* 80 (1961): 230–39; Jean Leclercq, "Les formes successives de la lettre-traité de Saint Bernard contre Abélard," RESB 4:279–83; Constant J. Mews, "The List of Heresies Imputed to Peter Abelard," R Ben 95 (1985): 73–110. For a summary of debate prior to 1976, see Edward F. Little, "The Source of the *Capitula* of Sens of 1140," in *Studies in Medieval Cistercian History II*, ed. John R. Sommerfeldt, CS 24 (Kalamazoo, MI: Cistercian Publications, 1976), 87–91.

[12] For evidence that they are part of the authentic text of Abael, see Mews, "List of Heresies," 94–96.

[13] CCCM 12:453–80. On this, see Eligius M. Buytaert, "The Anonymous *Capitula Haeresum Petri Abaelardi* and the Synod of Sens, 1140," *Antonianum* 43 (1968): 421–60; Nikolaus M. Häring, "Die Vierzehn *Capitula Haeresum Petri Abaelardi*," Cîteaux 31 (1980): 35–52. Buytaert traces the sources of the fourteen *capitula* in Abelard's writings (431–41). He also gives a synopsis of the contents of the three lists, correlating them with lists given by Abelard and with the contents of the body of Abael (443–45 = CCCM 12:468–69).

[14] For the details, see Leclercq, "Les formes successives," 265–83. Leclercq identifies nine nonstylistic changes in the body of the letter, none of which concern his teaching on the Cross (273–75).

our nineteen and were added to the letter-treatise; the latter was further revised without changing the *capitula*.[15]

Abelard complained that the *capitula* (of which he lists seventeen) were brought forward in malice or in ignorance.[16] In his *Apologia contra Bernardum* he states, "The devil, even though he wrongly interprets the Scriptures, nevertheless gives the words of Scripture whose meaning he is distorting. You, however, depart as much from my words as from their meaning."[17] Is Abelard's claim true? David Luscombe examines each of the nineteen *capitula* in the light of Abelard's known teachings and concludes that nine of them "fairly present Abelard's teaching."[18] The matter is not straightforward, however; Edward Little also examined them and concluded that "in the case of eight of the *capitula*, Bernard seems to have understood Abelard correctly: Abelard's meaning was reasonably close to what Bernard meant."[19] The difference is greater than it may appear at first sight, as they only agree about the correctness of six of the *capitula*.[20] To complicate matters further, Artur M. Landgraf raises the possibility that some of the *capitula* may have originated in lost works of Abelard.[21]

Of the nineteen *capitula* only one (the fourth) relates to the work of Christ, the statement that it was not in order to liberate us from

---

[15] This is a slightly abridged version of the process as set out in Mews, "List of Heresies," 105–6. Mews, "Council of Sens," 381–82, gives a proposed chronology of events from 1137 to 1143.

[16] Burnett, "Peter Abelard, *Confessio fidei 'universis,'*" 134–38.

[17] CCCM 11:361.

[18] David E. Luscombe, *The School of Peter Abelard* (Cambridge: CUP, 1969), 115–42, quotation at 132. These are *capitula* 4, 5, 7, 8, 11, 12, 13, 15, 19.

[19] Edward Little, "Bernard and Abelard at the Council of Sens, 1140," in *Bernard of Clairvaux: Studies Presented to Dom Jean Leclercq*, CS 23 (Washington, DC: Cistercian Publications, 1973), 58–66. These are *capitula* 4, 8, 9, 10, 11, 13, 15, 19. This article is based upon his doctoral dissertation of 1969, the same year as Luscombe's book.

[20] Nos. 4, 8, 11, 13, 15, 19. Luscombe approves nos. 5 and 7, which Little discusses on pp. 60–64, and no. 12, about which Little states that it is "not too clear" whether Bernard had understood Abelard (p. 59). Little approves nos. 9 and 10, which Luscombe discusses on pp. 128, 130–32.

[21] Artur M. Landgraf, "Probleme um des hl. Bernhard von Clairvaux," *Cistercienser Chronik* 61 (1954): 1–3.

the yoke of the devil that Christ assumed flesh.[22] From this one would gain the impression that the work of Christ was just one topic among many for Bernard, but in fact over half of the letter is devoted to it, ranging more widely than the specific issue raised in the *capitulum*.[23]

The precise redaction history of the *capitula* and their relation to the letter-treatise and to Abelard's writings remain a matter of controversy, but fortunately this is of little significance for our topic. Also controversial is what exactly happened at Sens and what exactly was sent to Rome and when. Fortunately, this is of even less significance for our topic, which is Bernard's teaching on the Cross in the letter-treatise rather than his actions at the Council of Sens.[24] Also, Luscombe and Little are both agreed that the fourth *capitulum*

---

[22] No. 4: "Quod Christus non assumpsit carnem ut nos a iugo diaboli liberaret," a slightly shorter version of William's seventh *capitulum*. No. 9 states that those who crucified Christ in ignorance did not sin, and no guilt is to be ascribed to whatever is done in ignorance. This refers to the Cross, but the issue is Abelard's understanding of ethics, not of the work of Christ. Luscombe, *School of Peter Abelard*, 130–32, clears Abelard of this charge; Little, "Bernard and Abelard at the Council of Sens," 59, does not.

[23] A. Victor Murray, *Abelard and St. Bernard: A Study in Twelfth Century "Modernism"* (Manchester: Manchester University Press, 1967), 87–88, rightly draws a contrast between the Council of Sens, which listed objectionable statements from Abelard, many of which are not in his extant works, and the letter-treatise, which goes to the heart of the issue and focuses on the nature of faith, the Trinity, and the work of Christ. Gillian R. Evans likewise notes how Bernard here places the emphasis where he thought it was needed, on redemption rather than trinitarian problems (*The Mind of St. Bernard of Clairvaux* [Oxford: OUP, 1983], 152).

By contrast, reading Jean Jolivet, "Sur quelques critiques de la théologie d'Abélard," *Archives d'histoire doctrinale et littéraire du moyen âge* 38 (1963): 22–51, one would never imagine that William or Bernard were particularly concerned about the work of Christ.

As is noted by Jean Rivière, "Le dogme de la rédemption au début du moyen âge III—rôle de saint Bernard," RSR 13 (1933): 190, it is only *this* letter against Abelard that focuses on redemption, the others focusing on faith, the Trinity, and the incarnation.

[24] For a summary of Abelard's responses to Bernard, see Verger, "Saint Bernard vu par Abélard et quelques autres maîtres des écoles urbaines," 161–75. For Berengar's response, see David E. Luscombe, "Berengar, Defender of Peter Abelard," RTAM 33 (1966): 319–37.

is one of those that go back to Abelard's own teaching.[25] Abelard himself, however, denied the *capitulum* in his *Confessio fidei universis*.[26]

What is Bernard's source for Abelard's teaching on the Cross? In particular, to what extent is he dependent upon William of Saint Thierry? Jean Leclercq argued, concerning Bernard's letter-treatise as a whole, that Bernard knew Abelard only via William. Bernard, normally so independent, in this instance chose to submit to the influence of his advisor. He relied upon William for his knowledge of Abelard and also borrowed William's arguments in responding to him.[27] In keeping with Leclercq's judgement, the footnotes of the *Sancti Bernardi Opera* edition of Abael 5.11–9.25 imply that Bernard was primarily dependent upon William.[28] That is simply not so. He uses the *Disputatio* in Abael 5.11 and 9.23 but cites the Romans commentary directly in Abael 7.18–8.19, 8.21–22, and 9.24. It is true that some of the passages from the commentary that he cites were first cited by William, but where William tends to paraphrase Abelard in the *Disputatio*,[29] Bernard goes back to the original and

---

[25] Luscombe, *School of Peter Abelard*, 137–39, argues that while Abelard's theory of redemption was defective, this *capitulum* was "somewhat too categorical, at least when compared with Abelard's Commentary"; Little, "Bernard and Abelard at the Council of Sens," 65, interprets it as a statement about God's power, which is not the issue on which Bernard focusses in Abael.

[26] Burnett, "Peter Abelard, *Confessio fidei 'universis*,'" 135: "Solum filium dei incarnatum profiteor ut nos a servitute peccati et a iugo diaboli liberaret."

[27] Leclercq, "Les lettres de Guillaume," 355–57.

[28] Constant Mews argues similarly. Mews, "List of Heresies," 83, inaccurately refers to "the very few passages of Abelard which Bernard (in Abael) had not copied from William's treatise." Similarly Mews, "Council of Sens," 366–67. Mews and Leclercq have probably made the mistake of too quickly assuming that what is true of the *capitula* is also true of Bernard's critique in Abael, extrapolating from their studies of the *capitula* to statements about the treatise itself. In his " *Sententiae* of Peter Abelard," 170–71, Mews states that "the only two texts (of Abelard) used by Bernard in his *Epist.* 190" were his *Theologia scholarium* and the *Liber sententiarum*, but then he states that Bernard "added reference to the commentary on Romans within the text of *Epist.* 190 after the list of nineteen *capitula* had been drawn up and attached to that letter-treatise."

[29] Or else William relied upon a source (such as the *Liber sententiarum*) that had paraphrased Abelard.

quotes him accurately. He also cites a number of passages not cited by William. It was William who pointed Bernard to Abelard's Romans commentary, but Bernard went back to the original and quoted it more widely and far more accurately than did William.[30]

B. The Text[31]

The early chapters of Bernard's treatise are devoted to Abelard's views on the relation between faith and reason (Abael 1.1), the doctrine of the Trinity (Abael 1.2–3.8), and faith as conjecture or opinion (Abael 4.9–10). He begins by announcing that in France "an old teacher has become a new 'theologian.'"[32] In his youth he played with dialectics; now he raves on about the Holy Scriptures" (Abael 1.1). "On the very threshold of his theology (or, rather, his stupidology)[33] he defines faith as conjecture [*æstimatio*]. . . . Far be it from us to think that anything in our faith or hope hangs on dubious conjecture, as he thinks. Rather, it is all based on solid and reliable truth, divinely established by oracles and miracles, fixed and consecrated by the virgin birth, the blood of the Redeemer, and the glory of the risen one. . . . How can anyone dare to call faith a conjecture unless they have not yet received the Spirit, are ignorant of the Gospel, or suppose it to be a fable?" (Abael 4.9; #600).[34] This

---

[30] The evidence for this will be found in the footnotes below.

[31] The translation/paraphrase is my own, with some reference to the translation of Samuel J. Eales.

[32] "Theologian" was a new word and one that Bernard uses in a mocking way. He uses the word only seven times: here and six times where he refers to Abelard as "our theologian" (Abael 1.2, 3.6; Epp 330, 331 [#638], 332, 338.1 [#640]).

[33] Bernard calls Abelard's *theologia* a *stultilogia*. On the source of the joke, see Leclercq, "Les formes successives," 277. Abelard blamed it on Bernard (Raymond Klibansky, "Peter Abailard and Bernard of Clairvaux: A Letter by Abailard," *Mediaeval and Renaissance Studies* 5 [1961]: 6).

[34] It is generally recognised that Bernard misunderstood what Abelard meant by "conjecture" (*existimatio*). See Elisabeth Gössman, "Zur Auseinandersetzung zwischen Abaelard und Bernhard von Clairvaux um die Gotteserkenntnis im Glauben," in *Petrus Abaelardus (1079–1142)*, ed. Rudolf Thomas (Trier: Paulinus-Verlag, 1980), 236, and the scholarship there cited.

was to be total war! "The blood of the Redeemer" is a major theme of the rest of the letter.

Abael 5.11 (#601). The first paragraph devoted to soteriology reveals the perspective from which Bernard attacks Abelard. He is accused of being a reckless investigator, attacking the mystery of our redemption. Bernard refers to Abelard's Romans commentary and to "libro quodam Sententiarum ipsius."[35] Abelard acknowledged that the tradition was unanimous on this question, yet he not only spurns this but brags that he knows better.

> "It should be understood," he states,[36] "that all our doctors since the apostles are agreed that the devil had dominion and power over humanity and possessed this justly [*iure*] because man, by the freedom of choice that he had, con- sented of his own accord [*sponte*] to the devil. They say that if someone conquers someone else, the vanquished justly becomes the slave of the victor.[37] In the same way, therefore, the doctors teach that the Son of God became incarnate because it was necessary for humanity (who could be lib- erated no other way) to be justly [*iure*] liberated from the yoke of the devil through the death of an innocent one. But it appears to us," he says, "that the devil never had any rights [*ius*] over humanity, unless perhaps God allowed him to act as a jailer, and it was not to liberate humanity that

---

[35] On the authorship of which, see above at nn. 7–9.

[36] The section from here to n. 38, below, is all found in *Disputatio* 7 (CCCM 89a:42) and is drawn from the *Liber sententiarum*. The only significant change is the addition by Bernard of the word "all" at the very beginning, which heightens the claim. Part of the first sentence is also found in the fourteen *Capitula haeresum Petri Abaelardi*, which also has the word "all" (CCCM 12:474). Since this list probably postdates Abael, it appears that Bernard is the one responsible for the addition. Murray, *Abelard and St Bernard*, 81, wrongly states that Bernard here is drawing only on the *capitula* and charges him with quoting inaccurately. Jean Rivière, *The Doctrine of the Atonement: A Historical Essay*, vol. 2 (London: Kegan Paul, Trench, Trübner and Co., 1909), 213, suggests that it originated in a lost work of Abelard's.

[37] This statement is of course historically inaccurate, as chap. 2A, above, has shown. See Rivière, "Le dogme de la rédemption au début du moyen âge III— rôle de saint Bernard," 193.

the Son of God took flesh."[38] Which should I judge to be
the more insufferable in these words—the blasphemy or
the arrogance? Which the more damnable—the temerity or
the godlessness? Surely the mouth that speaks such things
should more properly be beaten with sticks than refuted
by reasoning? Does not he whose hand is against everyone
deservedly provoke everyone's hand against himself? "All,"
he says, "think thus, but I do not." So what about you? What
can you produce that is better? What have you discovered
that is more exact? Of what greater secret do you boast, that
has been revealed to you, that has passed by so many saints,
that has escaped the notice of the wise? I suppose he will
serve up to us stolen waters and hidden bread [Prov 9:17].

Abael 5.12 (#602).

Tell us, what is it that is seen by you and by no one else?
Doubtless that it was not to liberate humanity that the Son
of God put on humanity. This is indeed seen by none but
you alone. You should see to it where you saw it[39]—for
you certainly did not receive it from a wise man, nor from
a prophet, nor from an apostle, nor from the Lord himself.
The master of the Gentiles received from the Lord what he
handed on to us; the master of all confessed that his teaching
was not his own. "I do not," he says, "speak from myself"
[John 14:10]. But you hand on to us your own teaching,
which you received from no one. Whoever speaks falsehood
speaks from himself. Keep your own ideas to yourself! It is
the prophets and apostles that I will listen to, the Gospel that

---

[38] "But it appears . . . jailer" is mostly a paraphrase of Abelard's *Romans Commentary* (CCCM 11:115.174–78, not CCCM 11:114 as in SBOp 8:26), the paraphrase being by William (Bernard's source here)—not Bernard, who quotes (William) closely. "It was . . . flesh" is a shorter version of William's seventh *capitulum*, on which see n. 4 above.

[39] Latin: "Hoc plane nemini, te excepto, videtur; tu videris ubi videris." "Tu videris" is an allusion to Matt 27:4 (thus aligning Abelard with Judas), and the translation takes this into account. See also "tu ipse videris" (Cicero, *De oratore* 1.58). I am grateful to David Wright and Graham Davies for advice on this phrase.

I will obey—not the gospel according to Peter [Abelard].
You, have you put together a new gospel? The church does
not accept a fifth evangelist. What do the law, the prophets,
the apostles, and apostolic men present to us as the Gospel
other than that which you alone deny—that God became
human to liberate humanity? And if an angel from heaven
preaches another gospel to us, let him be anathema [Gal 1:8].

Abael 5.13 (#603).

> But you do not accept the doctors who came after the
> apostles, because you see yourself as above all teachers.[40]
> You are not ashamed to say that they all understand [*sen-
> tiant*] the matter contrary to you, while they do not differ
> [*dissentient*] from each other. There is no point, therefore, in
> relating to you the faith and teaching of those whom you
> have already proscribed, so I will lead you to the prophets.
> Under the type of Jerusalem not the prophet but the Lord in
> the prophet speaks to his chosen people, saying, "I will save
> you and liberate you: do not fear."[41] From what power, you
> ask? You do not wish that the devil should have or has had
> power over humanity—and nor do I, I admit. But it is not
> because you and I do not wish it that he does not have such
> power. If you do not confess this, you are not even aware of
> it. Those "who have been redeemed by the Lord, whom he
> has redeemed from the hand of the enemy" [Ps 107:2], are
> aware of it and tell of it. You would not at all deny it if you
> were not in the hand of the enemy. You cannot give thanks
> with the redeemed who have not been redeemed yourself.
> If you had been redeemed, you would acknowledge the
> Redeemer and not deny redemption. Nor will he seek to
> be redeemed who is unaware that he is a captive.

Bernard then cites Psalms 107:6; 34:17; 106:10; 107:2, followed by
John 11:51-52. "Christ would not gather his people unless he had

---

[40] Bernard may well be thinking of Abelard's behaviour toward his teachers such
as William of Champeaux and Anselm of Laon.

[41] For the source of this quotation, see SBOp 8:27.

redeemed them. They were not only scattered but also held captive. Christ redeemed them and gathered them—'He redeemed them from the hand of the enemy' [Ps 106:10]. It says not 'of the enemies' but 'of the enemy.'" Who is this one mighty lord who was in control of not one but all countries? Clearly the devil.

Abael 5.14 (#604).

> But maybe you do not believe the prophets, who sing harmoniously concerning the devil's power over humanity. Come with me to the apostles, too. May you agree with them—having said that you do not share the view of those who came after the apostles—and perhaps to you will happen what one of them says of certain people: "Perhaps God will give them repentance to learn the truth, that they may escape from the snares of the devil, by whom they were held captive at his will" [2 Tim 2:25-26]. Paul it is who states that people are held captive by the devil at his will. You hear "at his will" and yet do you deny his power? If you don't believe Paul, come to the Lord himself and perhaps you will listen and shut up. He calls the devil the prince of this world [John 14:30] and the strong soldier with his possessions [Luke 11:21; Matt 12:29]—but do you say he has no power over humanity? . . . The Lord also said to those who were arresting him, "This is your hour and the power of darkness" [Luke 22:53]. That power did not escape the notice of him who said, "Who rescued us from the power of darkness and transferred us into the kingdom of his esteemed Son" [Col 1:13].
>
> The Lord, therefore, did not deny this power of the devil even over him, nor that of Pilate, who was a member of the devil, since he said, "You would not have had any power over me unless it had been given to you from above" [John 19:11]. . . . Not even [Abelard], I suppose, will object that the power given from above was unjust [*iniustam*]. Let him learn that the devil not only has power but has just [*iustam*] power over humanity and that it was to liberate humanity that the Son of God came in the flesh. But while the devil's power is just, his will is not. So neither the devil (who took

possession) nor humanity (that deserved it) but God (who proposed it) is just. What makes someone just or unjust is his will, not his power. The devil's power over humanity was not justly gained but wickedly seized, yet it was justly allowed. Thus, humanity was justly held captive, but this justice was not the devil's, nor humanity's, but God's.

Abael 6.15 (#605).

Humanity was justly enslaved but mercifully liberated; mercifully, but in such a way that a certain justice was not lacking in the very liberation. As was appropriate for the cure of those to be liberated, in showing mercy the liberator used justice rather than power against the usurper. For what could humanity, the slave of sin fettered by the devil, achieve of itself to restore the righteousness once lost? An alien righteousness is assigned [*assignata*] to him that lacked his own, and it happened like this. The prince of this world came and found nothing [sinful] in the Saviour. Nonetheless, he laid hands on the innocent one and so most justly lost those whom he held captive. Since he that owed nothing to death submitted to the injustice [*iniuria*] of death, he justly [*iure*] freed [*solvit*] from the debt of death and the dominion of the devil those who were liable to it. For by what justice [*iustitia*] could this be required of humanity a second time? Accordingly, it was man who owed the debt, man who paid it. As [Paul] put it, "If one has died for all, then all have died" [2 Cor 5:14]. As one bore the sins of all, so the satisfaction of the one is imputed [*imputetur*] to all. Nor is it a case that it was one that earned the forfeit and another that made satisfaction, for head and body together form one Christ. The head therefore made satisfaction for the members, Christ for his own body [*visceribus*]. This is in line with the gospel of Paul by which the falsehood of Peter [Abelard] is refuted. He who died for us will bring us to life together with him, "pardoning all our sins, nullifying the handwritten document with its verdict that was against us and hostile to us. He took it out of the way, fastening it to the Cross, plundering the principalities and powers" [Col 2:13-15].

Abael 6.16 (#606).

Would that I may be found among the spoils of which the enemy powers were despoiled and myself transferred to the possession of the Lord. If Laban pursues me and complains that I stole away from him secretly [Gen 31:25-28], he will hear that it was secretly that I drew near [*accessisse*] to him and for that reason it was secretly that I stole away [*recessisse*] from him. The secret cause of that sin [in Adam] made me subject to it; the plan of hidden righteousness stole me away from it. If I was sold freely, may I not be bought back [*redimar*] freely? If Assyria finds fault with me without cause [Isa 52:3-4], it is without cause that he demands to know the cause of my escape. If he says, "Your father enslaved you," I will reply, "But my brother has redeemed me." Why not an external [*aliunde*] righteousness since the guilt was external? One made me a sinner; the other justifies me from sin—one by his seed,[42] the other by his blood. Shall there be sin in the seed of the sinner but not righteousness in the blood of Christ?

But, it might be objected, let each one's righteousness be his own; what is it to you? All right. Let each one's guilt be his own; what is it to me? Can it be that the righteousness of the righteous will be upon him and the wickedness of the wicked will not be upon him [Ezek 18:20]? But it is not fitting for the son to bear the iniquity of the father and yet be denied a share in the righteousness of a brother. It was by a man that death came and by a man life. "As all die in Adam, so also will all be made alive in Christ" [1 Cor 15:21-22]. I do not hold fast to the former in such a way as not also to hold fast to the latter—to the former through the flesh, to the latter through faith. If by Adam I have been corrupted by original concupiscence, so likewise I have been imbued with the spiritual grace of Christ. What else is imputed [*imputatur*] to me from the sinner [Adam]? Against birth [from Adam] I set rebirth, the latter being spiritual while the

---

[42] That is, original sin transmitted by carnal propagation.

former is carnal. Equity does not allow them to compete as equals, but it is necessary that the spirit defeat the flesh and that the more efficacious cause be the one with the superior nature, so clearly the second birth is more beneficial than the first is injurious. The sin [*delictum*] certainly reaches me, but so does the grace. "But there is difference between the misdeed and the gift. For the judgement arising from the one misdeed led to condemnation, but grace led from many misdeeds to justification" [Rom 5:15-16]. Sin flowed from the first man, while the outflow of grace is from the highest heaven. Both come from a father—one from our first father, the other from the supreme Father. My earthly birth destroys me; does not my heavenly much more save me? I am not afraid of being spurned by the Father of lights, as I have been rescued from the power of darkness and am justified freely in the blood of his Son. Truly, "if it is he that justifies, who is there to condemn?" [Rom 8:33-34]. He that had mercy on the sinner will not condemn the righteous. I call myself righteous, but by his righteousness. What righteousness is that? "Christ is the end of the law, for righteousness to all who believe" [Rom 10:4]. "He was made righteousness for us by God the Father" [1 Cor 1:30]. The righteousness that he was made for me—is it not mine? If guilt was handed down to me, why should righteousness not also be granted [*indulta*] to me? And certainly what is given to me is more secure than what is inborn.

So, concludes Bernard, we should glory in God alone.

Abael 7.17 (#607).

This son of perdition, by attacking and mocking it, seeks to annul the righteousness that people have in the blood of the Redeemer. So much so that he thinks and argues that one can reduce to only one reason why the Lord of glory emptied himself, became less than angels, was born of a woman, lived in the world, experienced weakness, suffered shameful things, and finally returned to his own by the death of the Cross. He did this in order that by his life

and teaching he might bequeath to humanity a pattern of
life and that by his suffering and death he might set before
them the extremity of love. So, did he teach righteousness
but not give it? Did he demonstrate love but not impart it?
Is this the way in which he "returned to his own"?

Is this, Bernard wonders, the extent of the mystery proclaimed by
Paul [1 Tim 3:16]? Bernard proceeds to mock this "incomparable
doctor" for the way in which he has oversimplified the great mystery
of salvation. Such matters are made known by the Spirit, but the
Gospel is hidden from those who are perishing.

Abael 7.18 (#608). Bernard accuses Abelard of ridiculing the
things of the Spirit, mocking the apostle, attacking the Gospel, and
blaspheming the Lord. He should have believed what he could not
understand[43] rather than despise a holy mystery. Bernard responds
to some of Abelard's specific objections.

> "Since Christ liberated the elect alone, in what way did
> the devil hold possession of them more than he now does,
> whether in this age or in the future?"[44] We reply that it was
> precisely because the devil had power over God's elect and
> "they were held captive by him at his will," as the apostle
> says [2 Tim 2:26], that a liberator was needed to fulfil God's
> purpose for them. It was necessary for them to be liberated
> in this age so that God might have them free in the age to
> come. [Abelard] then asks, "Is it possible that the devil also
> tormented the poor man resting in Abraham's bosom like
> the rich man who was lost—and did he even have domin-
> ion over Abraham himself and the other elect?"[45] No, but
> he would have had if they had not been liberated through
> faith in him who was to come—as is written concern-

---

[43] Bernard was aware of Abelard's epistemological maxim, with which he engages
in 1.1.

[44] This sentence is drawn almost verbatim from the *Romans Commentary* (CCCM
11:114.139–40).

[45] *Romans Commentary* (CCCM 11:114.140–44) exactly, apart from the omission
of a brief phrase.

ing Abraham himself: "Abraham believed God, and it was reckoned [*reputatum*] to him as righteousness" [Gen 15:6]. Again, "Abraham rejoiced to see my day; and he saw it and was glad" [John 8:56]. Therefore, already then the blood of Christ was moistening Lazarus, lest he feel the flames, because he had believed in him that was to suffer. So also with all the elect of that time. Like us they were born under the power of darkness, because of original sin, but were rescued before they died—by the blood of Christ alone.

Bernard then appeals to Matthew 21:9.

Abael 8.19 (#609).

[Abelard] strives to teach and persuade us that the devil was not able or entitled to claim for himself any rights [*ius*] over humanity, except by God's permission—also that without any injustice to the devil God could have recalled [humanity's] exile, if he wanted to show mercy, and rescued him by a mere word, as if anyone denies this.[46] Then eventually he concludes: "Since the divine compassion could have liberated humanity from sin simply by giving the order, what was the necessity, reason, or need for the Son of God, having taken flesh, to endure so many and so great things: fasting, taunts, scourging, spitting, and finally shameful and most cruel death on the Cross, together with criminals [*iniquis*]?"[47] We reply: the necessity was ours, the hard necessity of remaining in darkness and the shadow of death. The need was ours—and also God's and the holy angels'. We needed him to remove the yoke of our captivity; he needed to fulfil the purpose of his will; the angels needed their number to be completed. Further, the reason for this act was the grace [*dignatio*] of the one who did it. Who denies that there were available to

---

[46] See Rivière, *Doctrine of the Atonement: A Historical Essay*, 2:218, for the inaccuracy of this claim.

[47] This sentence is a close quotation of the *Romans Commentary* (CCCM 11:116.202–9). It is quoted loosely by William in *Disputatio* 7 (CCCM 89a:43). Bernard has clearly gone back to the original.

the Almighty many other ways to our redemption, justification, and liberation?[48] This does not prejudice the efficacy of
the way that he chose. And maybe that way excels through
which we are more powerfully and vividly warned in the
land of forgetfulness, of torpor, of our falling, by the so many
and great sufferings [*gravaminibus*] of the one who restored us.

Bernard then states again that the inscrutable depth of salvation is a
mystery beyond our comprehension.

   Abael 8.20 (#610). "We are not permitted to probe the mystery
of the divine will, but we are permitted to experience the effect
of its working and to feel the fruit of its usefulness. And it is not
permitted to be silent about that which it is permitted to know."
Bernard justifies these principles with a quotation from Proverbs
25:2, though he reverses two words so that God is glorified by our
investigation of his speech [*sermonem*].[49]

It is a faithful word and worthy of all acceptance, since "when
we were still sinners we were reconciled to God through
the death of his Son" [Rom 5:8, 10]. Where there is reconciliation, there is also forgiveness of sins. For if, as Scripture
states [Isa 59:2], our sins separate us from God, there is no
reconciliation where sin remains. Now in what is the forgiveness of sins? "This cup," he says, "is of the new covenant
in my blood, which will be poured out for you for the forgiveness of sins" [Luke 22:20; Matt 26:28]. So where there
is reconciliation, there is the forgiveness of sins, and what is
that if not justification? So whether we talk of reconciliation, forgiveness of sins, or justification—or redemption or
liberation from the chains of the devil (by whom we were
held captive at his will)—it is by the intervention of the
death of the Only-Begotten that we come to be justified
freely by the blood of him "in whom," as he says again, "we
have redemption through his blood and the forgiveness of

----

[48] The simple answer to Bernard's question is of course "Anselm," who denied
precisely that. See chap. 2B above.

[49] Bernard bends the text of Scripture to argue for the investigation of doctrine,
a point one would rather have expected Abelard to be making!

sins, according to the riches of his grace" [Eph 1:7]. "Why," you say, "accomplish by blood what he could have done by a word?" You ask him. I am permitted to know that it is so, not why it is so.

Bernard concludes this paragraph by quoting Romans 9:20.

Abael 8.21 (#611).

These things appear to be stupid to [Abelard], and he cannot contain his laughter. Listen to his jeers. "How," he says, "does the apostle say that we are justified or reconciled to God by the death of his Son when God should have been more angry at humanity as they offended so much more by crucifying his Son than by contravening his first command by tasting a single piece of fruit?"[50] As if it were not possible in one and the same act both for the iniquity of the wicked to displease God and for the godliness of the sufferer to please him. He adds, "If that sin of Adam was so great that it could be expiated only by the death of Christ, what expiation will there be for the very act of murdering Christ?"[51] Briefly, that very blood which they shed and the intercession of him whom they murdered.

Again he adds, "Is it possible that the death of his innocent Son was so pleasing to God the Father that by it he was reconciled to us (who brought it about by sinning) and that it was on account of this that the innocent Lord was murdered? Would he not have been able much more easily to pardon sin if this greatest sin had not taken place?"[52] What pleased God was not Christ's death but his will in dying of

---

[50] This sentence is a close quotation of the *Romans Commentary* (CCCM 11:116.210–14). It is quoted loosely by William in *Disputatio* 7 (CCCM 89a:43; SBOp 8:35). Bernard has clearly returned to the original. On Abelard's use of humour at this point, see Clanchy, *Abelard*, 217–18.

[51] This sentence is a close quotation of the *Romans Commentary* (CCCM 11:116.216–117.220). It is not (pace SBOp 8:35) found in *Disputatio* 7 (PL 180:270A–B [= CCCM 89a:43]).

[52] These two sentences are an exact quotation of the *Romans Commentary* (CCCM 11:117.220–24). They are not (pace SBOp 8:35) found in *Disputatio* 7 (PL 180:270A–B [= CCCM 89a:43]).

his own accord and by that death eliminating death, effecting salvation, restoring innocence, conquering the principalities and powers, plundering the underworld [*inferos*], enriching heaven, making peace between things in heaven and on earth, and restoring all things. This death, which was so precious and needed to be accepted voluntarily against sin, could not happen except by sin—so God, while he did not take pleasure in it, made good use of the malice of the wicked and condemned death by the death [of Christ] and sin by the sin [of his killers]. And the greater their iniquity, the more holy is his will and the more powerful to save— for, by the mediation of so great a power, that ancient sin, great as it was, would necessarily yield to this one which was committed against Christ, as lesser yields to greater. This victory is not attributed to the sin or the sinners but to him that made good use of the sin, suffered bravely with sinners, and adapted to the use of godliness all that the cruelty of the ungodly undertook against him.

Abael 8.22 (#612).

So the blood that was shed was so great at pardoning that it also expunged that greatest sin, by which it was caused to be shed, and therefore left no doubt about the annihilation of that ancient sin, inasmuch as that was more trivial.[53] Then Abelard asks, "To whom does it not seem cruel and unfair that someone should demand the blood of an innocent one as payment for something or that it should be in any way pleasing to him that an innocent one is killed—let alone that God should consider the death of his Son so pleasing as by

---

[53] Murray, *Abelard and St Bernard*, 86, argues that this is a tacit reply to Abelard's query about the guilt of those who crucified Christ in ignorance, set out in the ninth *capitulum*. This is not plausible because that is not one of the thirteen *capitula* listed by William, and when Bernard first wrote the letter-treatise the nineteen *capitula* were not attached to it and had not been brought together at that point. (See nn. 14–15 above.) Furthermore, the reference to the greatness of this sin is not Bernard's reply to the ninth *capitulum* but an echo of Abelard's own words quoted in 8.21.

it to be reconciled to the whole world?"[54] God the Father did not demand the blood of the Son but nevertheless accepted it when it was offered. He thirsted not for blood but for salvation, because salvation was in the blood—salvation, clearly, and not (as Abelard understands and writes) simply a demonstration of love. For this is how he concludes his numerous accusations and onslaughts, which he godlessly and ignorantly spews out against God, saying that the whole reason that God appeared in the flesh was to educate or (as he later says) instruct us by his word and example, that the whole reason why he suffered and died was to exhibit or commend his love toward us.[55]

Abael 9.23 (#613).

Moreover, what was the use of him educating us if he did not restore us? Surely, instructing us is useless unless the body of sin is first destroyed in us so that we may no longer serve sin? If the only way that Christ benefited us was by exhibiting his virtues, it can then be said that Adam harmed us only by exhibiting sin, since the remedy that is provided is according to the nature of the disease. For "as in Adam all die, so in Christ shall all be made alive" [1 Cor 15:22]. As the one is, so is the other. If the life that Christ gives is nothing but education, then certainly the death that Adam gave will likewise be nothing but education, so that they both teach people—the one by his example to sin, the other by example and word to live well and to love him. But if, assenting to the Christian faith and not the Pelagian heresy, we confess that it is by generation, not education, that the sin of Adam has been transmitted [*traductum*] to us, let us also acknowledge that it is necessary for Christ to restore righteousness to us (and through righteousness, life) not

[54] This sentence is a close quotation of the *Romans Commentary* (CCCM 11:117.234–38).

[55] A summary of the argument of Abelard's Excursus (CCCM 11:117.242–118:274).

by education but by regeneration, so that "as through the
offence of the one to all humanity for condemnation, so
also through the righteousness of the one to all humanity for justification of life" [Rom 5:18]. If that be so, how
can Abelard say that the intention of and motive for the
incarnation was to illuminate the world with the light of
his wisdom and arouse it to love him?[56] Where would then
be redemption? Certainly, as he deigns to acknowledge, illumination and encouragement to love come from Christ,
but from whom come redemption and liberation?

Abael 9.24 (#614).

Grant that the coming of Christ benefits those who can
conform their lives to his and recompense him for his love—
then what about infants? What light of wisdom will he give
to those who have as yet scarcely laid hold of the light of
life? Whence will he arouse to the love of God those who
have not yet learned to love their mothers? Will the coming
of Christ be of no benefit to them? Will it be of no benefit
to them that they have been planted together with [Christ]
in the likeness of his death, by baptism, since prevented by
their age they are not yet able to know Christ or love him?
"Our redemption," he states, "consists in the utmost love
[*dilectio*] [aroused] in us by Christ's passion."[57] It follows that
infants have no redemption because they do not have that
utmost love. Or perhaps just as they have nothing to cause
them to love, so there is nothing to cause them to perish,
so that there is nothing in them requiring regeneration in
Christ inasmuch as nothing has harmed those whose generation is from Adam? If this is how he understands [*sapit*]
it, he is out of his mind [*desipit*] with Pelagius. Whatever he
thinks of these things, it is clear how much he is prejudiced
against the sacrament of human salvation and how much,
so far as he can, he purges the profound mystery from this

---

[56] A loose quotation from *Disputatio* 7 (CCCM 89a:50).
[57] A close quotation of the *Romans Commentary* (CCCM 11:118.256–57).

dispensation—for he attributes the whole of salvation to our commitment, none of it to regeneration; he locates the glory of our redemption and essence of salvation not in the power of the Cross, not in the value [*pretium*] of the blood, but in the improvement of our way of life. But "may I never boast except in the Cross of our Lord Jesus Christ" [Gal 6:14], in which is found salvation, life, and resurrection.

Abael 9.25 (#615).

Indeed, I admire three supreme points in this work of our salvation: the form of humility in which God emptied himself, the measure of love that extended even to death and the death of the Cross, the mystery [*sacramentum*] of redemption by which he endured [*sustulit*] the death that he suffered [*pertulit*]. The first two of these without the third are like painting on air.[58] An undoubtedly great and extremely necessary example of humility, a great example of love worthy of all acceptance—but without redemption these have neither foundation nor therefore stability. I want with all my endeavour to follow the humble Jesus; I long for him that loved me and gave himself for me to embrace [*amplecti*][59] me with the arms of the love that took my place [*vicariae dilectionis*]. But I need also to feed on the Paschal Lamb, for unless I eat his flesh and drink his blood, I will have no life in myself. It is one thing to follow Jesus, another to possess him, and another to feed on him. To follow is wholesome policy; to possess and embrace [*amplecti*] is a sacred joy; to feed on him is a blessed life. "For his flesh is truly food and his blood is truly drink. The bread of God is he that descends from heaven and gives life to the world" [John 6:55, 33]. What stability does joy or policy have without life? Truly no more than a painting without any substance. Therefore, neither the examples of humility nor the insignia

---

[58] Anselm argues that to call the incarnation and Cross appropriate without showing that they were necessary is like painting on air (*Cur Deus homo* 1.4).

[59] See *Amplexus Bernardi* (chap. 12H below).

of love are anything apart from the mystery [*sacramentum*] of redemption.

C. Assessment

Thomas Merton wrote eloquently about the importance of Bernard's letter-treatise and its defence of "the strict, literal, and objective value of Christ's redemptive death for man" for the history of Catholic theology. "Without this dogmatic basis the whole mystical theology of Saint Bernard would be completely incomprehensible." The purpose of Bernard's mystical teaching is to lead us to union with God, and "it was in order to bring us to this perfect union that Jesus died on the Cross."[60]

In this letter-treatise we have Bernard's fullest continuous account of the work of Christ on the Cross. He defends the traditional doctrine of liberation from Satan and does so by integrating it with other aspects of the work of Christ, especially those expounded in his *In Praise of the New Knighthood*. Our liberation from captivity to Satan must take account of God's justice. Satan loses his grip over us because Christ, the head, pays the debt for us, his body. Thus, Bernard's account of the defeat of Satan and his account of Christ on the Cross bearing the penalty for sin are not merely juxtaposed but integrated with each other.

How fair is Bernard's account of Abelard? His account of Abelard's teaching on the work of Christ, which is full and based on substantial and largely accurate quotation from his Romans commentary, is quite distinct from the *capitula*, which have been assessed above. Thus, for example, C. H. Talbot claimed that Bernard, in his attack on Abelard, "displayed a 'stupefying credulity,' attacked too impulsively, had not read Abelard's works thoroughly but relied upon the reports of friends."[61] There is a case to be answered where the *capitula* are concerned, but not where Abelard's teaching on the work of Christ

[60] Thomas Merton, *The Last of the Fathers* (London: Catholic Book Club, 1954), 57–58.
[61] Luscombe, *School of Peter Abelard*, 114, quoting C. H. Talbot, "San Bernardo nelle sue lettere," *San Bernardo*, 151–65, here 155.

is concerned. Here Bernard did not rely upon William's report but read the Romans commentary for himself. Or, at least, he read Abelard's Excursus on 3:19-26. There is no evidence that he read wider in the commentary, which is not to be confused with proof that he did not read any wider. If Bernard is guilty of confining his critique to that short passage, it can be said in his favour that this guilt is shared with the overwhelming majority of those who have commented on Abelard over the centuries.

Bernard's charges against Abelard can be considered in turn.

1. He accused Abelard of denying that the devil has *de iure* power over sinners [Abael 5.11–8.19; #601–9]. No one questions that this is in fact what Abelard says in the Excursus and elsewhere.
2. He accused Abelard of denying the Godward aspect of the work of Christ and did so by accurately quoting all or part of six of Abelard's eight questions on this topic [Abael 8.19–22; ##609–12]. He is not unfair to the latter's teaching in the Excursus, though Abelard himself is not wholly consistent with this in the rest of his commentary.[62]
3. He accused Abelard of reducing the work of Christ to exemplarism [Abael 7.17, 8.22–9.25; #607, ##612–15]. This is the most natural reading of the Excursus, though the teaching of the rest of the commentary is not always consistent with it.[63]
4. He accused Abelard of Pelagianism [Abael 9.23; #613], but there is no scholarly consensus about the accuracy of this accusation. Murray clears Abelard of the charge, but his case is spoiled by the fact that he treats the *Epitome* as a genuine work of Abelard.[64] Williams also examines the charge more

---

[62] See chap. 2C above.

[63] See chap. 2C above.

[64] Murray, *Abelard and St Bernard*, 131–34. (Mews, "The *Sententiae* of Peter Abelard," 130–68, argues that this work is a report on Abelard's teaching by a disciple.) For other serious weaknesses in Murray's account, see Buytaert, "The Anonymous *Capitula Haeresum Petri Abaelardi*," 455. Richard E. Weingart also defends Abelard against the accusation (*The Logic of Divine Love* [Oxford: OUP, 1970], 125–26), but by "Pelagianism" he appears to mean "exemplarism." Conversely, Reinhold Seeberg, "Die Versöhnungslehre des Abälard und die Bekämpfung derselben durch

probingly, asking what Abelard means by the term "grace." He
sees "the exaltation of divine grace at the expense of human
merit" as one of the two overarching themes of the Romans
commentary, but Abelard includes natural gifts and divine
revelation under the category of grace[65]—which was precisely
how Pelagius sought to justify his teaching. Quinn concludes
that Abelard's Excursus "offers no firm support" for the view
that he was Pelagian, but that it does suggest such a tendency.[66]

5. He accused Abelard of denying that the Cross benefits infants,
    since they are unable to appreciate the love there demonstrated
    [Abael 9.24; #614]. This is not an unreasonable charge against
    the teaching of the Excursus, taken on its own, but is refuted
    by teaching elsewhere in the commentary.[67]

6. Bernard argues against Abelard that the satisfaction made by
    the one is imputed to all, the head making satisfaction for
    the members (Abael 6.15; #605). Abelard himself later in his
    commentary refers to the imputation of righteousness and
    uses the head and members analogy.[68]

---

den heiligen Bernhard," *Mittheilungen und Nachrichten für die evangelische Kirche in
Rußland* 44 (1888): 147, convicts Abelard of Pelagianism, meaning exemplarism.
Bernard in 9.23 is referring not to exemplarism but to the denial of original sin
and of the internal workings of grace.

[65] Thomas Williams, "Sin, Grace and Redemption," in *The Cambridge Companion to Abelard*, ed. Jeffery E. Brower and Kevin Guilfoy (Cambridge: CUP, 2004),
260–61, 269–76.

[66] Philip L. Quinn, "Abelard on Atonement: 'Nothing Unintelligible, Arbitrary,
Illogical, or Immoral about It,'" in *Reasoned Faith: Essays in Philosophical Theology
in Honor of Norman Kretzmann*, ed. Eleanore Stump (Ithaca and London: Cornell
University Press, 1993), 292–95, quotation at 295.

[67] Murray, *Abelard and St Bernard*, 137; Rolf Peppermüller, *Abaelards Auslegung des
Römerbriefes* (Münster: Aschendorff, 1972), 110–17.

[68] *Romans Commentary* 4.22–23 (CCCM 11:152): "IDEO REPUTATUM EST, quia
scilicet confortatus est fide, dans gloriam Deo, plenissime sciens etc., hoc est etiam
haec fidei firmitas, si opera cessarent exteriora, imputatur ei a Domino pro iustitia,
ut uidelicet ad eum iustificandum sufficiat. . . . Totam autem humanae reparationis et salutis summam, tam in capite quam in membris." Cited by Murray,
Abelard and St Bernard, 129. Laurence W. Grensted isn't altogether fair when he
states that Abelard's "whole standpoint is that of an individualist who does not ap-

So how fair to Abelard was Bernard? His account can perhaps best be described as an unsympathetic reading of the Excursus. As such, it points clearly to the deficiencies of that piece. Some of these deficiencies are rectified in occasional passages in the rest of the commentary, but there is no doubt that the Excursus indicated where Abelard's heart lay. Also, the danger that Bernard perceived, a purely exemplarist account of the work of Christ, has proved to be real.[69]

---

preciate adequately either the solidarity of mankind in sin, or the solidarity of the redeemed in Christ" (*A Short History of the Doctrine of the Atonement* [Manchester: Manchester University Press and London: Longmans, Green and Co., 1920], 107).

[69] See Alister McGrath, "The Moral Theory of the Atonement: An Historical and Theological Critique," *Scottish Journal of Theology* 38 (1985): 205–20. If Rivière, *Doctrine of the Atonement: A Historical Essay*, vol. 2, 76–78, is correct, Abelard's teaching soon led to some adopting a purely exemplarist standpoint.

6

KEY PASSAGES III: SERMONS

Half of the passages in Bernard's writings referring to the Cross come in the sermons. These are not confined to one part of the liturgical year only but are spread across the whole year.[1] Some sermons are especially rich on the topic of the Cross, and three of these are included here. It is significant that these three include sermons on the Annunciation and the Resurrection. Bernard did not confine his treatment of the Cross to occasions that demanded it.[2] This chapter is especially relevant to Bernard's *preaching* of the Cross, and readers are free if they wish to defer reading it until we examine that topic,[3] but these three sermons are relevant to all of the exposition of Bernard's doctrine, and familiarity with them will enable the reader better to follow that exposition.

---

[1] SBOp 5:13–29. See appendix I for precise details.

[2] Other liturgical sermons that are rich in references to the Cross include Nat 1, 3, 5; Circ 3; Epi 1; Palm 3; Res 3; O Pasc 1; Asc 2; Clem; And 1, 2; Adv var 1; and Div 22, 33, 34. Jean Leclercq drew attention to this in his "La dévotion médiévale envers le crucifié," *La maison dieu* 75 (1963): 126. In his "Le mystère de l'ascension dans les sermons de saint Bernard," RESB 5:119, Leclercq correctly observes that there are more sermons devoted to the Ascension than the passion, but it is wrong to deduce from that that Bernard preached more often on (about) the Ascension than the passion (ET: "The Mystery of the Ascension in the Sermons of Saint Bernard," CSQ 25 [1990]: 11).

[3] See chap. 12F below.

A. *Sermo 1 in annuntiatione domini*[4]

The scriptural text for this sermon is taken from Psalm 85:9b–10, one of Bernard's favourite biblical passages for explaining the Cross of Christ.

Ann 1.1. The sermon begins not with the Cross but with the witness of our conscience, where we place our glory. This is the witness that the Spirit bears to our spirit and consists of three things:[5] the belief that [1] we can have no forgiveness of sins unless by God's pardon; that [2] we can do no good work unless it has been given to us; that [3] we cannot merit eternal life by any works unless that also is freely given to us. We are born with original sin, but [1] pardon comes about by God not imputing our sins to us. We can [2] perform no good works of ourselves since human nature could not even stand when first created whole.

Ann 1.2. [3] As for eternal life, human merits are not such that eternal life is owed to them as of right (*debeatur ex iure*) or that God would be guilty of any injustice (*iniuria*) were he to withhold it. There are two reasons for this. First, all our merits are gifts of God so that it is we that are indebted to God rather than vice versa. Second, our merits are negligible in comparison with the coming glory. Even David had to pray, "Do not enter into judgement with your servant" (Ps 143:2).

Ann 1.3. These truths are but the beginning and foundation of faith. It is good to believe [1] that only God is *able to* expunge your sins, but you need to go further and believe that your sins *are* forgiven

---

[4] I present the sermon through summary, paraphrase, and translation. The translations, indicated by quotation marks or indentation, are my own, with some reference to two earlier translations: Bernard, *Sermons for the Seasons of the Year*, trans. William B. Flower (London: John Masters, 1861), 179–89; and *St. Bernard's Sermons for the Seasons and Principal Festivals of the Year*, 3 vols., trans. Ailbe J. Luddy (Dublin: Browne and Nolan, 1921–25), 3:134–52. For a study of this sermon, see Jean Rivière, *Le dogme de la rédemption au début du moyen âge* (Paris: J. Vrin, 1934), 319–24; pp. 336–46 place Bernard's sermon in a historical tradition.

[5] These three things are traced through the text in square brackets to make clear the flow of the argument.

by him. This is the witness that the Holy Spirit bears in your heart. Thus, Paul judges that we are justified freely by faith (Rom 3:24, 28). Therefore, [2] concerning merits, it is not enough to believe that you cannot have them except through him, unless the Spirit of truth bears witness to you that you do actually have them. Thus also [3] concerning eternal life, you need to have the witness of the Spirit that you are going to attain it as a divine gift. These paragraphs comprise one of Bernard's clearest statements of justification by faith and Christian assurance.[6] The basis for this teaching is the work of Christ on the Cross, which is expounded in the rest of the sermon.

Ann 1.4 (#263). "These witnesses are exceedingly trustworthy. [1] Concerning the forgiveness of sins, I have the strongest proof—the Lord's passion, since the voice of his blood is much more effective than that of the blood of Abel, crying out the forgiveness of all sins in the hearts of the elect. He was handed over for our sins, and there is no doubt that his death is more powerful and efficacious for good than our sins for evil." [2] Concerning good works, we have the proof of his resurrection, and [3] concerning the hope of rewards, the witness of his ascension. These three are all taught in the Psalms: 32:2; 84:5; 65:4. This is true glory, an indwelling glory, from him who dwells in our hearts by faith.

Ann 1.5. This indwelling glory is found here and now where mercy and truth have met, where righteousness and peace kiss (Ps 85.10). We need both the mercy of God's prevenient grace and the truth of our confession of sin, as in 2 Samuel 12:13. We need fruits of repentance and works of righteousness. When these come together, we can safely glory.

Ann 1.6.[7] The first man lacked nothing when God first created him, having mercy to protect him, truth to teach him, righteousness to guide him, and peace to sustain him.

---

[6] On which, see chap. 12A, B below.

[7] For paragraphs 6–14, I have followed the standard text in SBOp, not the variant text given in the notes.

Ann 1.7 (#264). Unfortunately, the first man sinned and, like the man who went from Jerusalem to Jericho, was robbed and stripped of his clothes (Luke 10:30), as Adam himself complained (Gen 3:10[8]). "He could not be reclothed or recover the stolen clothes unless Christ parted with his. For just as he could only be made alive in his soul by the intervention of Christ's bodily death, so also he could only be reclothed by Christ being robbed of his." It is because the first man lost these four virtues (Ps 85:10) that the clothes of the second and new man were divided into four parts (John 19:23). The seamless robe that was not divided (John 19:24) refers to the image of God, freedom of choice (*libertatem arbitrii*), which cannot be lost. The likeness of God, virtues, is lost by sin.

Ann 1.8. Bernard then explains how each of the four virtues (mercy, truth, righteousness, and peace) was lost by the sins of Adam and Eve.

Ann 1.9 (#265). The result of human sin is that there is a serious contention between the virtues, as in the parable of Psalm 85:10, in that truth and righteousness were crushing the wretch, but peace and mercy, free from this zeal, judged rather that he was fit to be spared.

> Indeed these two virtues are siblings, just like the other two. The first pair persists in vengeance and in smiting the transgressor on all sides, augmenting present troubles with the threat of future punishment. The other two withdraw into the heart of the Father, returning to the Lord who gave them. For he alone was thinking thoughts of peace when all appeared to be full of suffering. For peace was not inactive, and mercy did not give him silence but spoke with a godly whisper, beating at the paternal heart: "Is it possible that God will abandon for ever or will never be yet more favourable? Is it possible that God will forget to show mercy or will hold back his mercies in his anger?" [Ps 77:7, 9]. And however much the Father of compassion appeared for a long time to dissemble, in order meanwhile to satisfy the zeal of righteousness and truth, the importunity of the supplicants was not fruitless but was heard in due time.

[8] A reference that is missed in SBOp 5:19.

Ann 1.10 (#266).

> Perhaps he can be said to respond thus to those importun-
> ing him: "How long will you pray? I am a debtor to your
> sisters, righteousness and truth, whom you see ready to
> execute vengeance on the nations. Let them be called, let
> them come, and let us confer together on this matter." The
> heavenly ambassadors therefore hastened, and when they
> saw the misery and severe injury of humanity, as the prophet
> says, "the angels of peace wept bitterly" [Isa 33:7]. For who
> strives for what makes for peace more faithfully than the
> angels of peace?

Following more of this vein, Bernard gives an account of how
truth and mercy each present to the Father that which is more useful
for their side. After modestly disclaiming inside knowledge of such
dialogue, Bernard suggests how it might have gone:

> "A rational creature requires compassion," says mercy, "since
> he has become miserable and extremely wretched. The time
> has come to have pity on him, for it is already overdue."
> Truth argues the contrary: "The word that you spoke must
> be fulfilled, O Lord. It is necessary for the whole Adam to
> die, together with all who were in him on the day when he
> tasted the forbidden fruit in his transgression." "But why,"
> says mercy, "but why did you give birth, O Father, to me
> who am so quickly to pass away? For truth herself knows
> that your mercy passes away and is nothing unless at some
> point you have pity." Truth likewise says, to the contrary,
> "Who is not aware that if the transgressor evades the sen-
> tence of death, previously spoken against him, your truth,
> O Lord, has passed away and has not endured for ever?"

Ann 1.11 (#267).

> One of the cherubim suggests that they should be sent to
> King Solomon since, he says, all judgement has been given
> to the Son. And it is in his presence that "mercy and truth
> have met" [Ps 85:10], rehearsing the same difference of
> opinion that we remember from above. "I admit," says truth,
> "that mercy has a good zeal—if only it were according to

knowledge. For what determines that it is the transgressor that should be spared rather than her own sister [truth]?" "Whereas you," says mercy, "spare neither but rage with such anger against the transgressor that you overwhelm your sister as well. What evil have I done to merit this? If you have anything against me, tell me; if not, why do you persecute me?" This is a grand controversy, brothers, a most complex dispute. Who in that situation would not have said that it would have been good for us if that man had not been born? That is how it was, most beloved; that is altogether how it was. It did not appear how both mercy and truth could be simultaneously maintained. Truth added that the merits of her case would redound upon the Judge himself, saying that one must especially take care that the word of the Father should not become ineffective, that the living and effective word should not in any way be made void. "Stop, I beg you," says peace, "stop speaking like this. Such a dispute is not proper for us. Contention between the virtues is shameful."

Ann 1.12 (#268).

Moreover, the Judge bent down and wrote on the ground with his finger, and these are the words that he wrote, which peace herself (being seated nearby) read in the hearing of all: the one says, "I am ruined if Adam does not die"; the other says, "I am ruined unless he obtains mercy. Let death become good and each have what she demands." All were astounded at this word of wisdom and at the beauty of agreement and judgement alike, since it was clear that there remained no occasion for a difference of opinion, since what each one demanded could take place, both that he should die and that he should obtain mercy. "But how shall that happen?" they ask. "Death is most cruel and most bitter; death is frightful, and the very mention of it is dreadful. How can it become good?" But he said, "The death of sinners is very bad, but the death of the saints can become precious. Will it not be precious if it is the door of life, the gate to glory?" "Precious," they say, "but how shall that happen?" "It can happen," he says, "if someone dies out of love, someone who is by no means obliged to die. For death will not be able to retain the innocent one, but the jawbone of Leviathan will be pierced, as it is written, the middle wall will be demolished, and the great chaos that has been established between death and life will be scattered. Without doubt, love that is as strong as death, indeed stronger than death, if she shall enter the house of that strong man, will bind him and certainly plunder his goods and by her very crossing will set a way in the depths of the sea so that those who have been set free may cross over."[9]

Ann 1.13 (#269).

This appeared to be a good saying, inasmuch as it was faithful and worthy of all acceptance. But where will it be possible to find that innocent one who is willing to die not as a debt, not because of ill merit, but of his good will? Truth went round the earth, and there was no one clean from baseness—not even an infant who had lived but one day upon the earth. Mercy also looked all through heaven and even in the angels found (I do not say perversity) insufficient love. Evidently, this victory was indebted to another than whom no one has greater love, that he might lay down his life for useless and undeserving servants. For though he no longer calls us servants, this is because of his boundless love and extraordinary favour. But we, even if we had done all that was commanded us, what else should we say but that we are useless servants? But who would dare to approach him about this matter? Truth and mercy return on the appointed day, most anxious because they had not found what they sought.

Ann 1.14 (#270).

Then peace comforted them, saying, "You know nothing, nor do you consider. There is no one who can do this good,

---

[9] The last two sentences form a huge complex of mixed metaphors that can only be understood by references to the passages of Scriptures that are alluded to: Job 40:19-21; 1 Cor 15:26; Eph 2:14; Luke 16:26; Song 8:6; Luke 11:21; Matt 12:29; Isa 51:10.

not even one. Let him who gave the advice provide the help."
The King understood this and said, "I regret [*paenitet me*] that
I made humanity. The punishment [*poena*] holds me, and it is
incumbent upon me to bear the punishment [*poena*] and do
penance [*paenitentiam*] for humanity, whom I created." Then
he said, "Behold, I come. This cup cannot pass away unless I
drink it." And he immediately summoned Gabriel and told
him, "Go and say to the daughter of Sion, behold your king."
He hastened and said, "Prepare your bed chamber, O Sion,
and receive your king." Mercy and truth preceded the coming king, as it is written: "Mercy and truth shall go before
your face" [Ps 89:14]. Righteousness prepares the throne, as
it is written: "Righteousness and justice [*iustitia et iudicium*]
are the preparation of your throne" [Ps 89:14]. Peace comes
with the King, so that the prophet who had said "there will be
peace on our earth when he will have come" [Mic 5:5] may
be found faithful. That is why, when the Lord was born, the
choir of angels sang, "Peace on earth to people of good will"
[Luke 2:14]. Then righteousness and peace, which previously
seemed to be not a little at odds, kissed each other. The former,
if it was the righteousness of the law, had not a kiss but rather
a sting, driving by fear rather than challenging by love. Nor
did it contain reconciliation, as now does the righteousness
that is known to be by faith. Otherwise, why was it that neither Abraham, nor Moses, nor the other righteous people of
that time were able at their death to lay hold of that peace of
eternal blessedness or to enter the kingdom of peace—except
that as yet righteousness and peace had not kissed each other?
Henceforth, most beloved, we should be more inflamed with
zeal to pursue righteousness, since righteousness and peace
have now kissed and have entered into an indissoluble treaty
of friendship. So whoever brings with him the testimony of
righteousness will be received by peace with cheerful face and
happy embrace, sleeping and resting in it.

Summary of Bernard's Teaching in Ann 1

The teaching of this sermon is in harmony with that found in the
treatises, though the manner of presentation is very different. Here

it is presented through an extended allegory involving mercy and
truth, righteousness and peace, all personalized. The main theme is
the tension between God's mercy, on the one hand, and God's truthfulness, his fidelity to his promise in Genesis 2:17, on the other. The
themes of justice, punishment, and debt, which are prominent in the
treatises, receive less attention in this sermon. Whereas the expositions
in *In Praise of the New Knighthood* and *On the Errors of Peter Abelard*
are relatively systematic, the exposition in this sermon is aimed at
making one basic point and presenting it in a vivid and memorable
way. Psalm 85:10, which is the basis for the allegory, is a verse that
Bernard repeatedly cites and alludes to when expounding the Cross.[10]

B. *Sermo in feria iv hebdomadae sanctae*[11]

The title (#284) of Bernard's sermon on Holy Wednesday is "The
Passion of Christ."

4 HM 1 (#285). The sermon begins with an exhortation to all
Christians to observe Holy Week so that they may appear to suffer
together with the suffering Christ. Bernard expects his hearers to
feel remorse, to be humbled, to forgive, to abstain, to restrain themselves, and to repent.

> Rightly so. The passion of the Lord is close, which until
> today shakes the earth, splits rocks, and opens tombs. Also
> near is his resurrection, on which you will celebrate a fes-
> tival to the Lord Most High—and would that your spirits
> may ascend with eagerness and passion to the highest of
> the mighty works that he has done. Nothing better could
> be done in the world than what the Lord did on these days;
> nothing more useful could be recommended to the world
> than to celebrate the memory of it with a perpetual annual
> ceremony each year with longing of soul and to express the
> memory of his abundant sweetness. Both events were for

---

[10] See chap. 11C below.

[11] SBOp 5:56–67. The translation/paraphrase is my own, with some reference
to the translations cited in n. 4, above, of William B. Flower (89–99) and Ailbe J.
Luddy (2:134–53).

our sake because in both is the fruit of salvation for us and in both is the life of our spirit. Marvellous is your passion, Lord Jesus, which drove back the passions of us all, which propitiated [*propitiata*] for all our iniquities and which has never been found ineffective for any disease of our [soul]. For what disease can be so fatal that it is not removed by your death?

4 HM 2 (#286).

In this passion therefore, brothers, it is appropriate to consider three things in particular: the deed, the method, and the cause. In the deed patience is recommended; in the method, humility; in the cause, love.[12] His patience was remarkable, as is clearly seen—when sinners forged his back, when he was so stretched out on the tree of the Cross that all his bones might be counted, when that strongest bulwark, which protects Israel, was pierced on all sides, when his hands and feet were stabbed, just as he was led like a lamb to the slaughter and like a sheep before its shearer did not open his mouth, murmuring neither against the Father who sent him, nor against the human race on behalf of whom he paid back what he had not plundered, nor indeed against the actual people, special to him, from whom he received so much evil in return for so many privileges. Some are punished for their sins and endure with humility, and this is reckoned to them as patience. Others are scourged not so much to be cleansed as to be tested and crowned, and a greater patience is entrusted to them. It must surely be judged that the greatest patience is found in Christ, who in the cord of his inheritance was sentenced to a cruel death by those to whom in particular he had come as a saviour, just as he had altogether no sin—neither from his own action, nor contracted, nor thus in anything in which it was able to arise. Doubtless, he it is in whom dwells all the fullness of the Godhead, not symbolically but bodily, in whom

---

[12] These three points are the topics for this and the next two paragraphs.

God is reconciling the world to himself, not figuratively but substantially, who finally is full of grace and truth, not cooperatively but personally, so that he may accomplish his work. "His work is alien to him," Isaiah says [28:21], because it was both his work (which the Father gave him to do) and alien to him that such a one should endure such things. So then, you have [an example of] patience in the deed.

4 HM 3 (#287).

On the other hand, if you pay careful attention to the method, you will realize that he was not only gentle but also humble of heart. Truly, "in humility he was deprived of justice" [Acts 8:33] since he responded neither to such great blasphemies nor to the falsest crimes with which he was reproached. "We saw him," says [Isaiah], "and there was nothing special to see in him" [Isa 53:2], nor was he attractive in appearance above the sons of men, but a reproach of men as if leprous—clearly a man of sorrows, buffeted and humbled by God so that there was no beauty or elegance in him. O hindmost and highest one! O humble and exalted one! O reproach of men and glory of angels! No one is more exalted than he, nor more humble. Finally, he was anointed with spittle, sated with reproaches, condemned to a most shameful death, and reckoned among the criminals. And that humility, which is to this measure, which is indeed beyond measure, shall it deserve [*merebitur*] nothing? So just as his patience is remarkable, so is his humility wonderful, both being without compare.

4 HM 4 (#288).

Yet the cause (which is love) gloriously recommends both [the deed and the method]. For because of his great love, with which God loved us, in order to redeem a slave, neither did the Father spare the Son nor did the Son spare himself. This love is truly great because it goes beyond measure and exceeds the limit, rising above all else. "A greater love no one has," he says, "than to lay down one's life for one's friends" [John 15:13]. But you had a greater love, Lord, laying it down for your enemies. For when we were still your enemies, through your death we were reconciled both to you and to the Father. Then what other love will be found that is, has been, or will be like this love? "Someone will reluctantly die for a righteous person" [Rom 5:7]; but you suffered for the unrighteous, dying for our misdeeds—you who came to justify sinners freely, to turn slaves into brothers, captives into joint heirs, exiles into kings. And truly nothing else illustrates this patience and humility so clearly as that he surrendered his soul to death and bore the sins of many, even praying for transgressors, that they should not perish. A trustworthy saying and worthy of all acceptance! It is because he willed it that he was offered. It is not merely that he willed it and was offered, but it was because he willed it. Clearly, he alone had the power to lay down his soul; no one took it from him. When he had taken the vinegar he said, "It is accomplished" [John 19:30]. There is nothing left to be fulfilled; there is no longer anything that I await. And inclining his head, having become obedient all the way to death, he surrendered his spirit. Who is able to sleep so easily, at will? To die is indeed a great weakness, but clearly thus to die is vast power. Truly, "the weakness of God is more powerful than men" [1 Cor 1:25]. People can in madness lay most wicked hands upon themselves and to their death, but this is not to lay down their soul—it is to violently attack it and break it rather than to lay it down at will. You, godless Judas, had the wretched ability not to lay down [*ponendi*] your soul but to hang [*pendendi*] yourself. Your most depraved soul departed, not surrendered [*tradente*] by you but dragged out [*trahente*] by the noose, not sent out [*emissus*] by you but lost [*amissus*]. He alone surrendered his soul to death who alone returned to life by his own power. He alone had the power to lay it down who alone had the equally free ability to pick it up again, having the authority over life and death.

4 HM 5 (#289).

Worthy therefore is love that is so priceless, humility that is so wonderful, patience that is so insuperable. Worthy clearly

is the sacrifice [*hostia*] that is so holy, so pure, so acceptable. "Worthy is the Lamb who was slain to receive power"
[Rev 5:12] to do that for which he came, to take away the
sins of the world. I say that the sin that prevailed on earth
was threefold. Do you suppose that I mean the lust of the
flesh, the desires of the eyes, and the pride of life? That is a
threefold cord which is not easily broken. Therefore, many
drag—or rather are dragged by—this cord of vanity, but
not without cause the former trio [patience, humility, love]
prevails in the elect. For how can the recollection of that
patience not prevent all passion [*voluptatem*]? How can the
contemplation of that humility not entirely squeeze out the
pride of life? For clearly worthy is that love, and meditation
on this so captures the mind, so claims the whole soul for
itself, that it altogether blows away the vice of curiosity. The
passion of the Saviour is powerful against these three things.

4 HM 6 (#290). "But I have been thinking of saying how the
power of the Cross likewise expunges another triple sin, and this
can perhaps be heard with greater profit. I shall call the first [sin]
original, the second personal, and the third unique [*singulare*]." Bernard then proceeds to explain original sin, which comes from the
first Adam, in whom all sinned, and affects the whole human race
and each individual, from the beginning of life to the end, bringing
many woes. Even Christ, born of a virgin, was likewise full of many
woes, assailed by snares, roughly interrogated, defamed with insults,
plagued with suffering, and assailed by mockery.

4 HM 7 (#291).

> Can you then doubt that this obedience suffices to absolve
> all the guilt of the first transgression? More indeed: "There
> is difference between the misdeed and the gift. For sin from
> one led to condemnation, but grace led from many mis-
> deeds to justification" [Rom 5:15-16]. Indeed, that original
> misdeed was utterly serious in that it corrupted not just the
> person but also the nature. But each one's personal sin is
> more serious, when having loosened the reins we every-

where present our members as the weapons of iniquity for sin and are fettered not just by an alien offence but also by our own. But most serious is that unique [*singulare*] sin, which was committed against the Lord of majesty, when godless men unjustly put to death a righteous man and laid sacrilegious hands on the Son of God himself, being most cruel homicides, or rather (if it is permitted to say it) deicides. How do the first two [sins] compare to the third? At this one the whole world order turned pale and became greatly terrified, and everything was almost returned to primeval chaos. Let us suppose that one of the nobility had attacked royal territory and laid it waste; let us suppose that another, who was the king's dinner guest and advisor, had strangled his only son with treacherous hands. Relative to the second, surely the first will appear innocent and blameless? Such are all other sins relative to this sin. And yet he bore this sin in himself,[13] he who made himself sin so that he might condemn sin by the sin [of his killers]. For through this all sin is annulled, original as well as personal, and even that unique sin itself is cast out by itself.

4 HM 8 (#292).

This is the chief argument, because the two lesser [sins] have been driven out, and it is [this]: "He bore the sins of many and prayed for transgressors" [Isa 53:12], that they should not perish: "Father, pardon them, because they do not know what they are doing" [Luke 23:34]. Your irrevocable word takes flight, O Lord, and it will not return to you void but will accomplish that for which you sent it. Behold now the works of the Lord, the wonderful things that he has ordained on the earth. He was beaten with whips, crowned with thorns, pierced with nails, fixed to the Cross, sated with reproaches, but, heedless of all this suffering, says, "Pardon them." On the one side many woes of the body, on the other many mercies of his heart; on the one side suffering, on the

---

[13] An echo of 1 Pet 2:24. The reference is missed in SBOp 5:61.

other pity; on the one side the oil of exultation, on the other drops of blood flowing into the earth. The mercies of the Lord are many, but so also are the woes of the Lord. Will the woes conquer the mercies, or will the mercies surpass the woes? Let your ancient mercies conquer, O Lord; let your wisdom conquer evil. For great is their iniquity, but is your pity not surely greater, O Lord? Much in every way. "Can it be that evil is rendered for good," he says, "because they have dug a pit for my soul?" [Jer 18:20]. Clearly, they dug a pit of impatience, providing many extremely great occasions for anger. But what is their pit compared with the depth of your gentleness? Rendering evil for good, they dug a pit; but love is not annoyed, it is not cast down, it never disappears, it does not fall into a pit, and it piles up good things for evil things that are rendered it. God forbid that flies that are about to die should banish the sweetness of the ointment that flows from your body, because there is mercy in your breast, and with him there is abundant redemption. Flies that are about to die are woes; flies that are about to die are blasphemies; flies that are about to die are the scoffing that a perverse and exasperating generation renders to you.

4 HM 9 (#293).

But what do you do? In the very raising of your hands, when the morning sacrifice was becoming the evening burnt offering, in that raising, I say, by the power of the incense that ascended to heaven, covered earth, and sprinkled the underworld, you cry out, being heard for your reverence, "Father, pardon them, because they do not know what they are doing" [Luke 23:34]. Oh, how ready you are to pardon! "Oh, how great is the multitude of your sweetness, O Lord!" [Ps 31:19]. Oh, how distant your thoughts are from ours! Oh, how your mercy is declared even on the ungodly! How amazing! He cries out, "Pardon"; the Jews cry out, "Crucify." "His words are softer than oil, and theirs are like darts" [Ps 55:21]. Oh, love that is long-suffering [*patiens*] and compassionate [*compatiens*]! "Love is long-suffering" is sufficient; "Love is kind" [1 Cor 13:4] is the pinnacle. "Do not be conquered by evil" is abundant love; "But conquer evil with good" [Rom 12:21] is superabundant love. It was not only God's patience but his kindness that brought the Jews to repentance, because kind love even loves, and loves ardently, those whom it bears with. Patient love ignores, hopes for, and puts up with the offender; but kind love that draws him, persuades him, and causes him to be converted from the error of his way finally covers a multitude of sins. O Jews, you are stones, but you are striking a softer stone, from which the ring of compassion resounds and the oil of love breaks out! How, O Lord, will you cause those who long for you to drink from the torrent of your pleasure, you who thus pour the oil of your mercy over those who are crucifying you?

4 HM 10 (#294).

It is clear, therefore, that this passion is most powerful to terminate every sort of sin. But who knows whether it has been given to me? It has been given to me because it could not have been given to anyone else. Perhaps to an angel? But he has no need of it. Perhaps to the devil? But he is not restored. Finally, it was not in the likeness of angels, and certainly not in the likeness of demons, but in human likeness that he was made; and being found in human appearance, he emptied himself, taking the form of a servant. He was a son and he became as a servant. Nor was it only the form of a servant that he took, so that he might be subject, but even of an evil servant, so that he might be beaten, and a servant of sin, so that he might pay the penalty [*poenam solveret*], although he had no guilt. "In the likeness," [Paul] says, "of men" [Phil 2:7], not man, because the first man was created neither in sinful flesh nor in the likeness of sinful flesh. Christ, however, immersed himself exactly and profoundly in the universal human wretchedness, lest the sharp eye of the devil should detect this mystery of godliness. Therefore, he was found in appearance, in every appearance, as a man, and where nature is concerned there appeared in him no sign of uniqueness. It is because he was thus found that he

was crucified. To a few, however, he did reveal himself, that
there might be some who believed; but from the rest he was
concealed, because "if they had known, they would never
have crucified the Lord of glory" [1 Cor 2:8]. He added
ignorance to that unique sin so that he might be able to
pardon the ignorant with some semblance of justice.

4 HM 11 (#295).

That ancient Adam, who fled from the face of God, left us
two things as an inheritance, namely, toil and sorrow: toil in
work, sorrow in suffering. He paid no attention to this in
Paradise, which he had received to work and take care of, to
work it with pleasure and to take care of it faithfully, both
for himself and for his posterity. Christ the Lord investigated
toil and sorrow that he might deliver them into his hands,
or rather himself into their hands, having been stuck fast in
the mire of the abyss, and those waters penetrated even to
his soul. "Look at my humility and my toil," he says to the
Father, "because I am a pauper and have been in toils from
my youth" [Ps 25:18; 88:15]. He toiled while enduring; his
hands served in toils. Concerning sorrow, see what he said:
"Pay attention and observe, all you who pass by, whether
there be any sorrow like my sorrow" [Lam 1:12]. "Surely he
bore our weaknesses and carried our sorrows" [Isa 53:4]—a
man of sorrows, poor and grieving, tempted in every way
but without sin. In life he was engaged in passive work, and
in death he endured an active passion, while he effected
salvation in the middle of the earth. So I will be mindful,
as long as I live, of those toils that he endured in preaching,
of his weariness in travel, of his trials in fasting, of his vigils
in prayer, of his tears in sharing our suffering. I will recall
also his sorrows, the jeers, the spittle, the blows, the mockery,
the reproaches, the nails, and the like, which in abundance
passed through and over him. His courage benefits me, as
does his likeness [to us], but only with the addition of my
imitation of him, that I might follow his footsteps. Otherwise that righteous blood, which was poured out upon the
earth, will also be required of me, and I will not be exempt

from that unique crime of the Jews, because I have been evidently ungrateful for such love, because I have insulted the spirit of grace, because I have considered the blood of the covenant impure, because I have trampled on the Son of God.[14]

4 HM 12 (#296). Bernard differentiates between those who suffer toil and sorrow either because they have no choice or for worldly ends and those who do so in order to follow Christ. The latter are those who "follow him wherever he goes" [Rev 14:4]. "Imitation of this sort is the strongest argument that the passion of the Saviour and his likeness to humanity serve to my advantage. Here is the savour; here is the fruit of his toil and sorrow."

4 HM 13 (#297). Bernard then draws the contrast between the ease with which God created the universe by a mere word and the difficulty with which he recreated us, outlining the hardships of the thirty-three years of Jesus' life, without explicit mention of his death.

4 HM 14 (#298). Finally, he extols the blessedness of those whose lives are motivated by righteousness. "For the Lord Jesus has embraced us by taking our toil and sorrow, so let us also cleave to him with vicarious embraces through righteousness and his righteousness, by aiming our works at righteousness, by enduring suffering for righteousness."

Summary of Bernard's Teaching in 4 HM

In this sermon there is a greater emphasis on the sufferings of Christ for us and the response that this should elicit from us. In particular, Christ's patience, humility, and love recommend these to us. At the same time it is clear from passing references that Christ endured suffering in order to pay the penalty for our sins. Bernard also focuses on the unique sin of deicide, an issue that had earlier been raised by Abelard.

[14] The last three clauses are taken straight from Heb 10:29. This reference is missed in SBOp 5:64.

C. *Sermo 1 in resurrectione domini*[15]

The title of this sermon is "The Taunts of the Jews."

Res 1.1 (#302).

> "The Lion of the tribe of Judah has overcome" [Rev 5:5].
> Wisdom has completely overcome wickedness, boldly
> reaching from end to end and sweetly regulating all things—
> boldly on behalf of me, sweetly for me. He overcame on
> the Cross the blasphemies of the Jews, he bound the strong
> soldier in his house, and he triumphed over the very rule
> of death. Where indeed are your taunts, O Jews? Where, O
> devil [*zabule*], are your instruments of captivity? "Where, O
> death, is your victory?" [1 Cor 15:55] The false accuser has
> been confounded; the plunderer has been despoiled. This
> is a new sort of power. Death, hitherto victorious, is struck
> dumb. What about you, O Jew, who the day before shook
> your sacrilegious head before the Cross? Why did you tor-
> ment with taunts the holy head of humanity, Christ? "Let
> Christ, the king of Israel," he said, "come down from the
> Cross" [Mark 15:32]. O poisonous tongue, word of wicked-
> ness, depraved speech! This is not, Caiaphas, what you said
> shortly before: "It is expedient for a person to die for the
> people and not for the whole race to perish" [John 15:50].
> You did not say that on your own nor speak from yourself,
> because it was not false. "If he is the king of Israel, let him
> come down from the Cross" [Matt 27:42]—this clearly is
> yours, or rather his who is false from the beginning. Why
> should it seem to follow that he should descend, if he is
> king, rather than ascend? So have you forgotten, O ancient
> serpent, how you once withdrew after being confounded
> when you presumed to say, "Throw yourself down" and "All
> these things I will give you if will fall down and worship

---

[15] SBOp 5:73–94. The translation/paraphrase is my own, with some reference
to the translation cited in n. 4, above, of William B. Flower (99–113). I have followed the standard text in SBOp, not the variant text given in the notes. On the
redaction history of this sermon, see Jean Leclercq, "S. Bernard prêcheur," RESB
4:81–93.

me" [Matt 4:6, 9]? So has what you read escaped you, O Jew, that the Lord reigned from the tree, so that you deny the king because he remains on the tree? But perhaps you have not heard that this declaration was destined not for the Jews but for the nations: "Say to the nations that the Lord reigned from the tree" [Ps 96:10].[16]

Res 1.2 (#303).

Rightly then did the Gentile procurator inscribe the royal title on the tree and the Jew was not able to undo the inscription of this title, as he wished, much less to hinder the Lord's passion and our redemption. "Let him come down," they say, "if he is the king of Israel" [Matt 27:42]. On the contrary, because he is the king of Israel let him not abandon the royal title, let him not lay down the imperial sceptre— the sovereignty being on his shoulder, as Isaiah predicted [9:6]. "Do not write," said the Jews to Pilate, "'King of the Jews,' but that he said, 'I am the King of the Jews.'" Pilate replied, "What I have written, I have written" [John 19:21-22]. If Pilate wrote what he wrote, shall Christ not complete what he began? "He himself began and will save us" [Hos 6:2]. But they say, "He saved others but he cannot save himself" [Matt 27:42]. On the contrary, if he comes down, he will save no one. Since one can only be saved by persevering to the end, how much less will one be able to be the Saviour [without persevering]? Therefore he saved others, for he had no need of salvation, since he is salvation. He works our salvation, and he does not allow the evening sacrifice to lack even the tail of the saving victim. He knew, O wicked one, what you are thinking. He will not give you the opportunity to steal from us perseverance, which alone is crowned. He will not cause to fall silent the tongues of preachers, of those who comfort the fainthearted and plead with each one, "Do not abandon your place"—which

---

[16] The words "from the tree" are not in the original Psalm text and are first found in Justin Martyr, *I Apology* 41 and *Dialogue with Trypho* 73.

would certainly be the outcome if they could reply that
Christ abandoned his place.

Bernard then argues that the disciples despaired and the Jews taunted,
but the devil could not hurt Christ with either weapon.

Res 1.3 (#304).

In the meantime he especially exhibits patience, recommends humility, fulfils obedience, and completes love. For
the four ends of the Cross are decorated with these four
jewels of virtue. Love towers over them, obedience is on the
right, patience is on the left, and humility, the root of the
virtues, is at the base. The accomplishment of the Lord's passion enriched the trophy of the Cross with these [virtues],
when humble at the Jew's blasphemies and patient at his
wounds he was afflicted inwardly by words and outwardly
by nails. For love was completed in that he laid down his
life for his friends, and obedience was accomplished when
he inclined his head and surrendered his spirit, having become obedient all the way to death. Whoever said, "If he
is the king of Israel, let him come down from the Cross"
[Matt 27:42] was busy [trying] to rob the church of this
dowry and to deprive her of the glory of Christ. The aim,
no doubt, was that there might be no pattern of obedience,
no incentive to love, no example of patience or humility,
but that these most agreeable words, sweeter than honey
and the honeycomb, might be obliterated from the gospel:
"No one has greater love than this, that someone lay down
one's life for one's friends" [John 15:13]; and to the Father:
"I have accomplished the work you gave me to do" [John
17:4]; and again to the disciples: "Learn from me because
I am gentle and humble in heart" [Matt 11:29], and "I, if I
am lifted up from the earth, will draw all things to myself"
[John 12:32]. This is what causes grief to the stratagem of
the poisonous snake—the bronze snake that was lifted up in
the desert, by looking at which the wounds that he inflicted
might be healed. Who else do we think incited Pilate's wife
to send to him, saying, "Have nothing to do with that righteous man, for I have suffered much today because of him

in a dream" [Matt 27:19]. The enemy was afraid even then; but now especially, feeling himself to be weakened by the power of the Cross, he is led by a tardy repentance, and those whom he incited to crucify him he now incites to urge him to come down from the Cross. Indeed, they say, "If he is the king of Israel, let him come down from the Cross, and we will believe him" [Matt 27:42]. This is clearly the stratagem of the snake, the invention of spiritual wickedness. The godless one had heard the words of the Saviour, "I have been sent only to the sheep that are perishing, the house of Israel" [Matt 15:24], and was aware how much zeal he seemed to have for the salvation of that people. Therefore, he very craftily instructed the tongues of the blasphemers and suggested that they say, "Come down and we will believe"—as if nothing was able to prevent him from coming down, who longed so much for them to believe.

Res 1.4 (#305). Christ cannot be swayed by Satan.

The aim of his crafty persuasion was not of course that they might believe but actually that our faith in him (if there was any) might by all means be destroyed. For as we read that "the works of God are complete" [Deut 32:4], how could we acknowledge a God who had left the work of salvation incomplete? But let us hear how Christ answers these things through the prophet. Do you seek a sign, O Jew? "Expect me in the day of my resurrection" [Zeph 3:8]. If you wish to believe, I have already shown you greater works. I have multiplied signs; I have healed people yesterday and the day before; today I must accomplish more. Was it not a greater thing to see evil spirits come out of possessed bodies and paralytics leap out of their beds than the nails that you thrust in spring back from my hands and feet? But this is the time to suffer, not to do; and as in vain you tried to anticipate the hour of my passion, so you will not be able to hinder it.

Res 1.5 (#306). The sign that was given was his resurrection, not his descent from the Cross. The Lion of the tribe of Judah has prevailed.

He who did not come down from the Cross came forth from the closed tomb. Whether this was truly greater, let our enemies judge, who took such care to defend the tomb, sealing the stone and posting sentries. Christ came out of the closed tomb. "But there is a place from which he was unwilling to proceed through closed doors—the prison of Gehenna. Accordingly, he shattered the iron bars and crushed all the bolts so that he might freely lead out his people, whom he had redeemed from the hand of the enemy, and so that processions of those who have been cleansed might come out through open gates, those who had "washed their robes and made them white in the blood of the Lamb" [Rev 7:14]. Entirely "white in the blood" because the cleansing water also flowed out with [the blood] in it, and he who saw it bears witness [John 19:34-35]—certainly "white in the blood" but in the milky blood of the tender lamb, white and ruddy, as you have in the Song of Songs: "My beloved," says the bride, "is white and ruddy, the pick of thousands" [5:10]. That is why the witness to the resurrection also appears in a white robe and with a face charged with lightning [Matt 28:3].

Res 1.6 (#307). The resurrection is the supreme miracle that confounds the Jews, who mockingly said, "If he is the king of Israel, let him come down from the Cross" [Matt 27:42]. Others who came back from the dead died again, but "'Christ rising from the dead dies no more; death will have no more power over him' [Rom 6:9]. Those who die a second time need to be revived again, but Christ, 'by dying, died once to sin; but by living, [he] lives to God' [Rom 6:10] and lives for eternity. Rightly then is Christ the firstfruits of those who rise again, who rose in such a way as never again to fall [Amos 5:2], who alone achieved immortality."

Res 1.7 (#308). Christ is unique in that he alone raised himself. Elisha raised someone else, but he himself lies in the tomb, "hoping to be raised by another, by him who triumphed over the reign of death in himself." This demonstrates that his uniqueness and his power is such that even while he was counted with the dead, he was free among them.

Res 1.8 (#309). This paragraph begins with the resurrection, noting that Christ "redeemed humanity on the Cross on the sixth day, the same day that he made humanity in the beginning." He is the victor over death,

> so let all of us who follow our head not cease to do penance [*agere paenitentiam*] for the whole of this day on which we were created and redeemed; let us not cease to take up our Cross, persevering in it as he himself persevered, until the Spirit says that we may rest from our labours. Let us listen to no one, brethren, not to flesh and blood, nor to any spirit who urges us to come down from the Cross. Let us remain on the Cross; let us die on the Cross; let us be taken down by the hands of others, not by our own fickleness. It was righteous men who took our head down; but let holy angels esteemed by him take us down so that when the day of the Cross has been manfully accomplished, we may rest pleasantly and sleep happily in our graves, anticipating the blessed hope and the coming of the glory of the great God, who will raise our bodies at length on the third day and make them like his glorious body.

But those who lie dead four days begin to stink.

Res 1.9 (#310). There is a contrast between the three days of God's appointment and the fourth day introduced by the corrupt sons of Adam. Christ is the Lamb who was slain but also the Lion of Judah that prevails. The wicked should fear his return, but his people will rejoice.

Res 1.10 (#311). Let those rejoice who are clothed with confession. Revelation 5 speaks of the scroll with seven seals, which only the Lion of Judah is able to unseal. "'And I looked and there was a Lamb standing in the middle of the throne, looking as if he had been killed' [Rev 5:6]. And he came and took the book from the right hand of the one seated on the throne and opened it. And there was great rejoicing and thanksgiving. John had heard the Lion and saw the Lamb. The Lamb was killed, the Lamb received the book, the Lamb opened it, and the Lion appeared. In short, 'Worthy is the Lamb who was killed,' say the elders, 'to receive power' [Rev 5:12]—not to lose his gentleness but to receive power, so that he may both remain a Lamb and be a Lion." In fact, he was himself the book that could not be opened.

Res 1.11 (#312). What of the seven seals? Bernard describes each in turn. The third is Christ's acceptance of the sign of circumcision, the remedy for sin and medicine for sickness. "The sixth is the seal of the Cross, where the Lord of glory hung between thieves and was lumped with the unrighteous [*cum iniquis deputatus est*]."

Res 1.12 (#313). There is no more room for tears, because "worthy is the Lamb who was killed." The Jews referred to him as a deceiver [Matt 27:65], and they were right. He is a deceiver—though godly rather than wicked. "He deceived you, O Jews, in the passion, for by the resurrection the conquering Lion of Judah grew strong and prevailed. 'For had they known, they would never have crucified the Lord of Glory' [1 Cor 2:8]." The resurrection confirms Christ's identity and witnesses against the Jews.

Res 1.13 (#314).

> What about what you said, "Let him come down from the Cross, and we will believe him" [Matt 27:42]? You wanted to break the seal of the Cross, promising that you would then come into faith. Behold, [the seal] has been opened, not broken—come in. Besides, if you do not believe in him when he rises again, you would not have believed in him if he had come down [from the Cross]. As the Cross of Christ caused you to stumble—"for the message of the Cross is indeed a stumbling block to Jews," says the Apostle [1 Cor 1:18, 23]—at least let the novelty of the resurrection arouse you. We find our glory in the Cross. To us who are being saved it is the power of God and, as we have shown, the fullness of all virtues. (Maybe the Jews will stumble also at the resurrection and, like the elder brother, refuse to come in.) Let us enter, brothers, and "feast on the unleavened bread of sincerity and truth, for Christ our Passover Lamb has been offered in sacrifice" [1 Cor 5:8, 7]. Let us embrace the virtues recommended to us on the Cross: humility and patience, obedience and love.

Res 1.14 (#315). This paragraph focuses on the resurrection and makes two passing references to the Cross. The resurrection of Christ was a transmigration, not a return. He did not return to this mortal life (after the accomplishment of the Cross) but rose into a new life. For by dying, he died once to sin; but by living, he lives not to the flesh but to God (Rom 6:10).

Res 1.15 (#316). Christ's resurrection was a Passover and not a return. Likewise, we should not return after Lent to our former bad habits. "We have shared Christ's sufferings, we have been once more planted with him through a baptism of tears, penitence, and confession. 'If, therefore, we have died to sin, how shall we still live in it?' [Rom 6:2]."

Res 1.16 (#317). "So those who love the world, the enemies of the Cross of Christ, who (having received his name) are called Christians in vain, long throughout the time of Lent for today, Easter Sunday, alas, so that they can more freely give way to pleasure." Bernard laments the indulgences and sins that reemerge on Easter Day. "What less respect is required by the time of the resurrection than the time of the passion? But it is clear that you respect neither. For if you suffer with him, you will also reign with him; if you die with him, you will also rise with him."

Res 1.17 (#318). Bernard cites Paul's words about many being weak and sick [1 Cor 11:30] through unworthy participation in the sacrament. If this leads you to refuse the sacraments, you have no life, because unless you eat Christ's flesh and drink his blood, you have no life in you [John 6:53]. Bernard applies this warning to transgressors.

Res 1.18. The last paragraph contains a concluding exhortation, without reference to the Cross.

Summary of Bernard's Teaching in Res 1

It is interesting that in a sermon on the resurrection there should be such an emphasis upon the Cross. The central theme is the Jews' challenge to Jesus to come down from the Cross. Bernard argues that Christ did not need to descend in order to prove his deity, since that is shown both by his miracles and by his resurrection. He also sees Christ as reigning from the tree. Bernard alludes to his work in despoiling Satan (Res 1.1) and redeeming us by his blood (Res 1.5), but his perseverance is presented primarily as a "pattern of obedience, [an] incentive to love, [an] example of patience or humility" (Res 1.3). An Abelardian emphasis upon the subjective effects of the Cross predominates, but it is one that is based on the objective redemption that Christ's sacrifice has produced.

PART III

Teaching on the Cross

7

REDEMPTION AND THE CROSS

A. Christ as the Second Adam

Irenaeus presented a picture of Christ as the Second Adam who recapitulates the First Adam, putting right what the latter had made wrong, which is one of the components of the "classical model."[1] Bernard does not have much to say about this, but he does say a little. He contrasts Christ and Adam, calling the former the "Second Adam."[2] Elsewhere he makes reference to the "First Adam"[3] and to the "old Adam."[4] He also twice refers to Christ as the "second man," as does Paul in 1 Corinthians 15:47,[5] but never as the "Last Adam" (1 Cor 15:45). He does, however, draw on Paul's contrast between the earthly and the heavenly man (1 Cor 15:47-49).[6] He also portrays Christ as the one who was able to erase the sin of the "first man" (#519).[7] The idea of Christ as Second Adam is also

---

[1] On the classical model, see chap. 2A above.

[2] Adv 2.2 (SBOp 4:171); Nat 3.1 (SBOp 4:258); Sept 2.1 (#239; SBOp 4:349); Ded 6.3 (SBOp 5:398; drawing on 1 Cor 15.47); Div 28.3 (#456; SBOp 6/1:206); Sent 3.110 (#539; SBOp 6/2:186). In Ep 542 (SBOp 8:509) Christ is the Second Adam by contrast with Abbot Adam.

[3] SC 20.3 (#22; SBOp 1:115); 4 HM 6 (#290; SBOp 5:60).

[4] Adv 5.3 (in the context of 1 Cor 15:49; SBOp 4:189); P Epi 1.3 (#231; SBOp 4:316); Par 7 (SBOp 6/2:299).

[5] #264, #586.

[6] Adv 5.3 (SBOp 4:189); Div 3.2 (SBOp 6/1:87); Sent 3.79 (SBOp 6/2:117).

[7] Here, as in ##264–70, the context is the conflict between truth, which demands our death on the basis of Gen 2:17, and mercy, which seeks our salvation (Ps 85:10). See chap. 11C below.

implicit in the parallels between Adam and Christ to be discussed further below,[8] although these parallels occur in his account of how Christ died for our sins. Finally, citing Hosea 6:2, Bernard contrasts our fallen state under Adam, our present state in Christ, and our future destiny with Christ (V Nat 2.2–3). Because the recapitulation perspective on the work of Christ places as much or more emphasis on the incarnation and the resurrection as on the Cross, it will not feature much in this book.

A similar perspective is that of the "Great Exchange." The idea, often used by Bernard, is that Christ took something less desirable from us in order to give us something more desirable in exchange. Bernard applies this basic idea in a number of different ways. The Son of God became man to make us sons of God (V Nat 1.2). Though he was rich, he became poor for us that we might be enriched by his poverty (2 Cor 8:9; #364).[9] Christ chose to exile himself from heaven in order to bring us back to heaven (#450). Just as we suffer from the disobedience of the old Adam, so we benefit from the obedience of Christ. The one stretched out guilty hands to the forbidden tree; the other stretched out guiltless hands on the saving tree (#231). Through his pure filial obedience, Christ offered sacrifice for the primal disobedience (#505). He shared God's wrath against us so that we might share God's grace with him (#545). He assumed the guilt (*meritum*) of our sins, in exchange bestowing upon us his righteousness (#148). Like the man going from Jerusalem to Jericho, we have been stripped of our clothes, and we can only be reclothed by Christ being stripped of his garments (#264). The sinless one was pierced with thorns for us, so we should be pierced for our own sins with him (#542).[10] This idea of an "exchange" comes out very clearly where Bernard compares Christ to a trader who exchanges gold for lead. The righteous one is given for a sinner, the

---

[8] See chap. 11F below.

[9] Bernard also cites 2 Cor 8:9 with the "for us" but omits the reference to our enrichment (#152 and #321; also V Nat 6.7, just after #195). He was more interested in Christ setting an example of voluntary poverty than in the idea of the Great Exchange.

[10] I have followed the emendation of the Latin text given in CF 55:383, n. 151.

Son of God is exchanged for a servant, the Creator is killed for a creature, the Lord is condemned for a slave. Bernard reflects on this in language that he also uses elsewhere: "What gracious compassion, what freely given and sure love, what surprising condescension, what marvellous sweetness, what unsurpassable clemency."[11] It may be a "Great Exchange" (the traditional term) from our perspective, but Bernard notes what a lousy deal (*vilis negotiatio*) it is from God's perspective (#477).

Another New Testament text relevant to this theme is 2 Corinthians 5:21, which states that Christ was made sin so that we might become the righteousness of God. Bernard cites this with a spin, stating that Christ *made himself* sin.[12] To what end? That he might unite penitent sinners with himself (#105); that he might condemn sin by the sin of his killers (Rom 8:3; #291).

In the latter half of the Middle Ages there was an increasing focus on the humanity, weakness, and suffering of Christ. Bernard played a central role in this development.[13] Leclercq sounds a warning here. Some have suggested a stark contrast between the early medieval emphasis on the objective achievements of the triumphant Christ and an emphasis emerging later in the Middle Ages on the weakness and suffering of the human Christ. Leclercq argues against this approach, citing evidence both from Bernard and from his contemporaries. What the Cross evokes for Bernard is not primarily the sufferings of Jesus but the fruit of this suffering, the redemption that he brought.[14]

---

[11] Elias Dietz, "Saint Bernard's Sermon 42 *De diversis*: Taking a Closer Look," CSQ 39 (2004): 119. As Dietz notes on p. 112, the identical wording is found in our #450, and very similar wording is found in our #134.

[12] See #38, #105, and #291.

[13] See Ulrich Köpf, "Die Passion Christi in der lateinischen religiösen und theologischen Literatur des Spätmittelalters," in *Die Passion Christi in Literatur und Kunst des Spätmittelalters*, ed. Walter Haug and Burghart Wachinger (Tübingen: Max Niemeyer, 1993), 25–30; Ulrich Köpf, "Schriftauslegung als Ort der Kreuzestheologie Bernhards von Clairvaux," in *Bernhard von Clairvaux und der Beginn der Moderne*, ed. Dieter R. Bauer and Gotthard Fuchs (Innsbruck and Vienna: Tyrolia, 1996), 194–99.

[14] Jean Leclercq, "La dévotion médiévale envers le crucifié," *La maison dieu* 75 (1963): 124–32, especially 129.

Until the end of the twelfth century there is no preoccupation with or prolonged meditation on Christ's sufferings, but the Cross remains primarily an objective reality outside of ourselves.[15] (Elsewhere Leclercq notes that Bernard's reputation as "doctor of the humanity of Christ" is based largely on pseudo-Bernardine texts from the late Middle Ages.[16]) Against Leclercq, Köpf points to texts from *Sermones in Cantica* 43, 45, 61, and 62 where Bernard does indeed focus attention on Christ's suffering, though admitting that Bernard's teaching there must be distinguished from further developments that took place in the later Middle Ages.[17]

It is hard to deny that Bernard played a role in the trend toward an increasing emphasis on the humanity of the suffering Christ and our subjective engagement with that. But if one examines the full range of Bernard's teaching across the whole body of his works, it is true that his emphasis remains upon the objective achievements of the Cross.

B. Christ Made Merciful through His Passion

The three main emphases of Bernard's teaching on the Cross concern its effects on God (the Cross puts us right with God), on Satan (bringing victory over Satan and death), and on ourselves (the Cross teaches and influences us).[18] All of these emphases have played a major role in interpretations of the Cross from apostolic times.

Basing himself especially on some passages in the Letter to the Hebrews, Bernard also draws attention to another aspect of the Cross, one that has not so often received attention—the effect that

---

[15] Leclercq, "La dévotion médiévale envers le crucifié," 132.

[16] Jean Leclercq, *Bernard of Clairvaux and the Cistercian Spirit,* CS16 (Kalamazoo, MI: Cistercian Publications, 1976), 106–7; Jean Leclercq, "General Introduction to the Works of Saint Bernard (III)," CSQ 40 (2005): 387. Ironically, Bernard's reputation as "mellifluous" was nourished especially by the emphasis of late medieval pseudo-Bernardine writings on devotion to the humanity of Christ (Jean Leclercq, "Études sur saint Bernard et le texte de ses écrits," ASOC 9 [1953]: 189–90).

[17] Köpf, "Schriftauslegung als Ort der Kreuzestheologie Bernhards von Clairvaux," 208–13.

[18] These three points are covered in chaps. 10–11, 8, and 9.

it had on Christ himself.[19] Christ was, in the words of Isaiah, a man of sorrows, acquainted with infirmity, who bore our weaknesses and carried our sorrows (Isa 53:3-4).[20] Although as Lord of the virtues he understood obedience, nonetheless he learned obedience through what he suffered (Heb 5:8; #75).[21] In another passage Bernard alters the text, stating that Christ learned compassion through what he suffered (#367).[22] When Hebrews also says that Christ became a merciful high priest through his bodily experiences (Heb 2:17), Bernard relates this to the suffering described in Isaiah 53:3-4.[23] Elsewhere Bernard gives the same teaching but without reference to Isaiah or Hebrews. What Christ knew theoretically from all eternity as God, he learned from experience in time—namely, human weakness and misery (#427). As Pelikan puts it, "Christ the teacher had, however, himself been a pupil first."[24]

This theme of learning through experience is expounded at length in Bernard's *Steps of Humility and Pride*. Only those who have suffered themselves can really sympathise with sufferers. Christ suffered in order to know compassion, and he shared our misery to learn mercy—in the same way that he learned obedience from the things he suffered. It is not that he did not previously know how to be merciful, his mercy being from eternity to eternity (Ps 103:17), but that he learned by experience in time what he knew from eternity as God (Hum 3.6; #116). At this point in Hum, Bernard backs off somewhat and suggests an alternative interpretation, that Christ learned obedience and mercy only in the sense that his body, the church, learned these things (Hum 3.7; #117). But then he reverts to his original interpretation, citing Hebrews 2:16-18, which clearly

[19] On the novelty or otherwise of Bernard's focus on the human sufferings of Christ, see the discussion of Leclercq and Köpf in chap. 7A above.

[20] #37, #75, #119, #192, #241, #287, #295, #363, #378, #495, #522, #561. These passages each contain all or some of the four points from Isa 53:3-4.

[21] See also #116 and #475.

[22] See also OS 5.10.

[23] See #42, #75, and #495.

[24] Jaroslav Pelikan, *The Growth of Medieval Theology (600–1300)* (Chicago: University of Chicago Press, 1978), 148–49.

refers to Christ, the head, not the church, the body. He learned
through the experience of suffering and temptation the lesson of
sympathy and mercy (Hum 3.8; #118). By suffering as described
in Isaiah 53:3-4, Christ learned from experience the mercy of a
fellow sufferer and the obedience of a fellow subject (Hum 3.9;
#119). While he has an eternal mercy, he has now added to this the
mercy that comes from sharing in our misery.[25] In his eternal mercy
he has infinite compassion for us, but it is only as we see him suffering in his passion that we fully realise this (Hum 3.12; #120). In
this exposition Bernard is of two minds. At times he affirms what
Hebrews states, that Christ actually learned obedience and mercy,
but at other times he suggests either that this refers to the church
(#117) or that what changes is not Christ's mercy but simply our
ability to believe in it (#120).

C. Salvation Not by the Cross on Its Own

Our topic is Bernard's teaching on the Cross, but it must not be
supposed that he confined Christ's work of salvation to that event.[26]
His *De laude novae militiae* is one of the key texts for his teaching on
the Cross, which he there discusses at length,[27] but in this work he
also tells us that "everything concerning Christ is good for us; everything is salvific and necessary—his weakness as well as his majesty."
Christ emptied himself and became weak, suffering hunger, thirst,
tiredness, and much else. By doing this, he provided a model and a
pattern for us to follow. So while his death freed us from death, his
life freed us from error and his grace from sin, Christ himself thus
being an example and mirror of life and instruction for us (#152).[28]
Bernard makes similar points elsewhere, relating both the Cross and

---

[25] See also #84: it is through his wounds that Christ can sympathise with our
weakness.

[26] A point made by Leclercq, "La dévotion médiévale envers le crucifié," 126.

[27] See chap. 4A above.

[28] A passage to which Joël Regnard, "Il nous sauve non seulement par sa mort
mais aussi par sa vie," Coll 58 (1996): 41, draws attention.

salvation to other phases of Christ's incarnate life.[29] His conception, every stage of his life, his death, his resurrection, his ascension, and his sending of the Spirit were all for us and work together for our salvation (#353). "Christ died for our offences, rose again for our justification, ascended for our protection, sent the Spirit for our consolation, and at some time will return for our perfection. He demonstrated his mercy in death, his power in resurrection and both in the remainder" (#131). A few examples from Bernard's writings will show how at every stage Christ was effecting our salvation.

Annunciation. When the angel confronted Mary with the news that she was to give birth to the one who will be the price of our salvation, her consent was necessary for our redemption to proceed (#177).

Conception. Christ's conception by the Holy Spirit purifies our evil conceptions. In his nine months in the womb he was cleansing our ancient wound.[30]

Nativity. Bernard observes how talking about the mystery of the nativity leads one to ponder the passion. Christ's birth is not effective for us without his death on the Cross, since it was there that he gave himself as a ransom, the price of our redemption (Ps 49:8; #201). It was for us and for our salvation that he was born and likewise that he died and was buried (#208–9).

Circumcision. It was at his circumcision that Christ began to shed his blood for our salvation, since it was for our sins, not for his own, that he was circumcised (#214). He did not need circumcision for himself, but he accepted the wound to heal our wounds. Though he was without sin, he did not spurn being counted as a sinner (#216). We are to imitate the patience, humility, and love that he displayed in his circumcision (#218). Christ the head accepted on behalf of the members of his body the cure that he did not need for himself (#220).

---

[29] For a comprehensive study of the significance of every event in the life of Christ, from his incarnation to his ascension, see Alberich Altermatt, "Christus pro nobis: Die Christologie Bernhards von Clairvaux in den 'Sermonum per annum,'" AC 33 (1977): 64–143.

[30] Pent 2.4, immediately preceding #353.

Epiphany. The gifts of the magi included myrrh, pointing forward to his death (#227–29).

Life. While the death of Christ delivers us from death, it is his life that gives us a pattern of how to live (#146). In all his manner of life Christ strove against sin, by word and example, but it is by his Cross and resurrection that the battle is won (#197).

Descent into the underworld. The faithful who died before the death of Christ faced no festive joy but only a dark prison.[31] Christ by dying for his friends descended into the underworld (*infernum*; #182) and plundered it (#611). He brought out of prison the prisoners sitting in darkness and shadow of death (#202) and led out from the prison of Gehenna his people that he had redeemed from the hand of the enemy (#306). While he went once to the underworld (*inferos*) to deliver people (1 Pet 3:19), this is not something that he will ever do again (#108).

Resurrection. Bernard focuses often upon the Cross, but it should not be imagined that the Cross on its own would be effective without the resurrection. Christ defeated Satan both by strategy and by strength—by strategy in that the adversary laid hands on the innocent one, thus forfeiting his rights over humanity, by strength in rising from the dead (#271). Bernard repeatedly cites Romans 4:25 to the effect that Christ was raised for our justification.[32] Just as we are united with Christ's death by baptism, so also through his resurrection we walk in newness of life (Rom 6:4-5).[33] Being risen with Christ, we should seek the things that are above (Col 3:1; Res 1.18). His death teaches us how to die with peace of mind, since by rising again he brings the hope of resurrection from the dead (#146).

Pierre-Yves Emery claims that Bernard, in his theology of redemption (though not elsewhere), sees the death of Christ as salvific in isolation from its essential relation to the resurrection.[34] It is certainly true that Bernard, like the apostle Paul, associates our

---

[31] #423 and #583.
[32] #2, #66, #131, #263, #315 (variant text only), #317, and #659.
[33] #153, #315, ##348–49, and #504.
[34] SCh 367:45–46.

justification especially with the Cross, but his repeated citation of Romans 4:25 shows that he was not insensitive to the link that Paul also saw with the resurrection. Emery gives the impression that his unease is as much with Paul as with Bernard. Leclercq is right when he claims that Bernard never separated the two aspects of the one mystery, the Cross and the resurrection, the suffering and the glory.[35] "To the fruits of the passion, which she has taken from the tree of the Cross, [the bride] wishes to add some of the flowers of the resurrection, whose fragrance may especially entice the bridegroom to revisit her more frequently" (#129).

Ascension.[36] Christ's ascension, like all else that he did, was done on account of us (*propter nos*) and on our behalf (*pro nobis*; #343). As a result, he is now in the presence of the Father on our behalf.[37] Furthermore, because he has ascended, he is able to send the Spirit.[38] We should follow him in his ascension, which means seeking the things that are above (Col 3:1; #349). He ascended for our glorification, and the ascension is a witness to our hope for reward (#263).

Pentecost. When Christ left earth, he sent the Spirit, who applies to us the benefits of Christ's Cross and resurrection (#353–55).[39]

D. How Central Is the Cross?

While Bernard did not confine the salvific work of Christ to the Cross, the Cross was for him clearly central. Or was it? Here Bernard speaks with two voices. On the one hand, Jesus cannot be known except as hanging on the Cross (#523). Bernard's philosophy is to know Christ and him crucified, to view him on the Cross as his Saviour (#65). The faithful recognise their total need of Jesus and him crucified (#129). Bernard often cites 1 Corinthians 2:2 about resolving to know Christ and him crucified, sometimes

---

[35] Leclercq, "La dévotion médiévale envers le crucifié," 127.

[36] Bernard also echoes the Johannine concept of the Cross as Jesus' exaltation or ascension (##346–47).

[37] Asc 2.5, between #339 and #340.

[38] Asc 3.5, 9; 4.1.

[39] Pent 1.2–6; 2.6–8, which includes #352 and ##354–55.

adding "only" or "nothing but."[40] On the other hand, however, such
a resolve is not for those who are mature (#233). Knowing Christ
and him crucified is for spiritual children and for beasts (who feed
on milk and hay, respectively), which to be transcended by the spiritual adult, though Bernard adds that animals and people, children
and adults, all derive nourishment from the same heavenly source
(#143).[41] Nineteen times he cites Paul's comment about glorying
only in the Cross of Christ (Gal 6:14).[42] Indeed, it is the mark of
the true Christian to glory only in the Cross (#590), but here again,
this is a stage to be left behind. The faithful soul "sighs eagerly for
his presence, rests sweetly in the memory of him, and glories in the
disgrace of the Cross, until it is fit to see the glory of God in his
revealed face" (#133). Focus on the sufferings of Christ is a stage
that can be transcended through the Spirit (#25).[43] This point is
sometimes made by citing 2 Corinthians 5:16 (no longer regarding
Christ according to the flesh) together with John 6:63 (the flesh
being of no profit).[44] The mystic can reach the point of viewing God

[40] #67, #143, #194, and #233 with "only" or "nothing but"; #65, #129, #377,
#447, #502, and #588 without. He elsewhere simply cites the phrase "Christ and
him crucified" (#15, #90, #376, #585, and #634). For a study of these passages,
see Sr. Brigitte, "Jésus et Jésus crucifié chez saint Bernard," Coll 57 (1995): 219–37.

[41] See Reinhold Seeberg, *Lehrbuch der Dogmengeschichte*, vol. 3, 2nd/3rd ed.
(Leipzig: A. Deichert, 1913), 128.

[42] #37, #163, #194, #219, #244, #347, #486, #523, #531, #532, #546, #590,
#614, and #651, with "only"; #132, #133, #314, #364, and #420 without. In Vict
1.1 Bernard alludes to the verse, but without mentioning the Cross (SBOp 6/1:30).

[43] On this passage, and the role of Lam 4:20 in particular, see Sven Grosse, "*Spiritus ante faciem nostram Christus Dominus*: Zur Christozentrik der Mystik Bernhards
von Clairvaux," *Theologie und Philosophie* 76 (2001): 185–205.

See also Adolf Harnack, *History of Dogma*, vol. 6 (New York: Russell and Russell,
1958), 13: "It might have been expected that for one who became so absorbed in
the picture of the suffering Christ, it would have been impossible to repeat the
direction given by Origen and Augustine, that we must rise from the word of
scripture, and from the Incarnate Word, to the 'Spirit.'"

[44] See #25, #143, #233. In #447, 2 Cor 5:16 is cited without John 6:63 and
without the idea of no longer viewing Christ this way. Both verses are cited elsewhere without being applied to the question of our attitude to the Cross: 2 Cor
5:16 in #57, #107, #111, #398, #499, and #591; John 6:63 in #42, #330, #438,

face to face, which excludes the frailty of Christ's suffering humanity, since there was no beauty in his frailty (Isa 53:2; #69).[45] Bernard
speaks with two voices, being torn between a biblical, Cross-centred
piety and an Origenist mysticism.[46] It would be wrong, though, to
present these as two equal voices. Only five of our 669 passages refer
to leaving the Cross behind, though these do come in significant
works.[47] Cave's judgement is fair: "Like other Catholic mystics, St.
Bernard sometimes speaks as if in the highest range of experience
the earthly life and death of Jesus was forgotten, but, in general, it
was the life and death of Jesus on which he delighted to meditate."[48]

Bernard's teaching that the mystic can leave the Cross behind raises
the question of the influence of Origen.[49] Leclercq notes Bernard's
knowledge of Origen's biblical commentaries and suggests that he
prepared for his *Sermones in Cantica* by a diligent reading of Origen.[50]

---

and #586. These passages are also cited in other passages that do not belong to our
669 relating to the Cross. For further reading on this, see Jean-Marie Déchanet,
"La christologie de S. Bernard," in *Saint Bernard théologien*, ASOC 9, no. 3-4 (July–
December 1953): 86–91.

[45] See also #68.

[46] The problem is not his failure to recommend a constant focus on Christ's
passion but his teaching that those who are mature leave this behind—presumably forever. By contrast, the Apocalypse shows us the slain lamb by the throne of
God the Father in heaven (Rev 5:6, 9, 12). Bernard cites these verses (especially in
##310–11 and #313) but does not consider their implication for the present issue.

[47] See #25, #69 (SC), #133 (Dil), #143 (Tpl), and #233 (P Epi).

[48] Sydney Cave, *The Doctrine of the Work of Christ* (London: University of London
Press and Hodder and Stoughton, 1937), 143.

[49] On this, see Luc Brésard, *Bernard et Origène, commentent le Cantique* (Forges:
Abbaye Notre-Dame de Scourmont, 1983); Luc Brésard, "Bernard et Origène:
Le symbolisme nuptial dans leurs oeuvres sur le Cantique," Cîteaux 36 (1985):
129–51; Jean Daniélou, "Saint Bernard et les pères grecs," in *Saint Bernard théologien*, ASOC 9, no. 3-4 (July–December 1953): 46–51; Henri de Lubac, *Medieval
Exegesis*, vol. 1 (Grand Rapids, MI: Eerdmans; and Edinburgh: T&T Clark, 1998),
168–69, 204–6.

[50] Leclercq, "General Introduction to the Works of Saint Bernard (III)," 374. See
André Wilmart, "L'ancienne bibliothèque de Clairvaux," Coll 11 (1949): 117–18,
for the availability of Origen. For the patristic sources of SC, see Jean Leclercq,
"Aux sources des sermons sur les Cantiques," RESB 1.275–98. For Origen and
Bernard on the Cross in SC, see Brésard, "Bernard et Origène," 138–39.

He took his inspiration from Origen, imitated him, and preached like him.[51] He could, however, be critical of the Alexandrian and reprimands him in these sermons for his suggestion that the demons can be saved (#74). Elsewhere he preached a sermon on Origen's statement that Christ still grieves over our sins. He defends it as hyperbolic, expounding his own view of the completeness of Christ's work (Div 34; ##468–72).[52] Origen appears to have influenced Bernard's specific teaching that we should move beyond attachment to the crucified Christ,[53] but in general McGinn rightly argues that while Bernard knew and used Origen, his thought is fundamentally rooted in Augustine and Gregory the Great.[54]

E. Redemption

"Redemption" and "reconciliation" are two terms that should be considered at this stage because they each relate to more than one aspect of Bernard's teaching on the work of Christ. First, Christ is the Redeemer. Bernard frequently refers to Christ as the one who has redeemed us.[55] Sometimes this comes in the context of 1 Corinthians 1:30: "Jesus Christ, whom God has made for us wisdom, righteousness, sanctification, and redemption."[56] Christ is the most abundant Redeemer, who brings abundant redemption, an eternal redemption (Heb 9:12).[57] Most of the time Bernard simply refers to Christ's redemption, but sometimes he spells out more specifically what this means.

[51] Jean Leclercq, "Saint Bernard et Origène d'après un manuscrit de Madrid," RESB 2.385.

[52] There is also a passing reference to Origen in 1 Nov 4.3 (SBOp 5:317).

[53] Sven Grosse, "Der Messias als Geist und sein Schatten: Leiblichkeit Christi und Mystik in der Alten Kirche und bei Bernhard von Clairvaux," AC 58 (2008): 170–222, argues for Origen's influence on Bernard over this issue.

[54] Bernard McGinn, *The Growth of Mysticism*, vol. 2 of *The Presence of God: A History of Western Medieval Mysticism* (London: SCM, 1995), 492, n. 86.

[55] E.g., #6, #31, #40, #96, #179, #202, #478, #496, #517, #541, #542, #549, #557, #589, #603, #606, #610, and #613.

[56] See #26, #32, #33, #85, #152, #236, #247, #297, #394, #606, and SC 22.4–5, immediately before #29. This translation of 1 Cor 1:30 is based on the Vulgate.

[57] See #135 and #558.

In modern English usage, redemption has become a rather general concept, but the Latin *redemptio* conveyed more explicitly the ideas of ransom and buying back, ideas that in Bernard are often explicit and vividly expressed. From whom or what has Christ redeemed us? He has redeemed us from death and from Satan (#22). He has redeemed his unique bride from the yoke of the devil by his blood (#540).

The term "redemption" also covers our relationship with the Father. Christ died in order to reconcile us to the Father, his blood being the price of our redemption (#22). God sent Christ as a redemption through his sacrifice of himself, which was pleasing to God and brought reconciliation. "Redemption" is a general term that embraces victory over death and Satan as well as the restoration of our relationship with God.

How has Christ redeemed us? Primarily by his death. We are redeemed by his passion.[58] More specifically, it is by his blood that he has redeemed us.[59] Bernard cites a variety of texts in order to make this point: Romans 3:24-25 and Ephesians 1:7 (#610); Hebrews 9:12;[60] 1 Peter 1:18-19;[61] Revelation 5:9.[62] The blood of Christ is the price of our redemption (Ps 49:8).[63] Bernard remarks how precious is the soul that can be redeemed only by the blood of Christ (#578) or by the Cross of Christ (#567).

Elsewhere, without using the word "redemption" but echoing Acts 20:28, Bernard states that we have been bought with the price of the blood of Christ (#101) and that he paid for the fruit of his Cross by his own precious blood (#189). Neither passage states from whom/what we have been bought. Bernard three times cites Matthew 20:28,

---

[58] See #499, #614, and #615.

[59] See #92, #237, #334, #355, #433, #504, #540, #544, #555, #600, #628, and #652.

[60] See #235, #237, #334, and #558.

[61] See #355, #563, and #621. There is possibly an echo of 1 Pet 1:18-19 in #433, but without the mention of redemption.

[62] See #399, #544, and #555. The allusion to Rev 5:9 in these passages, which is tenuous, amounts to no more than that he has redeemed us *in sanguine suo*. I have excluded #237 and #621, where the point being made is found in another passage that is more explicitly cited.

[63] See #22, #201, #235, #477, and #637.

that the Son of Man came to give his life as a ransom (*redemptio*) for many, but two of these times he omits the word "ransom."[64]

Bernard's doctrine of redemption is expressed mostly in individual terms, but he also applies it to the church. Christ redeemed his unique bride from the yoke of the devil by his blood (#540). He died to behold the church without spot or wrinkle (#638). Christ redeemed his bride with his own blood.[65] He preferred the life of his body the church to that of his own body.[66] And, with a homely touch for the recipients of his letter, Bernard states that Christ preferred to die for Rievaulx Abbey than to lose it (#582).

F. Reconciliation

The second term is "reconciliation." Like "redemption," it is an all-embracing term, and it also is mentioned often, but by no means exclusively, with reference to the Cross.[67] Bernard refers repeatedly to Christ's work of reconciliation.[68] Christ is the peacemaker (*pacificus*).[69] Bernard uses a variety of biblical texts to refer to this. While we were yet enemies, we were reconciled to God through the death of his Son (Rom 5:10).[70] Christ has made peace by his blood, reconciling earth and heaven (Col 1:20; see also Eph 1:10).[71] He is himself our peace and has broken down the barrier between us and God (Eph 2:14).[72] God was in Christ reconciling the world to himself (2 Cor 5:19).[73] The voice with which he cried out to the Father and yielded

---

[64] See #73 and #373 (without) and #587 (with).

[65] #628 and #652.

[66] #446 and #496.

[67] In SC 16.2 Bernard states that while we were sinners Christ reconciled us to God, echoing Rom 5:8, 10. There is no explicit mention of the Cross, so it is not one of our 669 passages; but not long after he turns to the Cross (##16–17), and he was probably thinking of it in 16:2, even though he doesn't mention it explicitly.

[68] E.g., #1, #5, #31, #224, #271, #490, and #549.

[69] See #48 and #479.

[70] See #21, #251, #288, #450, #541, #585, and #610.

[71] See #35, #236, #358, #381, #396, #566, and #611.

[72] See #1, #35, #268, #396, #413, and #427.

[73] See #2, #84, #286, and #566.

his spirit to him (Matt 27:50; Luke 23:46) was a voice of reconciliation commending us to the Father (#515).

"Redemption" is a term Bernard applied both to our release from Satan and death and to the restoration of our relationship to God. "Reconciliation" is also a term that has a variety of applications. Obviously, it is not used to describe our status vis-à-vis Satan, to whom we are not reconciled, but it does refer to the removal of the barrier between ourselves and God. There remains an ambiguity, though. Does God need to be reconciled to us, or is it only we who need to be reconciled to God?[74] In other words, is the barrier between us and God purely on our side (our hostility toward him), or is there a barrier on his side? There is no doubt that for Bernard there is a barrier on both sides. We will see this more fully when we turn to Christ's death for our sins and the objections that have been raised against that,[75] but it can also be seen from what Bernard states about reconciliation.

In at least one passage Bernard refers to reconciliation on our part.[76] Repentance—light and easy now, but not so later—is needed for us to be reconciled to God. Here and now there is no one who cannot be reconciled to God; after death it will be impossible to be reconciled to God (#224).[77] The thief on the cross (Luke 23:39-43) is an example of our need to confess our sins, repent, and persevere.[78] He is the sole example in Scripture of a deathbed conversion, lest anyone presume to delay until then (#492).

---

[74] Interestingly, where Daniel L. Akin, "Bernard of Clairvaux: Evangelical of the Twelfth Century (A Critical Analysis of his Soteriology)" (PhD thesis, University of Texas at Arlington, 1989), 123, states that "God is reconciling himself to the world," the abridged version in Daniel L. Akin, "Bernard of Clairvaux and the Atonement," in *The Church at the Dawn of the 21st Century: Essays in Honor of Dr. W. A. Criswell*, ed. P. Patterson, J. Pretlove, and L. Pantoja (Dallas: Criswell Publications, 1989), 120, states that "God is reconciling the world to himself." The change is probably stylistic.

[75] See chaps 10 and 11 below.

[76] There are probably other passages in contexts where Bernard is not referring to the Cross.

[77] See #108 and #567 for the impossibility of finding pardon after death, without the use of the word "reconcile."

[78] See #473, #476, #515, #546, and #560.

Mostly, though, Bernard teaches that the Cross brings reconciliation by removing a barrier on God's side. Christ is the holy sacrifice (*hostia*), pleasing to God, for the reconciliation of us all, having redeemed us by his blood (#237). In order to reconcile us to the Father, Christ suffered death and defeated it, pouring out his blood as the price of redemption, placating the offended Father (#22). Since our sins separate us from God (Isa 59:2), reconciliation with God requires the forgiveness of sins (#610). It is by his sacrifice that Christ reconciles humanity to God since only thus is God placated (#430). Through this sacrifice we are reconciled to God in the blood of the Mediator (#431). Bernard often refers to Christ as Mediator.[79] We are reconciled to God through Christ, who is both the Mediator of reconciliation and the pledge (*obses*) of it (#208). Bernard can appear to teach that reconciliation with God follows the defeat of Satan (#431),[80] but immediately before this he states that defeating the devil would not be effective without a sacrifice for sin, since without that we cannot be reconciled to God (#430). Ultimately, the defeat of Satan is based upon reconciliation with God rather than vice versa, as we will see in due course.

Christ is Mediator and Mary is Mediatrix. Her role relative to Christ is comparable to that of the moon relative to the sun (#370). Mary has reversed the harm caused by Eve. Whereas Adam could complain about being given forbidden fruit by the woman that God gave him (Gen 3:12), now we must thank God that the woman that God gave us has fed us with a blessed fruit (#371).[81] Mary is a martyr as described by Simeon (Luke 2:35).[82] The sword could not penetrate the flesh of the Son without passing through the heart of his mother (#369).

The reconciliation that Christ brings is not solely between us and God. The Cross also brings people together who were previ-

---

[79] See #208, #367, #427, #431, #519, and #522.

[80] Satan unjustly imposes punishment on the innocent Christ, so he is himself justly condemned, and thereupon (*inde*) we are reconciled through that sacrifice, in the blood of the Mediator.

[81] For the content of this paragraph so far, see also O Asspt 2.

[82] For Luke 2:35, see also #529 and SC 29.8.

ously alienated. Bernard makes this point using words other than
"reconciliation." He repeatedly affirms the statement of John 11:52
that the Cross gathers into one those who were scattered abroad.[83]
Unsurprisingly, this thought comes especially in the letters. By leaving his monastery, Adam is scattering again what Christ gathered
together (#559), as also is Abbot Arnold (#557). Conversely, a group
of young men who together embraced the monastic life have been
gathered together by Christ into one (#589). In the diocese of Metz
a great wolf is seeking to scatter the sheep that Christ had gathered
together (John 11:52; #623). Gerard of Angoulême by unscrupu-
lously seeking the role of a papal legate is tearing asunder the church
for which Christ's side was torn apart. He is dividing those whom
Christ saved by uniting, and he shows himself to be not a Christian
but Antichrist (#591). Arnold of Brescia is an enemy of the Cross of
Christ by sowing discord, fabricating schism, disturbing the peace,
and dividing unity (#619).

Bernard complains to some bishops in the curia that hardly was
the wound of the Leonine schism healed before others were re-
opening it, once again nailing Christ's body on the Cross (#622). In
this context he repeatedly refers to the seamless robe of Christ (John
19:23-24)[84] and to the dividing of his garments by the soldiers (Ps
22:18; Matt 27:35).[85] Without using the actual word, Bernard makes
it clear that an important aspect of the Cross is the reconciliation
that it brings between people, as is seen in the unity of the church.

---

[83] See #329, #559, #589, #603, and #623.
[84] See #125, #242, #264, #337, #338, #547, #551, #622, and #639.
[85] See #264, #278, #622, and #639.

8

CHRIST AS TEACHER / MORAL INFLUENCE: THE USWARD ASPECT

A. The Cross as a Demonstration of Love

Bernard is best known for his opposition to Abelard's subjective interpretation of the Cross as the way in which God changes us. In his Excursus (8.1) the latter famously presents the Cross as a demonstration of God's love that evokes a response on our part:

> Now it seems to us that this is how we have been justified by the blood of Christ and reconciled to God: his Son took our nature upon himself and persevered in it to death, instructing us by both word and example. Through this unique act of grace displayed to us he has bound us to himself yet more by love, so that our hearts might be inflamed by the great kindness of divine grace and true love should no longer dread enduring anything for him.[1]

The idea of the Cross as a demonstration of love evoking a response was not in itself at all original.[2] Bernard had no quarrel with this.[3] In

---

[1] See chap. 2C above.

[2] See, e.g., Michael T. Clanchy, *Abelard: A Medieval Life* (Oxford: Blackwell, 1997), 287; Reinhold Seeberg, "Die Versöhnungslehre des Abälard und die Bekämpfung derselben durch den heiligen Bernhard," *Mittheilungen und Nachrichten für die evangelische Kirche in Rußland* 44 (1888): 152.

[3] "St. Bernard was far from abandoning to Abelard the monopoly of the moral aspect of the Atonement" (Jean Rivière, *The Doctrine of the Atonement: A Historical Essay*, vol. 2 [London: Kegan Paul, Trench, Trübner and Co., 1909], 69).

fact, Bernard wrote as much on the subjective effects of the Cross as did Abelard, and much more eloquently.[4] The difference between them was that Bernard saw it as just one implication of the work of Christ on the Cross and resisted any attempt to limit the meaning of the Cross to this alone.[5]

The Cross demonstrates the love of God the Father,[6] and nowhere is this seen more clearly than in the mystery of the incarnation and passion (#458). It is because God loved the world that he gave his Son (John 3:16).[7] God showed his love for us in that it was while we were sinners that Christ died for us (Rom 5:8).[8] So great was his love that he did not spare his own Son but gave him up for us (Rom 8:32).[9]

The Cross also demonstrates the love of the Son. One of Bernard's favourite biblical texts was John 15:13: there is no greater love than to lay down one's life for one's friends.[10] Christ, however, did this for those who were his enemies. He even prayed for those who crucified him (Luke 23:34),[11] as prophesied in Isaiah 53:12 (#292).[12] Not only did the Father not spare the Son (Rom 8:32), but the Son did not spare himself (#288). He loved me/us and gave himself up for me/us (Gal 2:20; Eph 5:2).[13] Modifying Romans 5:8, Bernard

---

[4] Ulrich Köpf, "Zentrale Gedanken der monastischen Theologie Bernhards von Clairvaux," *Cistercienser Chronik* 111 (2004): 54, states that Bernard pays more attention than Abelard to the religious subject.

[5] On the question of whether Abelard did in fact reduce the work of Christ to its subjective effects, see chap. 2C above.

[6] For more on this, see chap. 11D below.

[7] See #128, #134, and #648.

[8] See #288, #344, #458, #525, #541, #585, and #610. In #136 Bernard uses the verse to state that *Christ* shows his love to us through the Cross.

[9] #16, #128, #175, #183, #288, #354, #434, #474, #541, and #585. It is also quoted in V Nat 1.3 without mention of the Cross.

[10] #23, #84, ##128–29, #133, #182, #194, #251, #253, #269, #288, #304, #458, #486, #499, #501, #542, and #545.

[11] #3, #31, #156, #180, #186, #277, ##292–93, #508, and #576.

[12] The end of Isa 53:12 is also cited in #99, #157, and #175.

[13] The only difference at this point between the two texts is the reference to *me* (Gal 2:20; #615 and #661) versus *us* (Eph 5:2; #304). Passage #354 could be either.

states that *Christ* showed his love to us through the Cross (#136).[14] This involved great cost. We have been saved *for* nothing (*pro nihilo*) but not *by* nothing (*de nihilo*). Redemption is free so far as we are concerned, but it was very costly for Christ (#255).

B. The Cross Evokes Our Response

This demonstration of love evokes a response on our part.[15] Given Christ's great love to us when we were so undeserving, he deserves our love in response, since we owe him a great debt of gratitude.[16] Bernard is grateful to God for the gift of creation, but even more for what Christ suffered to pay the price of our redemption. On the Cross he endured so much—and while we were still his enemies. This shows how much he loved us and thereby claims, wins, demands, and binds our love for him (#21).[17] God deserves our love because he created us and much more because he also restored us by the death of his Son (#541). Related to this is the contrast that Bernard repeatedly draws between the ease with which God created the world by a word and the great hardship with which Christ won our salvation.[18]

On our behalf and for our salvation, Christ became, in the words of Isaiah 53, one with no beauty (53:2)[19] who was despised and rejected (53:3)[20] and deemed to be leprous and smitten by God (53:4).[21] Psalm 22 also states that he was despised (22:6)[22] and mocked (22:7; #71), and this is described in the gospels.[23]

---

[14] See n. 8 above.

[15] Bernard frequently cites John 12:32 (#28, #31, #112, #196, #304, ##346–47, and ##465–67) but, following the Vulgate, reads this to state that the crucified Christ draws to himself all things (*omnia*) rather than all people.

[16] #7, #128, #151, #238, #255, #448, and #457.

[17] Similarly #136.

[18] #7, #21, #136, #255, #297, #355, and #448.

[19] #37, #38, #41, #69, #287, #345, #375, #378, #390, and #502.

[20] #41, #287, and #522.

[21] #37, #287, #375, #376, and #378.

[22] #38, #287, #304 (v. l), #322, and #661.

[23] Matt 27:42: #47, #78, #112, ##302–7 and #314; Mark 15:32: #302.

Bernard spells out all that Christ has done for us from his conception and especially in his passion (##353–54). What more should he have done for us? Not to be moved by all this is to be hard, hardened, and obdurate (*duri, et indurati, et obdurate*; #355).[24] Bernard repeatedly asks what more Christ could have done, echoing Isaiah 5:4.[25] So what can we do that would be an adequate recompense for the great price that Christ paid for us (#530)—all the more so since he gave himself for us when we least deserved it (#128)? Christ deserves our love because he died for us—it is shameful to look with ungrateful eyes on the Son of God dying for us (#585).[26] When we reflect with faith upon Christ's love as shown in his passion, it leads us to mourn our sins and to obey God (#537). We need to recognise how much we owe to Christ Jesus. He, the King of Glory, was crucified for a despised slave, for a worm. While we were still God's enemies he chose to be exiled from heaven to restore us (#450). Even if I dedicate myself totally to him, compared with what he has done it is like a drop of water compared to a river, a grain of sand compared to a mountain (#451).

Bernard repeatedly refers to what we owe to Christ for what he has done, but he also recognises the inadequacy of a sense of obligation. Who has a greater claim on my life than he who gave his life for me, who at the cost of his own life purchased eternal life for me? But we serve him willingly, out of love, which is a more effective motivation than fear, a sense of obligation, or desire for reward (#594). What can I do but live for him who did that (#595)? In his third sermon for Christmas Day, Bernard spells out in detail all that Christ has suffered for us and asks how we should respond. The gravity of the remedy shows how serious is our plight, how great our danger. Not to repent is simply insane (#205 in the context of #204–7).

---

[24] See #457 for a similar thought.

[25] #31, #355, #448, #458, #474, and #486. This is also found in #593, but not referring to the Cross.

[26] Bernard also observes that this grateful response of love is possible only because the Holy Spirit effects it in us (#585).

Bernard repeatedly speaks of what Christ has done *for us* or *because of us* (*pro nobis, propter nos*).[27] The fact that the objective work of Christ was for our benefit provides the basis for our subjective response. We meditate on and respond to what he has done for us on the Cross.[28]

Bernard brings together most of the themes discussed so far in this chapter in one of his *Sentences*:

> It is clear that [Christ] had love for everyone, because he loved us so much that he laid down his life for us. Though innocent, he died for us, even though he found nothing in us worthy of his love. If the Lord died for his servant, what should the servant do for his Lord—the one who had been redeemed for his Savior? Let them take up the cup of salvation and invoke his name [#542].[29]

C. The Cross as an Example to Follow

The Cross is a demonstration of the love of God and Christ that demands a response on our part. It is also portrayed as an example to be followed, and indeed one reason why the Cross was necessary was to set us such an example. Why was Christ obedient even to death (Phil 2:8)? By suffering for us, he left us an example to follow (1 Pet 2:21; #117).[30] Bernard spells this theme out at length in his Sermon 60 *de diversis*. Christ descended from heaven and ascended there again in order teach us how to ascend to heaven, to point out

[27] See Alberich Altermatt, "Christus pro nobis: Die Christologie Bernhards von Clairvaux in den 'Sermonum per annum,'" AC 33 (1977): 116–29.

[28] See Ulrich Köpf, "Schriftauslegung als Ort der Kreuzestheologie Bernhards von Clairvaux," in *Bernhard von Clairvaux und der Beginn der Moderne*, ed. Dieter R. Bauer and Gotthard Fuchs (Innsbruck and Vienna: Tyrolia, 1996), 194–99; and a briefer account in Ulrich Köpf, "Die Passion Christi in der lateinischen religiösen und theologischen Literatur des Spätmittelalters," in *Die Passion Christi in Literatur und Kunst des Spätmittelalters*, ed. Walter Haug and Burghart Wachinger (Tübingen: Max Niemeyer, 1993), 28–30.

[29] Bernard of Clairvaux, *The Parables and the Sentences*, trans. Michael Casey and Francis Swietek, CF 55 (Kalamazoo, MI: Cistercian Publications, 2000), 383–84.

[30] 1 Pet 2:21 is also cited to this end in #486 and #517. In Ep 159.1 we have the example of one who was obedient to death.

the way for us (Div 60.1). He descended in three stages: by taking flesh in the incarnation, by going to the Cross, and by dying. Likewise, he ascends in three stages: resurrection, power of judgement, and being seated at the Father's right hand. By doing this, he left us an example to follow (Div 60.2; #486). Bernard then sets out the practical implications of this (Div 60.3–4).

We should follow Christ's example, and Bernard makes this point in general terms by citing Revelation 14:4: that we should follow the Lamb wherever he goes.[31] He also specifically urges us to imitate Christ's passion.[32] There are various ways in which we can do this. If we meditate[33] on the Cross and follow Jesus' example by mortifying our earthly members, we have eternal life (#132). We should imitate him who prayed, "Not my will but yours be done" (Luke 22:42; #323), who was obedient to Father unto death (Phil 2:8; #534). Meditating on all that he suffered for us is good, but it benefits us only if we also imitate his example by following in his footsteps. Otherwise we share in the guilt of those who crucified him (#295). His death teaches us how to die with peace of mind in the hope of resurrection from the dead (#146). Bernard encourages Hugh, a new convert to the monastic life, to resist any temptation from his family to turn back. He quotes the brutal advice of Jerome to ignore their pleas and with dry eyes flee to the banner of the Cross. Cruelty for Christ's sake is the most loyal path (#636).

Christ's death brings us many benefits and also gives us an example and pattern for life here and now (#545). Bernard goes on to compare remembering and imitating Christ's death to the waters of Siloam, in which we can wash like the man born blind (John 9:7, 11), an illustration that he develops at length. By remembering Christ's death with affection and imitating it with devotion, we share his

---

[31] #170, #348, #383, #384, #387, and #517. Also see SC 8.3 and Miss 1.7, 3.7. Bernard also cites the verse for the idea of following wherever he goes, but without mention of the lamb: #240 and #296.

[32] #151, #186, #280, and #324.

[33] See Köpf, "Zentrale Gedanken der monastischen Theologie Bernhards von Clairvaux," 61: Bernard may not have a fully developed *Passionsmystik*, but he does at least speak of a *Passionsmeditation*.

suffering and in due time will share his glory (#545). By following the example of Christ, who was obedient to death (Phil 2:8), we shall by the merit of obedience gain eternal life (#665).

D. Opposition to Abelard

As we have seen, Bernard held as fully as Abelard to the subjective effects of the Cross. It demonstrates the love of God and of Christ, evoking a loving response on our side. It sets an example for us to follow. His problem with Abelard was not that the latter taught this but with Bernard's perception that Abelard sought to reduce the Cross to this only, as can be seen clearly from his letter-treatise.

> This son of perdition . . . thinks and argues that one can reduce to only one reason why the Lord of glory emptied himself, became less than angels, was born of a woman, lived in the world, experienced weakness, suffered shameful things, and finally returned to his own by the death of the Cross. He did this in order that by his life and teaching he might bequeath to humanity a pattern of life and that by his suffering and death he might set before them the extremity of love. (Abael 7.17; #607)

To this Bernard's response is "So did he teach righteousness but not give it; did he demonstrate love but not impart it; did he thus return to his own?" (Abael 7.17; #607).

Again, he summarises Abelard's teaching as being that "the whole reason that God appeared in the flesh was to educate or (as he later says) instruct us by his word and example, that the whole reason why he suffered and died was to exhibit or commend his love toward us" (Abael 8.22; #612). To this Bernard responds:

> What was the use of him educating us if he did not restore us? Surely, instructing us is useless unless the body of sin is first destroyed in us so that we may no longer serve sin? If the only way that Christ benefited us was by exhibiting his virtues, it can then be said that Adam harmed us only by exhibiting sin, since the remedy that is provided is accord-

ing to the nature of the disease. . . . Certainly, as he deigns
to acknowledge, illumination and encouragement to love
come from Christ, but from whom come redemption and
liberation? (Abael 9.23; #613)

In line with this, Bernard proceeds to accuse Abelard of Pelagianism—of the denial of original sin and of the internal working
of grace (Abael 9.23–24; ##613–14). If we believe in original sin
and the internal working of grace, it makes no sense to limit the
work of Christ to education and illumination. Thus to limit it would
mean that the Cross is of no benefit to infants (Abael 9.24; #614).
To affirm the humility of Christ's incarnation and the love shown
in his death without also affirming the objective redemption that he
brought is like painting on air. "An undoubtedly great and extremely
necessary example of humility, a great example of love worthy of all
acceptance—but without redemption these have neither foundation
nor therefore stability" (Abael 9.25; #615).

As a response to Abelard's Excursus, this is not unreasonable, but
in the remainder of his Romans commentary Abelard affirms many
of the points that Bernard accused him of denying.[34]

---

[34] See chap. 2C and 5C for this.

9

CHRIST AS VICTOR OVER SATAN AND DEATH

*C*hristus Victor is a major theme in Bernard's theology of redemption and is found throughout his writings. Christ is
the one who has conquered the enemy and set the captives
free.[1] What enemy? Bernard mentions two. We see death dead and
death's author defeated (#129).[2] Christ destroyed the power both
of the devil and of death (#505). By accepting death, he defeated it,
paying for our redemption; he conquered all things, having hoodwinked Satan (#22). The defeat of the devil and the defeat of death
are not unconnected; Satan's power over us was "the power of death,"
as Bernard indicates by citing that phrase from Hebrews 2:14.[3] We
will first examine Christ's victory over Satan.

A. Victory over Satan

Christ has defeated Satan.[4] He has rescued us from the kingdom
of darkness (Col 1:13),[5] on the Cross triumphing over the princi-

---

[1] See #11 and #353.
[2] See also #477.
[3] #302 and #442.
[4] E.g., #171, #258, and #408.
[5] #30, #102, #158, #441, #604, and #606. Not all of these explicitly relate the
rescue to the Cross.

palities and powers (Col 2:15).[6] With reference to Matthew 12:29 and Luke 11:21-22, Bernard repeatedly describes Christ as the one who has bound the strong man and despoiled him, thus setting his captives free.[7] He has redeemed his unique bride from the yoke of the devil by his blood (#540).

In fact, Bernard says relatively little about Christ's victory over Satan,[8] with one key exception. His fullest and most famous exposition of this theme comes in his letter-treatise,[9] where he responds to Abelard's Excursus. In order to assess his remarks we first need to clarify precisely what Abelard taught.[10] Does Satan exercise power over us? If so, is that merely brute power or a lawful dominion? If the latter, does he *justly* exercise it? Abelard's position is not as clear as one might wish, due in part to the fact that he asks questions as often as giving answers. While he questions the extent and nature of Satan's power, he certainly does not deny it. He questions Satan's dominion over the elect while admitting his dominion over the unrighteous (Excursus 4). Dominion implies a legal form of power. He gives the example of a slave who voluntarily places himself under the power of another, which appears to concede Satan's power, yet shortly afterward he states how unjust it is for a seducer to gain privilege or power over his victim (Excursus 5.2–4). He then concedes the possibility that God himself may have handed sinners over to the devil for punishment (Excursus 6.1). Thus, on the question of Satan's dominion Abelard asks more questions than he gives clear answers.

---

[6] #336, #396, #605, and #611.

[7] #19, #169, #197, #302, #360, #362, #430, #440, #442, #449, #522, #531, #536, #549, and #604.

[8] More material, relating to the issue of the deception of Satan, is found in section B below.

[9] On this, see Jean Rivière, *The Doctrine of the Atonement: A Historical Essay*, vol. 2 (London: Kegan Paul, Trench, Trübner and Co., 1909), 215–23.

[10] On this, see Jean Rivière, *Le dogme de la rédemption au début du moyen âge* (Paris: J. Vrin, 1934), 96–113; Richard E. Weingart, *The Logic of Divine Love* (Oxford: OUP, 1970), 82–88, 136–39.

When it comes to Satan's rights, however, he is clearer.[11] Any right
that the devil has to punish us is given to him by divine permission.[12]
While God might have permitted Satan the role of jailer or torturer,
which implies a God-given status, God can at any point withdraw
this without acting unjustly. In particular, and this is the key point
for Abelard, the ransom price that redeems us was paid not to Satan
but "to him in whose power we were—that is, to him who handed
us over to his torturer, that is, God" (Excursus 7.7). God owed Satan
nothing and was not obliged to square it with him before liberating us. In article 3 of his *Confessio fidei universis*, his response to the
"points of indictment" cited against him, Abelard professes that it
was in order to liberate us from bondage to sin and from the yoke
of the devil that the Son of God became incarnate.[13]

Bernard's opposition to Abelard in his letter-treatise is not helped
by the fact that the treatment of redemption starts with gross misrepresentation. Bernard quotes from William of Saint Thierry Abelard's
alleged statement that "it was not to liberate humanity that the Son
of God took flesh" (Abael 5.11; #601). What was William's source?
It looks as if William has abbreviated the seventh of his "points of
indictment" supposedly gathered from Abelard's writings: "That it
was not in order to liberate us from the yoke of the devil that Christ
took flesh and suffered."[14] This has been crucially abridged, enabling
Bernard to accuse Abelard of denying not just that we need liberation and redemption *from the devil*, but that we need any liberation
or redemption at all. Bernard returns repeatedly to the accusation

---

[11] Although it remains true, as Rivière notes, that while appearing to mean
to deny Satan's rights, Abelard ends by expressing himself in terms that logically
imply them (*Le dogme de la rédemption au début du moyen âge*, 100).

[12] Weingart, *Logic of Divine Love*, 137, summarises Abelard's view as that "the
prince of evil does possess *de facto* power in holding sinners captive and punishing
them, but solely by the permission of God." William of Saint Thierry similarly
held that the devil's power over humanity is not by right but is justly permitted by
God (E. Rozanne Elder, "The Christology of William of Saint Thierry," RTAM
58 [1991]: 88–89).

[13] Charles S. F. Burnett, "Peter Abelard, *Confessio fidei 'universis'*: A Critical Edition of Abelard's Reply to Accusations of Heresy, *Medieval Studies* 48 (1986): 135.

[14] See chap. 5, n. 4.

that Abelard denied that the purpose of the incarnation was to liberate humanity (Abael 5.12; #602 [twice]; Abael 5.14; #604). Later, though, Bernard contradicts this claim by quoting Abelard's statement that Christ liberated the elect (Abael 7.18; #608).[15] Abelard also concluded his Excursus with the statement that "Christ's passion . . . liberates us from bondage to sin." The claim that Abelard denied that the purpose of the incarnation was to liberate humanity is simply false, as Bernard demonstrated by his own quotations in his letter-treatise. This initial misrepresentation, which leads to the charge that Abelard is setting himself up as a fifth evangelist (Abael 5.12; #602), and the charge that Abelard has not himself been redeemed (Abael 5.13; #603), is followed by a more careful analysis of accurate quotations taken from Abelard's Romans commentary, but by this stage the reader (or intended listener[16]) has already been predisposed to view him as a heretic.

Bernard then proceeds to argue from both testaments that the devil has power over humanity and holds us captive (Abael 5.13–14; ##603–4). This power is given him from above (John 19:11) and therefore is not unjust. It is true that Satan seized it wickedly and that *his* will is not just, but God justly allowed him to hold this power, and it is just that we are held captive (Abael 5.14; #604). While our bondage is just, our liberation is merciful—though not *contrary* to justice. God uses justice rather than power to free us. Satan has a part to play in this inasmuch as he "laid hands on the innocent one" and so justly lost his captives. This does not involve any transaction between God and the devil; rather, by bringing about the death of Christ, Satan enables him to die for the sins of all and thus make satisfaction for their sins (Abael 6.15; #605). It is by restoring our relationship with the Father that Christ liberates us from Satan. Bernard goes on to answer Abelard's specific questions about the

[15] Bernard's charge against Abelard might have been strengthened by his quotation of Abelard's claim that "the divine compassion could have liberated humanity from sin simply by giving the order" (Excursus 7.1), were it not that Bernard claimed that no one denied this. He proceeds himself to concede that "there were available to the Almighty many other ways to our . . . liberation" (#609).

[16] See chap. 5, n. 10.

extent of Satan's power over the elect, responding that it was by the blood of Christ shed for them that they were liberated from it (Abael 7.18; #608).

Bernard accurately reports Abelard's teaching that Satan "was not able or entitled to claim for himself any rights [*ius*] over humanity, except by God's permission," and that God could have saved us by a mere word without doing any injustice to Satan. He does not dissent from this, though he also insists that Christ's work was necessary—for us, for God, and for the angels (8.19; #609).[17] He then goes on to speak of the fruit of the Cross in terms of reconciliation with God, forgiveness of sins, and justification. "So whether we talk of reconciliation, forgiveness of sins, or justification—or redemption or liberation from the chains of the devil (by whom we were held captive at his will)—it is by the intervention of the death of the Only-Begotten that we come to be justified freely by [his] blood" (Abael 8.20; #610).

In response to Abelard, Bernard affirms the reality of Satan's power over humanity without claiming that the devil actually has any rights over us. His concern was to establish not Satan's rights but his moral domination of sinners.[18] So how does his teaching differ from Abelard's? Indeed, *does* it differ from Abelard's? Bernard is ferocious in his attack on Abelard on the issue of Satan's power and our liberation from it, (falsely) accusing him of denying that Christ came to set us free (Abael 5.11; #601), of setting himself up as a fifth evangelist (Abael 5.12; #602), and of not having been redeemed himself (Abael 5.13; #603)—but this is all dependent upon his initial false accusation. In fact, Abelard and Bernard are broadly agreed that Satan has

---

[17] For more on this, see chap. 11B below.

[18] Jean Rivière, "Le dogme de la rédemption au début du moyen âge III—rôle de saint Bernard," RSR 13 (1933): 194. Daniel L. Akin, "Bernard of Clairvaux: Evangelical of the Twelfth Century (A Critical Analysis of His Soteriology)" (PhD thesis, University of Texas at Arlington, 1989), 100; Daniel L. Akin, "Bernard of Clairvaux and the Atonement," *The Church at the Dawn of the 21st Century: Essays in Honor of Dr. W. A. Criswell*, ed. P. Patterson, J. Pretlove, and L. Pantoja (Dallas: Criswell Publications, 1989), 110, mistakenly charges Bernard with teaching that God *owes* Satan a ransom.

power over humanity—though maybe with differences concerning the devil's power over *the elect*. Bernard reports Abelard's statement that Satan has no rights over us, except by God's permission, but forebears from himself claiming, here or elsewhere, any stronger rights for Satan.[19] He does, however, repeatedly affirm that Satan's power over us is *just* (Abael 5.14–6.15; #604–5), a stronger statement than Abelard's concession that God might have permissively granted the devil the right to punish us.

So does this mean that there was no difference between them? On the question of our bondage to Satan, there is little difference. Furthermore, both are agreed that the prime need is for our relationship with God to be restored, which will resolve our unhappy bondage. But *how* is our relationship with God restored? It is at this point, the question of *how* we are liberated from the devil, that the significant differences emerge. In his response to Abelard, Bernard repeatedly raises the question of reconciliation with God by the Cross (Abael 6.15–7.17, 8.20; ##605–7, #610). Furthermore, this discussion of liberation from Satan leads into a discussion of how the Cross reconciles us with God (Abael 8.21–9.25; ##611–15). At that point, we earlier concluded,[20] Bernard presents us with "an unsympathetic reading of [Abelard's] Excursus," an interpretation of the work of Christ that is radically different from his own. We shall examine this more fully in the following two chapters, which treat of the Godward aspect of the work of Christ.

What does Bernard teach positively about Christ's victory over Satan in this letter-treatise? Christ is the one who binds the strong man (Satan) to despoil him of his possessions (Luke 11:21; Matt 12:29). This he does not by brute force but according to justice. Satan unjustly laid hands on the innocent Christ and so justly lost his captives. "Since he that owed nothing to death submitted to the injustice [*iniuria*] of death, he justly [*iure*] freed from the debt of death and the dominion of the devil those who were liable to it." Christ

---

[19] Rivière, *Doctrine of the Atonement*, 220–23, also sees more common ground between Bernard and Abelard than is commonly recognised.

[20] See chap. 5C above.

pardoned all our sins, "nullifying the handwritten document with its verdict that was against us and hostile to us. He took it out of the way, fastening it to the Cross, plundering the principalities and powers" (Col 2:13-15; Abael 6.15; #605). The result is that we are redeemed or liberated from the chains of Satan, by whom we were previously held captive. This happens because we are reconciled with God—our sins are forgiven and we are justified—by the Cross of Christ (Abael 8.20; #610). It is not that we are put right with God because we have been liberated from Satan, but vice versa.

This point is illustrated by an incident described in the *First Life of Bernard*, written soon after his death. Bernard was at death's door, and the devil was accusing him of his sins. Bernard's reply is significant:

> I admit that I am myself neither worthy nor able to obtain the kingdom of heaven by my own merits. But my Lord has obtained it by a double right: by inheritance from the Father and by the merit of his passion. Being content with the former, he gives the latter right to me. I claim it for myself on the basis of his gift and so will not be put to confusion.[21]

B. Deception

Some of the early Church Fathers held that Satan was tricked into accepting Christ in our place, not realising that he could not hold onto the sinless one who was also God. Bernard continues this tradition, but with a difference. Christ defeated Satan both by strategy and by strength—by strategy in that the adversary laid hands on the innocent one, thus forfeiting his rights over humanity; by strength in rising from the dead (#271). Christ tricked the serpent with a holy deception, Christ's humanity being the trap that deceived him (#22). In this context Bernard often cites 1 Corinthians 2:8: had the rulers of this age understood [Christ's deity], they would not have crucified the Lord of glory.[22] The Jews referred to him as a deceiver

---

[21] *Vita prima* 1.12.57. On this, see Franz Posset, "The 'Double Right to Heaven': Saint Bernard's Impact on the Sixteenth Century," CSQ 38 (2003): 263–73.

[22] #47, #56, #144, #156, #294, #313, #379, #522, and #576. Sometimes Bernard applies this verse to the Jewish authorities, sometimes to Satan.

(Matt 27:63), and they were right. He was a deceiver—though godly rather than wicked (#313).

How is it that Christ's humanity deceived Satan? This is spelled out at length in one of Bernard's *Sentences*. Christ the Mediator concealed his divinity from the enemy, for the prince of this world would not have knowingly crucified the Lord of glory (1 Cor 2:8). Satan saw only the weakness of Christ's flesh. He was roused to envy by Christ's righteousness and miracles and to the hope of victory by the weakness of Christ's flesh. Satan, the ancient deceiver, was himself deceived into imposing a cruel death upon Christ, with the result that the righteous one unjustly suffered death, the punishment for sin. There was no need for him to endure this, and so he shared the benefits with sinners, their guilt being absolved by the punishment of his innocence (#522). Bernard takes up the theme of Satan being deceived but understands by this that Satan unwittingly facilitated Christ's death for our sins on the Cross, the absolution of our guilt by his penal death. Here again, it is not that we are put right with God because we have been liberated from Satan, but vice versa.[23]

The same theme is expounded in Bernard's sermon on the seven gifts of the Holy Spirit.[24] Satan brings about his own defeat by offering Christ as a sacrifice. This is a sufficient sacrifice for the sins of humanity, humanity having no way to placate God on its own. Christ offered to the Father his sinless humanity and was thus able to reconcile us to God. Victory normally involves remaining alive and defeating one's opponent, but to have defeated the devil this way would have meant that no sacrifice for sin would have been offered to God and therefore that humanity would not have been reconciled to God (#430). Life attacks death and defeats it by dying. Satan is justly condemned for unjustly imposing the penalty of death upon

---

[23] Rivière, *Doctrine of the Atonement*, 219–20, argues that Bernard's teaching on the deception of Satan and Satan's misuse of his rights is inconsistent with the teaching of Abael concerning Satan's rights. Rivière does not take into account the fact that the key point for Bernard is not that Satan has overstepped his rights but rather that he has facilitated the death of Christ on the Cross for our sins.

[24] On this, see Jean Leclercq, "Introduction to Saint Bernard's *Sermones varii*," CSQ 43 (2008): 158–59.

the innocent one, and at the same time poor sinners are reconciled to God by that sacrifice, by the blood of the Mediator (#431).

Bernard does not expound the deception of Satan purely in terms of Satan overstepping his rights. By bringing about Christ's death, Satan enabled him to placate God the Father, which we could not have achieved (#22). So when Bernard states that Satan forfeited his rights over humanity by laying hands on the innocent one (#271), he means that Satan's action enabled Christ to die for our sins. Bernard's teaching about liberation from Satan is not separate from his teaching about Christ's death for our sins, but both teachings are integrated into a coherent whole.

C. Victory over Death

For Bernard the defeat of Satan is closely connected with the defeat of death. Christ tasted death for everyone (Heb 2:9)[25] and thus destroyed Satan, who held power of death (Heb 2:14).[26] He destroyed both the devil's power and death (#505), so we see death dead and death's author defeated.[27] Death is defeated and destroyed by Christ's death[28]—not of course in isolation from the resurrection, since Christ conquered death by enduring it and rising again (#484). We are made alive by Christ's passion (#478), and it was Christ's passion that opened the tombs (Matt 27:52).[29]

How does this happen? Death is the work of the devil but also the penalty of sin, and Christ has conquered all three: death, the devil, and sin (#404). Bernard expounds this in his twentieth sermon on the Song of Songs. Christ's love was strong because he endured death and expelled it from human nature. He defeated death and deceived Satan, the seducer of the universe. In order to reconcile us to the Father, he endured (*subit*) death and conquered (*subigit*) it, shedding his blood as the price of our redemption (Ps 49:8). He took death

---

[25] #9 and #251.
[26] #302 and #442.
[27] #129 and #477.
[28] #202, #302, ##307–9, #326, #353, #431, and #509.
[29] #285 and #299.

upon himself and so satisfied the Father (#22). Death is defeated—by virtue of the fact that by the Cross Christ has satisfied the Father and reconciled us to him. Christ's death frees us from death—it is the death of my death, because he died that I might live. How can I fail to live, for whom Life has died? (#152). Christ drank of death so that death should not drink of humanity. Through his death we get relief from our death because it no longer leads to hell (#545). Before Christ's passion the dead faced only the darkness of the grave (#583). Now, however, the death of Christ has overcome death and put it to flight, which he did by bearing the punishment of our sin, thus paying the debt of death and restoring life (#148).

Just as he spoke of Christ deceiving the devil, so also Bernard used the patristic fishhook analogy,[30] but of death personified rather than of Satan. Death is dead, having swallowed the hook by laying hands on the innocent one (#39). Death gobbled up the hook and thenceforth was held by the one it had appeared to hold (#403). As with the deception of Satan, the mythological imagery is interpreted in terms of the Godward aspect of the Cross. Sin is the cause of death, and so it is by taking our punishment upon himself, and thus paying our debt, that Christ provides the remedy for death, the consequence of sin (#147).[31] Death is defeated, but this is by resolving the issue of sin. Death is the consequence of sin, so by removing the cause, the consequence is eliminated.

D. Relation to Other Models

In his letter-treatise we have Bernard's fullest defence of the traditional doctrine of liberation from Satan. Bernard achieves this defence by integrating the doctrine of liberation from Satan with other aspects of the work of Christ, especially those expounded in his *In Praise of the New Knighthood*. Our liberation from captivity to Satan must take account of God's justice. Satan loses his grip over us

---

[30] See chap. 2, n. 8.

[31] The Latin word *poena* is rendered as "penalty" or "punishment," according to context. It should be remembered that in Latin, unlike English, there is no distinction between these.

because Christ, the head, pays the debt for us, his body. Thus, Bernard's account of the defeat of Satan and his account of Christ on the Cross bearing the penalty for sin are not merely juxtaposed but integrated with each other. Furthermore, Satan is defeated because sin has been dealt with, not vice versa. Death is defeated because Christ has dealt with our sin, not vice versa. The dramatic battle on which Bernard focuses the most attention is not that between God and Satan or between God and death but the "grand controversy" between the virtues, truth and righteousness demanding our condemnation, mercy and peace urging forgiveness, to which he devotes his first sermon on the annunciation (##265–70). The controversy is resolved not by any dealings with the devil but by Christ bearing the punishment due to humanity (#270).[32]

---

[32] For more on this theme, see chap. 11C below.

10

CHRIST DIED FOR OUR SINS: THE GODWARD ASPECT

Contrary to the views of some,[1] the aspect of the Cross to which Bernard devotes the most attention is its Godward aspect, which focuses on what Paul stated to be of prime importance, that Christ died for our sins (1 Cor 15:3).[2] Caiaphas rightly prophesied that Christ would die for his people (John 11:50–52).[3] Bernard cites Matthew 1:21, that the baby was called Jesus because he would save his people from their sins.[4] Bernard uses a wide range of biblical language and imagery in his exposition of this aspect of the work of Christ, and he also uses the language of redemption and reconciliation.[5] Christ bore our sins, bore our punishment, and paid the price that we owed. Christ was crowned with the thorns of our sins (#390). The crown of thorns pierced

---

[1] Such as Robert Linhardt, *Die Mystik des hl. Bernhard von Clairvaux* (Munich: Natur und Kultur, 1923). He claims that Bernard viewed redemption less from the divine than from the human side; less as a vicarious propitiation of the Father or a ransom from the devil, more as a restoration of human nature and the image of God; less as a legal transaction, more as an act of pure mercy (105–6). He claims that Bernard's prime interest was the restoration of human nature, that ransom from the devil was an ongoing concern especially in response to Abelard, but that while he taught propitiation, it was not important for him (110). The evidence of the present study suggests otherwise.

[2] On Bernard's use of this verse, see n. 9 below.

[3] #41, #98, #302, #329, #589, and #603.

[4] #173, #174, #212, #214, #223, and #530;V Nat 1.2; Div 53.2.

[5] On these last two, see chap. 7D–E above. Some of the material there set out will be repeated here, where it is relevant.

him physically on the outside and on the inside with the spiritual thorns of our sins (#542).[6] He was the Lamb of God who offered himself as a sacrifice to God. The Cross, propitiating God, serves as a satisfaction for our sins. As well as talking about the death of Christ and about the Cross, Bernard also talks about Christ's wounds and about the shedding of his blood.

It should be recognised that while these different ways of speaking of the Cross come under the general heading of the Godward aspect, there are several different sets of imagery—in particular, as we shall see, Christ offered himself as a sacrifice; he paid the price for us, paying off our debt; and he bore our punishment. These must be seen as distinct themes or pictures. One example will suffice to make this point. If we think of the Cross as a sacrifice, it is clear in the New Testament and in Bernard that this sacrifice is offered to God. Similarly, if the Cross is a satisfaction for our sins, this is offered to God. But what about the Cross as a price to be paid to ransom us? To whom is the ransom paid? To Satan? To God? The New Testament does not push the metaphor that far, and, as we shall see, neither does Bernard.[7] So what we have here is not one coherent picture but a number of complementary pictures making the same point in different ways. Here, as in other contexts, there is a danger in mixing metaphors.

One implication of this is the danger of absolutising any one metaphor. As we shall see, Bernard sees the Cross as propitiating or placating God the Father. But does that mean that the Father was reluctant to forgive us and needed to be bought off? Such questions were raised by Abelard and are raised even more insistently today. We will consider these in the following chapter.

A. Christ Bore Our Sins

On the Cross, one bore the sins of all (#605). He who was innocent died for us (##541–42), for the guilty (*pro nocente*; #522), for

---

[6] For more on the crown of thorns, see #228, #292, #446, and #479.

[7] Lest it be objected that the price of ransom relates only to the model of victory over Satan, it should be noted that we are ransomed from slavery to *sin* (#547 and #550).

the ungodly (*pro impio*; #149), for sinners (#545). This truth Bernard expresses in the language of various passages of Scripture. Christ bore the sins of many (Isa 53:12).[8] He died for our sins (Rom 4:25 with 1 Cor 15:3)[9] and gave himself for them to deliver us from the present evil age (Gal 1:4; #548).[10] Christ died for the ungodly (*pro impiis*; Rom 5:6)[11] and for the unrighteous (1 Pet 3:18; #450). The righteous one died for the ungodly (*pro impiis*; 1 Pet 3:18 with Rom 5:6; #474). He was numbered with transgressors and bore the sins of many (Isa 53:12);[12] he bore our sins in his body on the tree (1 Pet 2:24; #48). He fixed our sin(s) to the Cross (Col 2:14).[13] Thus he made purification (*purgatio*) for sins (Heb 1:3)[14] and by his passion most powerfully removed every kind of sin (Heb 9:28; #294). In a variation of 2 Corinthians 5:21, Bernard speaks of Christ as the one who made *himself* sin.[15] By the sin of those who crucified him, he condemned sin in the flesh (Rom 8:3).[16]

To summarise the key points, Christ is the one who died for us, who died for our sins. He bore our sins and made purification for them.[17]

---

[8] #99, #175, #292, and #458.

[9] #2, #66, #131, #214, #288, #315 (variant text only), and #659. When citing Rom 4:25, Bernard consistently replaces the *traditus est* with the statement that Christ "died" for our sins, echoing 1 Cor 15:3. Rom 4:25 is also cited in #263 and #317, referring to the resurrection only.

[10] Elsewhere Bernard cites Gal 1:4 to the effect that Christ gave himself up for us, without specifying that it was for our sins (#100, #128, and #425).

[11] #219 and #251. See also #149: *pro impio*.

[12] #43, #99, #175, #216, #273, and #287, of which only #99 and #175 include bearing the sins of many. Christ also bore our infirmities and carried our sorrows (Isa 53:4): #75, #119, #192, #241, #295, and #561.

[13] #58, #404, and #435. In Col 2:14 it is a document that is fixed to the Cross, but the document relates to the consequences of our sins.

[14] #145, #216, #220, #225, #231, #357, and #597.

[15] #38, #105, and #291.

[16] #114, #291, #611, and #657.

[17] He hurled all of our sins into the depths of the sea (Mic 7:19; V Nat 3:1, without explicit reference to the Cross).

B. The Cross as Sacrifice

Christ was offered for us on the Cross because he was the only sacrificial victim that would suffice to redeem us (#281). On the Cross he played a dual role as both priest and sacrificial victim (#527). He offered *himself* as a saving sacrifice (*hostia*), exposing his body to punishments and insults (#283). Bernard graphically states that Christ on the Cross offered the evening sacrifice with raised hands (Ps 141:2; #648). Being so holy, so pure, and so acceptable, he is clearly a worthy sacrifice (*hostia*; #289). He is the holy sacrifice (*hostia*), pleasing to God, for the reconciliation of us all (#237). The Son of God offered himself to God as an oblation and an offering (*hostia*) in the odour of sweetness. The Father smelled and accepted this new and godly sacrifice (#428). Bernard repeatedly cites Hebrews 9:14 for the statement that Christ "offered *himself*."[18] Because of sin, humanity was unable to please God. Reconciliation to God was not possible without the offering in sacrifice of an adequate sacrificial victim. As an incarnate human being, the Son was able to offer himself to God as a sacrifice and thus bring reconciliation. Defeating the devil would not bring reconciliation with God without the offering of a sacrifice for sin (#430). We are reconciled with God through that sacrifice (*hostia*), in the blood of the Mediator. As God, he had the right to rule, which he also provides for us by the price of his sacrifice (#431).

Christ's sacrificial death has ongoing application. Just as Christ was both priest and sacrificial victim on the Cross, so also is he daily both priest and sacrificial victim on the altar (#527). Each day he is in a certain manner (*quodam modo*) offered in sacrifice while we proclaim his death—just as he is being born when we faithfully commemorate his birth (#195). The repentant thief on the Cross prefigures those who, aware of the contrast between their unrighteousness and God's righteousness, offer themselves to God on the Cross of penitence as a fat and rich burnt offering (#515).

In addition to referring to the Cross as a sacrifice, Bernard repeatedly refers to Christ as the Lamb of God, the Paschal Lamb. Not all of the references to Christ as a lamb refer explicitly to his death on

---

[18] #185, #238, #374, and #428.

the Cross (though it could be argued that they all do so implicitly), but most do, and they thereby point to his death as a sacrifice. The same can be said of references to the blood of Christ.

C. Christ the Lamb of God

As Christ's death is seen as a sacrifice, so he is seen as the sacrificial Lamb. He is the Lamb of God that takes away the sins of the world (John 1:29).[19] This metaphor clearly refers to the Old Testament sacrificial system, but there are two more specific Old Testament references that Bernard has in mind when calling Christ the Lamb. In Isaiah 53, one of Bernard's key texts for the topic of the Cross,[20] verse 7 states that the servant was led like a lamb to the slaughter and kept silent like a sheep before its shearers. This is quoted with minor differences in wording in Acts 8:32, and Bernard cites these two verses many times.[21] Bernard also cites 1 Peter 2:23, which loosely alludes to Isaiah 53:7.[22]

Secondly, Christ is our Passover Lamb, our Paschal Lamb, who has been sacrificed (1 Cor 5:7; *pascha* [#314], *agnum paschalem* [#615]). As well as twice stating this explicitly, Bernard twice implies it by quoting the statement that no bone of his body is broken (John 19:36).[23] 1 Peter 1:19 calls Christ a Lamb without spot or blemish (*incontaminati et immaculati*), probably a reference to the requirement of the Paschal Lamb (Exod 12:5), and Bernard cites this Petrine text.[24] He also refers repeatedly to Christ as the Lamb without blemish (*sine macula*),[25] but here Bernard is citing not Exodus 12:5 (*absque macula*)

---

[19] #47, #124, #144, #188, #193, #211, #225, #289, #351, #356, #543, and #553.

[20] See chap. 3C and appendix II.

[21] #103, #186, #277, #322, #354, #432, and #553 blend them; #530 follows Isaiah; #286 and #508 follow Acts; #124, #170, and #216 are too loose to be tied to one rather than the other.

[22] #277 and #322.

[23] #439 and #455. John 19:36 refers back to Exod 12:46.

[24] #329, #625, #642, and #654.

[25] #193, #216, #225, #233, and #454. SBOp sometimes mistakenly refers these to Exod 12:5.

but Leviticus 9:3 (*sine macula*), which does not refer to the Paschal Lamb. A word of caution is needed at this point. Bernard's use of 1 Peter 1:19 is no proof that he was consciously thinking of Jesus as the Passover Lamb, and, conversely, his use of *sine* rather than *absque* should not be interpreted as a deliberate intention *not* to refer to the Paschal Lamb. What can be said is that he twice refers to Christ as the Passover Lamb and that he regularly attributes to him properties that relate to that lamb.

Related to the lamb's lack of blemish is the statement of Isaiah 53:9 that there was no deceit in his mouth, quoted with some change in 1 Peter 2:22. Bernard a number of times blends these two passages.[26] He also, more often, quotes Peter's statement in the same verse that Christ committed no sin.[27]

The association of Christ as Lamb with his sacrificial offering is seen in the statement that he is "the Lamb that was slain" (Rev 5:6, 9, 12).[28] Bernard refers to the precious blood of the Lamb (1 Pet 1:19)[29] and to those who have washed their robes in the blood of the Lamb (Rev 7:14).[30] More specifically, Bernard states that the holy places in Palestine were adorned by the blood (*cruor*) of the immaculate Lamb.[31] He also states that pastors will have to give an account of their ministry to the Lamb of God, who died for the flock (#569). Christ was manifest as a Lamb in his passion but became a lion in his resurrection (#484).[32]

---

[26] #41, #138, #251, #358, and #553. He does this also in Sent 3.111, with no mention of the Cross.

[27] In addition to the passages cited in the previous note, #105, #124, #144, #186, #216, #221, #273, #454, #461, and #470.

[28] #289, #310, #311, and #313.

[29] #547 and #551. 1 Pet 1:19 is cited without reference to the Lamb in #355, #621, and #658.

[30] #221, #306, #329, #388, #507, #547, #552, and #649. These all refer at least to the blood of the Lamb. In #186 the verse is cited without mention of the Lamb.

[31] #642 and #654.

[32] Bernard also refers to the marriage feast of the Lamb (Rev 19:9) in the context of the Cross (#400 and #545).

Christ's role as the Lamb of God has practical implications for discipleship. We are called to follow the Lamb wherever he goes (Rev 14:4).[33]

D. The Blood of Christ

Bernard refers frequently to the blood of Christ. As with the references to the Lamb, this also relates to the picture of Christ's death as a sacrifice. We have already seen his references to the precious blood of the Lamb (1 Pet 1:19), to those who have washed their robes in the blood of the Lamb (Rev 7:14), and to the adornment of the holy places by the blood of the Lamb.[34]

Christ has redeemed us. How? By his blood. Bernard uses a number of scriptural texts to make this point. We have redemption through Christ's blood (Eph 1:7; #610). Unlike other priests, it was by his *own* blood that he redeemed us (Heb 9:12),[35] obtaining an eternal redemption (Heb 9:12; #558). We are redeemed by his blood (Rev 5:9),[36] by his precious blood (1 Pet 1:18-19).[37]

Christ has redeemed his unique bride from the yoke of the devil by his blood (#540).[38] His blood is the price of our redemption,[39] or

---

[33] #170, #348, #383, #384, #387, and #517. The verse is cited without mention of the Lamb in #240 and #296.

[34] Similar to the last of these is the statement that the Holy Land has been dedicated by Christ's own blood (Heb 9:18; #642, #654, and #663). Bernard also refers to those who, keeping the blood of Christ in sight, embrace death for Christ (#528), and he states that the martyrs are sprinkled with the blood of the slain Christ (#553).

[35] #235, #237, #334, and #558. In #257 it is cited without the reference to redemption. The English translation of #540 states that it was by his "own" blood (CF 55:369), but there is no equivalent to "own" in the Latin (SBOp 6/2:193).

[36] #399, #544, and #555. The allusion to Rev 5:9 in these passages amounts to no more than that he has redeemed us *in sanguine suo* and is tenuous. I have excluded #237 and #621, where the point being made is found in another biblical text that is more clearly cited.

[37] #355, #433, #621, and #658. In the last of these the word is *empti* rather than *redempti*. In #433 it is *emerat*.

[38] See also #628 and #652: Christ redeemed his bride with his blood.

[39] #22 and #235.

(more generally) just the price (*pretium*).[40] In other words, we have been acquired by his blood (Acts 20:28).[41] The blood of Christ is of greater value than the price for which we were sold into slavery to sin—namely, the pleasure of sin.[42] The blood that flowed from his side is the price of the satisfaction that placates the Father (#30).

It is through the blood of Christ that we are justified (Rom 3:24-25; 5:9).[43] Just as there is sin in the seed of the sinner, so there is righteousness (*iustitia*) in the blood of Christ (#606). He brings peace through his blood (Col 1:20).[44] We are washed from our sins by his blood (Rev 1:5)[45] because Christ's blood is more powerful than that of Abel and proclaims forgiveness (Gen 4:10; Heb 12:24).[46] Our sin cannot be expunged by the blood of calves or goats (#356), so our only hope is for Christ's blood to cry out for us so that we may be forgiven (#31).

Bernard often cites verses that link water and the blood of Christ, such as John 19:34[47] and 1 John 5:6.[48] Sometimes he adds to these a third, the Spirit, taking this either from 1 John 5:6-8 or from an alternative reading of 1 John 5:6.[49] A good example of this is found in his first sermon on the octave of Easter, whose title refers to the

---

[40] #189, #254, #504, and #614. CF 55:135 translates *sanguis spectat ad pretium* as "the blood looks to reward" (#504). That Bernard is thinking of the price of redemption can be seen from the parallel phrase that follows, *Sanguis Domini nos redemit*. This is clearly the meaning in the passage of Ambrose that he is quoting (SCh 52:172).

[41] #101 and #189. Both of these allusions to Acts 20:28 are rather tenuous, especially the second.

[42] #547 and #550.

[43] #606 and #610 (both); #541 (Rom 5:9 only).

[44] #35, #236, #358, #381, #396, and #566. Bernard always omits the words *crucis eius*.

[45] #175 and #385. In #145 and #198, Rev 1:5 is quoted without the reference to blood.

[46] #263 and #559. For further allusion to Gen 4:10, see #17, #96, and #625; to Heb 12:24, see #431 and #512.

[47] #306, #329, #400, #402, #512, and #591. The verse is also cited with reference to blood only in #439, to water only in #231, #334, #392, and #544.

[48] #76, #328-30, #400, #440, #599, and #649.

[49] #328, #330, ##332-35, #401, and ##503-4.

three witnesses in heaven and on earth. Christ came by water and
blood, and the Spirit bears witness to him. John adds "not by water
alone but by water and blood," thus pointing to Christ's superiority
over Moses: Moses came by water alone but Christ came by both,
as is witnessed by the fact that both flowed from his side (1 John
5:6; O Pasc 1.4; #328). Deliverance from Egypt was effected by the
blood of the Lamb, signifying that we are saved by the blood of the
immaculate Lamb (O Pasc 1.5; #329). So also today Christ comes
to us by water and blood and also by the witness of the Spirit. These
refer, respectively, to baptism, martyrdom, and love. We need the Holy
Spirit because without the love that he sheds in our hearts (Rom 5:5)
nothing is of value (1 Cor 13:1-4; O Pasc 1.6; #330). In addition to
once-for-all baptism, water signifies compunction of heart and tears.
As well as literal martyrdom, blood signifies the extended martyrdom
of daily mortification (O Pasc 1.7; #331). Only the Spirit abides,
because water and blood will not inherit the kingdom of God; but
we cannot now have one without the other, because these three are
one (1 John 5:8; O Pasc 1.8; #332). Bernard continues to draw out
practical applications from 1 John 5:6-8 in his second sermon on the
octave of Easter, concluding that we have the threefold testimony if
we abstain from sin, bear fruits worthy of repentance, and perform
works of life (O Pasc 2.5; #335).[50]

Bernard also refers to the blood of Christ in the context of the
Eucharist.[51] Christ gave his apostles wine and established the sacrament of his blood (#126). The cup is the new covenant in Christ's
blood and is poured out for us (Matt 26:28; Luke 22:20).[52] He refers
to eating Christ's flesh and drinking his blood, in the words of John
6:53-55.[53] He explains that the sacrament and the phrase "eating

[50] See also ##399–402 for a shorter extended treatment of the theme.

[51] In ##570–71 he discusses a situation where the prayer of consecration had
been said with no wine in the chalice.

[52] For new covenant, #610; for "pour out," #181, #214, and #610. The reference to the blood of the covenant in #295 is a quotation from Heb 10:29, not a
reference to the Last Supper.

[53] #73, #107, #132, #247, #262, #318, #524, and #615. He also cites these
verses referring to flesh only: #53 and #282.

his flesh and drinking his blood" signify sharing in his sufferings (#262).[54] He also refers to being guilty of the blood of the Lord, echoing 1 Corinthians 11:27 (#334).[55]

To summarise, we are redeemed by the blood of Christ, which is the price of our redemption. So far as I am aware, Bernard only once refers to the blood of Christ when explicitly speaking of redemption from Satan (#540). By contrast, he links the blood of Christ with justification and the forgiveness of sins, clearly referring to our relationship to God. Talk of blood is also closely linked to that of sacrifice, and there is no question but that it is God to whom the sacrifice is offered. As always, Bernard is interested in the practical outworking, in terms of embracing martyrdom and sharing in Christ's sufferings.

E. The Wounds of Christ

Bernard speaks of the wounds of Christ. He refers to the piercing of Christ's hands and feet, using the language of Psalm 22:16,[56] and to the nails that pierced him.[57] He also refers to the lance that pierced his side (John 19:34).[58] Bernard identifies "the dove in the clefts of the rock" of Song of Songs 2:14 with the wounds of Christ in general[59] and with the wound in his side in particular (#250). He also refers to the incident of Thomas (John 20:25, 27; ##54–55)[60] and to the day when people will look upon him whom they have pierced (Zech 12:10; John 19:37).[61]

Bernard's teaching on the wounds of Christ is found especially in his sixty-first sermon on the Song of Songs. The title to this an-

[54] Similarly #247.

[55] In #301 he talks of giving thanks for "the body and blood of the Lord," again echoing 1 Cor 11:27.

[56] #84, #91, #201, #202, and #286.

[57] E.g., #129, #439, and #446.

[58] #84, #129, #201, #250, #369, #439, #446, #544, #591, and #622.

[59] #68, #82, #83, #87, and #89.

[60] Also with a passing mention in #372.

[61] #121, #187, and #591. See also an allusion to Rev 1:7, which quotes Zech 12:10, in #545.

nounces that the "clefts of the rock" in which the dove dwells (Song 2:14) are the wounds of Christ (#82). Having introduced Song 2:13-14 (SC 61.1–2), Bernard announces that the correct interpretation of the clefts is that given by "someone else,"[62] that they refer to the wounds of Christ, Christ being the rock. They are the one secure resting place for the weak. We may have sinned greatly, and our conscience may be disturbed (*turbabitur*), but it is not perturbed (*perturbabitur*), because we remember the wounds of Christ, who was wounded for our transgressions (Isa 53:5;[63] SC 61.3; #83). Whatever may be lacking in our merits we can take from the heart of the Lord. The Lord's mercy flows out from the clefts, from the five wounds of Christ, which declare that God is in Christ reconciling the world to himself (2 Cor 5:19). Christ's wounds declare God's heart, his steadfast love and mercy (SC 61.4; #84). Our merit is the Lord's mercy, and we do not lack merit while he does not lack mercy. Against our sins we can set God's treasury of tenderness and wealth of goodness, which are stored in the clefts of the rock (SC 61.5; #85). The Lord is lofty in his kingdom but delightful in the Cross (SC 61.6; #86). The church does not flee the ugliness of Christ's wounds but rejoices in them. Her devotion is focussed on them, and she lingers there in continual meditation.[64] She need not fear him by whose stripes she is healed (Isa 53:5).[65] Meditation on the wounds of Christ enables her to endure even martyrdom. The soldier is strengthened by the wounds of his commander and by the example that he has set (SC 61.7; #87). As the martyrs discovered for themselves, considering his wounds enables us not to feel our own. The martyr's soul is safe in the clefts of the rock, in Christ's wounds that are open to enter. This is where martyrs derive their courage (SC 61.8; #88).

---

[62] Oluf Schönbeck, "Saint Bernard, Peter Damian, and the Wounds of Christ," CSQ 30 (1995): 275–84, argues that this refers not to Gregory the Great (as in CF 31:142) but to someone in the tradition found in Peter Damian.

[63] Also cited in #37 and #378.

[64] In the following sermon Bernard affirms that persevering meditation on Christ's wounds is the greatest cure for wounds of conscience (#91).

[65] Also cited in #37, #378, and #439.

As always, Bernard makes practical application of his teaching on the wounds of Christ. He also urges a novice, when tempted, to look to the bronze serpent on the staff (*ligno*)[66] and to draw life from the wounds of Christ. The nails that cleaved his hands and his feet must also pass through ours (#635).

To summarise, Bernard sees in the wounds of Christ the basis for confidence before God[67] and the encouragement to endure even to the point of martyrdom.

F. Christ Paying the Price

Bernard often, in different contexts, speaks of Christ paying a price: Christ is the price of our salvation (#177) and indeed the price of the world (#191). To what sort of price is he referring? There is more than one answer to this:

- Bernard refers repeatedly to the "price of *redemption*," using a phrase from Psalm 49:7-8,[68] this price being paid by Christ's blood.[69] We have been bought at a price (1 Cor 6:20; 7:23).[70] The blood of Christ is of greater value than the price for which we were sold into slavery to sin—namely, the pleasure of sin.[71]

- Christ is the one who has paid our *debt* for us.[72] Echoing Psalm 69:4, Bernard says that Christ is the one who repaid what he had not stolen.[73] It was man that owed the debt and a man who paid it. "As one bore the sins of all, so the satisfaction of the one is imputed to all" (#605).[74]

---

[66] Num 21:8-9; John 3:14. Bernard also refers to this in #304 and #376.

[67] See chap. 12B below.

[68] #22, #201, #235, #477, and #637.

[69] #22, #235, and #637.

[70] #433, #625, and #658 (1 Cor 6:20); #162 (1 Cor 7:23).

[71] #547 and #550.

[72] E.g., #147, #148, #150, and #427.

[73] #152, #216, #286, #344, #458, and #491. In #469, in the context of discussion of the Cross (#468 and ##470–72), Bernard applies this verse to the situation where one bears the burden of penitence for the sins of one's neighbours.

[74] On the echoes of Anselm, see section J below.

- In *De laude novae militiae* Bernard ties together the concepts of *debt* and *merit*. Our spiritual death is the reward for our fault (*culpae meritum*), and our bodily death is the debt of punishment (*poenae debitum*). "Christ submitted to the punishment, though innocent of the fault. He died of his own accord, only in the body, and merited life and righteousness for us. If he had not suffered bodily, he would not have paid the debt; if he had not died voluntarily, his death would have had no merit.[75] Death is merited by sin and is a debt owed because of sin, as we said. So in remitting sin and dying for sinners, Christ nullified the merit and paid the debt" (Tpl 11.21; #147). We can be sure that Christ has removed death, "because he that did not deserve [*non meruit*] to die endured it. How can the debt that he has already paid for us be required again of us? He bore the punishment of our sin [*peccati meritum*] and gave us his righteousness by paying the debt of death and restoring life" (Tpl 11.22; #148).

- Christ's blood is the price of *satisfaction* to placate the Father (#30), and, as we have just seen, the debt that Christ paid in bearing the sins of all is counted as satisfaction for all (#605).

- Christ confers on us the *ius regnandi* by the price of his *sacrifice* (#431).

"Paying a price" naturally relates to the idea of redemption, of buying back. Yet Bernard also speaks of the payment of a debt, a slightly different picture. In addition, he speaks of "price" once in terms of the satisfaction offered to God and once in terms of the sacrifice offered to God.

What was the price that Christ paid? It was his blood.[76] It is by his blood that he acquired us (Acts 20:28).[77] Again, the price was his

---

[75] This is the one place in this passage where the word "merit" is used positively to refer to what Christ achieved, rather than negatively to refer to what we deserved and Christ nullified. In #137 Bernard states that Christ "gave himself as merit for us."

[76] #189, #254, #504, and #614.

[77] #101 and #189. Both of these allusions to Acts 20:28 are rather tenuous, especially the second.

passion (#222), his laying down his life for us.[78] When we think about
the greatness of the reward that awaits us, we must consider the great
worth of the price that was paid (#89). Since such a great price was paid
for us, we should be prepared in turn to die for love of Christ (#530).

The ideas of a price to be paid and a debt to be repaid are prominent in Bernard's thought. But to whom were we indebted, and to
whom was the price paid? Abelard poses this question and responds
that "the price of blood paid to redeem us" was paid to God, his
prime point being to deny that it was paid to Satan.[79] Bernard quotes
verbatim almost all of Abelard's questions about the need for the
Cross but significantly ignores this point. He never states in so many
words to whom the price was paid, exercising the same restraint
as the New Testament, but it is clear that for Bernard nothing was
offered to Satan.[80] In Bernard's view, Satan loses his power over us
because the punishment imposed by God (not by Satan) has been
paid and we have been reconciled with God. Death is defeated because the issue of sin has been resolved. Death is the consequence
of sin, so by removing the cause, the consequence is eliminated.

G. Christ Bearing Our Punishment

The debt that is owed is understood by Bernard to be death, the
penalty for sin.[81] Christ accepts the punishment (*multari*) of death and
the shame of the Cross (#7).[82] He identifies with sinful humanity

---

[78] #53 and #73.

[79] Excursus 7.7. See chap. 2C above. Richard E. Weingart, *The Logic of Divine
Love* (Oxford: OUP, 1970), 138, wrongly exonerates Abelard of ever suggesting
that a ransom or price was paid to God.

[80] Daniel L. Akin, "Bernard of Clairvaux: Evangelical of the Twelfth Century (A
Critical Analysis of His Soteriology)" (PhD thesis, University of Texas at Arlington,
1989), 100, 112; Daniel L. Akin, "Bernard of Clairvaux and the Atonement," *The
Church at the Dawn of the 21st Century: Essays in Honor of Dr. W. A. Criswell*, ed. P.
Patterson, J. Pretlove, and L. Pantoja (Dallas: Criswell Publications, 1989), 110,
mistakenly charges Bernard with teaching that a ransom is paid *to* Satan.

[81] *Poena* can, of course, be translated "punishment" or "penalty." Where it is a
question of something being paid, the word "penalty" is more appropriate.

[82] See also #217: on the Cross Christ's whole body *in poenam . . . distensum est*,
which is usually translated "in pain" (e.g., CF 51:141). Given the theological con-

"so that he might pay the penalty [*poenam solveret*], although he had no guilt" (#294). He offered himself as a sacrifice, exposing himself to punishment (*suppliciis*) and insults (#283), and he put on the garment of our curse (Gal 3:13; #114).[83] Bernard cites Isaiah 53: it was for our iniquities that Christ was wounded (Isa 53:5);[84] the Lord laid our iniquity upon him (Isa 53:6; #42). Christ provides the remedy for death, the consequence of sin, by paying our debt, by taking our punishment upon himself. He "submitted to the punishment [*poenam*], though innocent of the fault" (#147).[85] He has reconciled us to God by his death, delivering us from the punishment due to us in justice (*puniens iustitia*; #549). Bernard poetically represents Christ as stating, "I regret [*paenitet me*] that I made humanity. The punishment [*poena*] holds me, and it is incumbent upon me to bear the punishment [*poena*] and do penance [*paenitentiam*] for humanity, whom I created." When Christ took our punishment upon himself, justice and peace kissed one another (Ps 85:10; #270).[86]

The punishment (*poena*) of sin was unjustly imposed on Christ by Satan, who was thereby condemned, and we in turn are reconciled to God (#431). This drama involves the two aspects of death: it is both the work of the devil and the punishment (*poena*) for sin (#404). Satan the deceiver was himself deceived into imposing death, the punishment (*poena*) for sin, on the sinless one. The punishment of the innocent one outweighs the punishment due to the disobedient.[87] The death that he did not need to suffer was imputed to sinners. The punishment inflicted on the innocent one brings absolution to the guilty (#522). So through the Cross Christ dissolves our guilt, removes our disgrace, and ends our punishment (*supplicium*; #545).

---

text, it is likely that Bernard also had in mind that on the Cross Christ was bearing our *poenam*. Christ also endured the Cross, despising the shame (Heb 12:2; #259).

[83] In #529 Bernard speaks of Christ doing this for the Virgin Mary in particular.

[84] #37 and #83. Another part of Isa 53:5 is cited in #42.

[85] See also #145: Christ "did not tremble at the punishment in order to snatch us away from eternal disgrace and restore us to glory."

[86] Similarly ##427–28. On Ps 85:10, see chap. 11C below.

[87] *Poena innocentiae meae . . . poena inoboedientiae humanae.* In CF 55:244 *poena* is translated as "suffering," which is not unreasonable, but the translation also brings out the fact that this suffering is penal: "[suffering] due for humanity's disobedience."

The cup that Jesus tasted on the Cross but did not want to drink (Matt 27:34) was the damnation of the wicked (#513). Bernard also refers repeatedly to the cup to which Jesus gave his assent in the Garden of Gethsemane (Matt 26:39, 42; Mark 14:36; Luke 22:42; John 18:11).[88] To what does that cup refer? Bernard twice points to an answer. It was, unsurprisingly, a cup of suffering (#545). More particularly, drinking the cup is related to the principle that under the rule of justice no sin can be left unpunished (#519). The cup that Jesus faced, then, was to bear the punishment due to us.

Christ bore our punishment on the Cross. What was that punishment? Death. What sort of death? In one place Bernard appears to state that this was physical death only (#147), but other passages point to a different conclusion. As just stated, the cup that Jesus tasted on the Cross but did not want to drink (Matt 27:34) was the damnation of the wicked (#513). On the Cross he experienced abandonment by the Father (Matt 27:46; #377).

Harnack famously stated that "that which we really miss in Abelard—that Christ bore our penalty—is also wanting in Bernard."[89] The evidence that we have seen shows that this is not merely a mistaken interpretation; it is simply untrue. By contrast, Rivière, having stated that Bernard had little concern to explain the doctrine of redemption and confined himself to reiterating the statements of the Fathers, claims that "the idea which has his preference is that of penal substitution."[90] We shall need to assess this claim when we have seen all that Bernard had to teach on the Godward aspect of the Cross.

H. The Cross as Propitiation for Our Sins

Because of sin, we are separated from God and subject to death (Tpl 11.19). Bernard repeatedly speaks of Christ's work as placating or appeasing (*placo*) the Father. By accepting death, Christ satisfied

---

[88] #140, #270, #324, #511, #519, and #542.

[89] Adolf Harnack, *History of Dogma*, vol. 6 (New York: Russell and Russell, 1958), 80.

[90] Jean Rivière, *The Doctrine of the Atonement: A Historical Essay*, vol. 2 (London: Kegan Paul, Trench, Trübner and Co., 1909), 70.

the Father. By patiently enduring death, he appeased the offended Father and reconciled us to him (#22). Christ's blood is the price of satisfaction to placate the Father (#30). Mary offers Jesus as a holy sacrifice (*hostia*), pleasing to God (*Deo placentem*), for the reconciliation of us all (#237). The Son of God offered himself as an oblation and an offering (*hostia*) to God. The Father smelled the odour of his sacrifice and accepted it (#428). Satan was defeated because, by bringing about Christ's death, he inadvertently offered a sacrificial victim that was able to placate the Father, something that human beings could not have achieved (#430).

Bernard uses the word "propitiation" (*propitiatio*) to describe Christ's work of placating the Father.[91] He quotes 1 John 2:1-2, which states that Jesus Christ the righteous is our advocate with the Father and the propitiation for our sins,[92] in connection with which he states that Christ intercedes for transgressors (Isa 53:12).[93] How marvellous is the passion of Jesus that propitiated (*propitiata*) for all our iniquities (#285). Christ was broken in body on the Cross, thus propitiating (*propitians*) the Father (#76). Bernard also quotes 1 John 4:10: God sent his Son as the propitiation for our sins (#541).

Propitiation conveys the idea of turning away wrath, and that idea is also stated by Bernard. The Son of God brought (*attulit*) the grace of God and took away (*abstulit*) the wrath of God. He shared God's wrath with us in order that we might share God's grace with him (#545).[94] Although by nature we are children of wrath, through the redemption of Jesus Christ we are made children of mercy. Jesus has reconciled us to God by his death, delivering us from the punishment

---

[91] In Pre 9.19 Bernard refers to the *propitiatio Dei* as our consolation. If we offend God, we need someone to plead for us who is appropriate for the one who needs to be appeased. There is no mention of the Cross at this point, but that comes in the following section (#156).

[92] All: #157. 2:2 only: #175. 2:1 (Advocate) only: Pent 1.4 (of the Holy Spirit) and PP 3.3.

[93] #157 and #175.

[94] Later in #545 he refers to the cup that the Father gave to him (John 18:11), which may plausibly be identified with the cup of God's wrath, though that is not a link that Bernard explicitly mentions.

due to us in justice (#549). On the Cross he experienced abandonment by the Father (Matt 27:46; #377).

Robert Linhardt claims that while Bernard taught that Christ
propitiated the Father, this doctrine was not important for Bernard.[95]
The passages cited in this section certainly demonstrate that Bernard
taught the doctrine; the question of how important it was for him
can only be properly assessed in the light of the rest of his teaching
on the Godward aspect of Christ's work. We shall return to that
question at the conclusion of this chapter.

Talk of propitiation can easily raise the spectre of a vengeful Father
who is reluctant to forgive until persuaded to do so by his Son. This
is an issue that will be discussed in the following chapter,[96] but it
is also answered in some of the passages just considered. Christ is
the propitiation for our sins (1 John 2:2) offered to the Father, but
Father and Son are equal and united in mercy and will (#175). It
is because he already loved us that God the Father sent his Son as
the propitiation for our sins (1 John 4:10). God's prior love for us is
further demonstrated from Romans 5:8-10 (#541). Indeed, in one
passage Bernard speaks of Christ suffering in order to reconcile sinners to *himself* (rather than to the Father). On the Cross he hungered
and thirsted for righteousness and exacted from himself so great a
satisfaction for our sins (#186).

I. The Cross as Expiation for Our Sins

There is a difference between propitiation and expiation. Strictly
speaking, it is persons who are propitiated, and the Cross deals with
the break in our relationship with the Father caused by our sin. It
is sin or guilt that is expiated, not a person. Bernard's own usage
conforms to these definitions. He uses the words *expio* or *expiatio*
only fourteen times[97] and never chooses to use them of the Cross.
In his letter-treatise he quotes a question of Abelard's: "If that sin of

---

[95] Linhardt, *Die Mystik des hl. Bernhard von Clairvaux*, 110.

[96] See chap. 11D below.

[97] It also appears as an incorrect variant reading in #112 (SBOp 2:254).

Adam was so great that it could be expiated only by the death of Christ, what expiation will there be for the very act of murdering Christ?" (#611).[98] In his response he doesn't himself use the word.

So how does Bernard use the words "expiate" and "expiation"? We must flee from the vision of God's wrath to a place of refuge, to his zeal of mercy (*zelus misericordiae*); it is that mercy that effectually expiates. But does not love expiate (1 Pet 4:8)? Yes, powerfully (SC 69.6). If the patriarch Joseph was guilty of pride in talking about his dreams, this sin could be expiated by what he suffered (Hum 10.37). In hell our offence (*culpa*) is eternally punished but will never be able to be expiated (Conv 6). For those who after baptism have sinned seriously with their lips, there is no second baptism, and Christ will not be crucified a second time for them. They must expiate the curse of their own lips by their own lips (#455). Bernard also three times refers to purgatory as the place of expiation. The *infernus expiationis* is the place for souls in need of purification after death—by contrast with hell, where our sin cannot be expiated by any punishment (#425). The *regio expiationis* is where our sins are expiated by suffering (Div 42.5). The *regio expiationis* is one of five regions described in Sent 3.91. Here the souls of those who will be saved are punished. Elsewhere, discussing the fate of those living before Christ, Bernard notes that Gentile adults were expiated by faith and sacrifices (Bapt 1.4; here and here only, what is expiated is not a sin but the sinner). Finally, Bernard urges that those at Genoa guilty of various sins should desist from them and even expiate and erase them by their good works (Ep 129.3).

In short, Bernard himself (unlike Abelard) never refers to Christ's work in terms of expiation,[99] though he does once talk of God's zeal of mercy expiating. Generally, the word in its various forms is used of our part in offering satisfaction for postbaptismal sin, whether in this life or in purgatory.

---

[98] A close quotation of Excursus 7.3. See chap. 2C above.

[99] Akin, "Bernard of Clairvaux: Evangelical of the Twelfth Century," 105–6; Akin, "Bernard of Clairvaux and the Atonement," 111–12, is misled here by relying on the translation of #145 in CF 19:153, which gratuitously adds "in order to expiate our sins."

J. The Cross as Satisfaction for Our Sins

Bernard uses the concept of satisfaction to expound the death of Christ, though less frequently than any of the other concepts thus far described in this chapter.[100] There are just eight passages where the idea of satisfaction is applied to the Cross. Christ satisfied the Father by accepting death, thus reconciling us to the Father (#22).[101] He surrendered himself to death and out of his side flowed his blood, the price of satisfaction to placate the Father (#30). He is the righteous one who makes satisfaction for sinners (#149). On the Cross he hungered and thirsted for righteousness and exacted from himself so great a satisfaction for our sins (#186). God may be exasperated by the horror of our villainy, but he is pacified by sorrow of the satisfaction of his Son (#659). The idea of satisfaction is associated especially with appeasing or placating the Father and thus reconciling us to him. God found no way to forgive our guilt without a fitting satisfaction (#427).

Bernard also considers, in the context of satisfaction, how Adam and Christ each affect us. We have been imprisoned by the sin of another (Adam), and so also it is the satisfaction of another (Christ) that has prepared our return (#424). "As one bore the sins of all, so the satisfaction of the one is imputed to all. Nor is it a case that it was one that earned the forfeit and another that made satisfaction, for head and body together form one Christ. The head therefore made satisfaction for the members, Christ for his own body" (#605).

Bernard understands the Cross in terms of satisfaction, but he does not confine the term to the Cross. Old Testament sacrifices provided satisfaction for sins of ignorance (Lev 5:17-19; Bapt 4.16). He also occasionally uses the term for the satisfaction that we might

---

[100] Apart, of course, from expiation. Linhardt, *Die Mystik des hl. Bernhard von Clairvaux*, 112, correctly notes that Bernard prefers to talk of reconciliation more than satisfaction. Akin, "Bernard of Clairvaux: Evangelical of the Twelfth Century," 95; Akin, "Bernard of Clairvaux and the Atonement," 107, mistakenly claims that for Bernard the motif of satisfaction is "primary or foundational."

[101] Satisfaction is just one of the many pictures used in this passage, which include the deception of Satan, the conquest of death, his blood as the price of redemption, and the appeasement of the Father.

make for our sins. Our sins create a gulf between us and God (Isa 59:2), and this is closed by our making satisfaction (*satisfacimus*; SC 4.2). Abstinence is a good thing if understood as satisfaction for sins (SC 66.6). One way that we can "follow the Lamb" is by making satisfaction to cleanse our impurity (#170).

Bernard saw no contradiction between the satisfaction that Christ has offered and that needing to be offered by us, as he speaks of the latter in the context of the former. He refers to the worthy satisfaction of penitence (#426) shortly after reference to the satisfaction made by Christ (#424). In the context of a discussion of Christ's work on the Cross (##222–26), Bernard refers to the satisfaction that we can make, which is most agreeable and, though little, is not to be underestimated (#224). In the light of Christ's work on the Cross (#477), he speaks of the satisfaction that we can make for those in purgatory by our own personal sacrifice (Div 42.5). There is, however, no question of us making a full satisfaction for our sins. Those who realise how sinful they are extract from themselves the severest satisfaction, but they are aware of the inadequacy of this and flee from justice to mercy (Hum 5.18). The debt we owe is too great to be repaid by our penitence (#452).[102]

The modest number of passages portraying the Cross as satisfaction for our sins poses the question of Bernard's relation to Anselm's *Cur Deus homo*. How does Bernard's argument compare with that of Anselm? Was he influenced by Anselm's work? Did he even know it? The first of these questions is relatively straightforward. The second and third are much harder to answer. Leclercq explains why: it is difficult to discern Bernard's patristic sources because he almost never declares them. Indeed, far from citing them, when he writes he does not even remember where he derived the ideas.[103] Since he

---

[102] On the other hand, having given an account of how Christ has paid the debt that we cannot pay (##450–52), Bernard goes on to speak of the debt of *poenitentia* that we owe (#452). Similarly, he argues, on the basis of Heb 6:6 and 10:26, that we ourselves need to expiate sins committed after baptism (#455), though no one is able to offer sufficient satisfaction for one's own sins (#456).

[103] Jean Leclercq, "S. Bernard et la tradition biblique d'après les Sermons sur les Cantiques," RESB 1:318.

never mentions Anselm by name,[104] any verdict about influence is likely to be tentative.

There are two passages that especially echo Anselm's argument. The first is from a sermon on epiphany. The Son of God, in order to reconcile us to God, needed to know both the weakness of humanity and the power of deity. The latter he knows from eternity; the former he learned from experience, from his time on earth. There was a problem because God did not find a way in his secret plan (*consilii*) to forgive our guilt without a fitting satisfaction, but humanity had nothing worthwhile to pay. God saw our misery and the claims of justice and managed to preserve justice (*aequitatem*) but exalt mercy above all. There is a huge contrariety between God and humanity, but the Son of God serves as the Mediator. He assumes mortality that he might learn human misery, while retaining truth so that he might preserve the justice of the Father. He mediates between mortal deceit and immortal truthfulness, being mortal but true. He had a plan to rescue humanity and knew the justice (*iudicium*) by which he might preserve the honour of the royal majesty—since the honour of the king loves justice (Ps 99:4; Epi var 4; #427). The Father's command meant that humanity must be punished by death, but he decided that they should do penance before death lest they should be punished after death. This way mercy and truth meet one another (Ps 85:10) because it was not contrary to the divine sentence (Gen 2:17). In death, which could not be avoided, human righteousness kisses peace. The Son of God offered himself to God as an oblation and an offering (*hostia*) in the odour of sweetness. The Father smelled and accepted this new and godly sacrifice (Epi var 5; #428).

The other passage is in Bernard's sermon on the seven gifts of the Holy Spirit. The devil held us firmly in his grip, and we needed deliverance. Because of sin, humanity was unable to please God. Satan, by bringing about Christ's death, inadvertently offered a sacrificial victim that was able to placate the Father, something that we could not have achieved. What could the Son offer to the Father,

---

[104] CETEDOC, *Thesaurus Sancti Bernardi Claraevallensis: Index formarum singulorum operum; Concordantia formarum* (Turnhout: Brepols, 1987).

with whom he had all things in common? He needed to offer him something but had nothing from his deity to offer him. So he assumed human nature, free of sin, to abolish the written code against us (Col 2:14),[105] and thus he reconciled us to the Father. Defeating the devil would not bring reconciliation with God without the offering of a sacrifice for sin (Doni 1; #430).

These passages echo Anselm's argument that Christ needed to be both human and divine in order to redeem us, but there is also much that is different. The word "satisfaction," which lies at the heart of Anselm's argument, occurs only once (#427), and the problem to be resolved is the need to preserve God's truth and justice (##427–28) rather than the need to restore his *honour*. The need was for a sacrifice that would placate the Father (#430). Again, Bernard's argument that Christ needed to be human in order to experience our misery is missing from *Cur Deus homo*. The word "honour" does appear at the end of #427, but it is not linked with the idea of satisfaction, and for Bernard God's honour is preserved by God acting justly. Apart from this passage Bernard mentions God's honour only twice in the context of the Cross. One passage, quoting Malachi 1:6, refers to God being honoured, the issue being our honouring of God, not what Christ has done on our behalf (#333).[106] In the second passage, Bernard talks of the will of the Father being honoured by Christ completing the work of redemption on the Cross (#542), the issue being Christ submitting to the Father's will, not the restoring of God's lost honour.[107] Thus, Bernard hardly ever uses even the word "honour" in connection with Christ's saving work and never uses it in Anselm's sense of Christ restoring God's lost honour.[108] This

---

[105] Bernard cites Col 2:14 for the cancelling of the written code (*chirographum*), which is of our damnation (#301 and #386), against us (*adversum nos* [Vulg]; #396, #430, and #605), and contrary to us (*contrarium nobis* [Vulg]; #396, #428, and #605).

[106] Similarly, in SC 16.6, following on from #17, Bernard states that God as Creator demands that we honour him.

[107] Elsewhere, without mentioning the Cross, he states that in reconciling us to our offended Lord, zeal for God's honour should not cause us to be crushed, nor should his honour be defrauded by excessive goodwill to sinners (Ann 2.2).

[108] Checked with the aid of CETEDOC, *Thesaurus Sancti Bernardi Claraevallensis*.

conclusion should occasion no surprise since, according to Burns, twelfth-century accounts of Christ's saving work were developed "almost without regard for [Anselm's] proposal."[109]

Given the differences between Bernard and Anselm, how likely is it that Bernard was influenced by Anselm's *Cur Deus homo*? A number of scholars claim that he clearly was influenced. Kleineidam states that Bernard took up Anselm's newly coined term *satisfactio* in order to sharpen up his own teaching on redemption.[110] The problem is that it does not sharpen up his teaching—he makes little use of the term, and it appears to mean no more than that the Father is placated or appeased. Grensted claims that the passage quoted above from #605 clearly shows the influence of Anselm's language, but then he adds that Bernard has not actually grasped or adopted the latter's satisfaction theory.[111] Because Grensted's latter point is undoubtedly correct, it throws doubt on why the mere use of the word "satisfaction" to describe the significance of the Cross should prove Anselm's influence, given that satisfaction language predated Anselm. Rivière recognises that there is no compelling evidence that Bernard had read Anselm's work for himself but argues that he was manifestly influenced by Anselm, whether directly or indirectly.[112] Here again, the problem is that while Bernard occasionally uses the word "satisfaction," he does not use it to express Anselm's theory, as Grensted notes.[113] Finally, Gillian Evans, who came to Bernard from

[109] J. Patout Burns, "The Concept of Satisfaction in Medieval Redemption Theory," *Theological Studies* 36 (1975): 285. His article focuses on scholastic theology and makes no mention of Bernard, but his conclusion makes the lack of influence upon the latter the more plausible.

[110] Erich Kleineidam, "Wissen, Wissenschaft, Theologie bei Bernhard von Clairvaux," *Bernhard von Clairvaux: Mönch und Mystiker*, ed. Joseph Lortz (Wiesbaden: F. Steiner, 1955), 153.

[111] Laurence W. Grensted, *A Short History of the Doctrine of the Atonement* (Manchester: Manchester University Press; London: Longmans, Green and Co., 1920), 111.

[112] Jean Rivière, "Le dogme de la rédemption au début du moyen âge III—rôle de saint Bernard," RSR 13 (1933): 203–6.

[113] It may be that Rivière means no more than to affirm that Bernard follows Anselm in teaching an objective Godward dimension to the work of Christ, though he does appear to be claiming rather more.

having studied Anselm, also argues for Anselm's influence. She lists a number of places where this influence can be discerned: Bernard's emphasis on the gravity of Adam's offence and on *convenientia* and *decentia*, his use of the image of painting on air, his teaching that angels cannot be restored, and his teaching on the necessity for the incarnation and Cross.[114] (She also recognises significant points of difference, especially the acknowledgement of the devil's rights and the positive role given to Christ's human life.[115]) She concludes that Bernard "had certainly read the *Cur Deus Homo*" and that he "had been reading Anselm."[116] One has to ask, though, how many of the parallels that she discerns need to have come from Anselm and how many could have another source, such as Augustine.[117]

Given the important differences between the two writers and given the sparsity of Bernard's use of "satisfaction" with reference to the Cross and his failure to interpret the Cross in terms of God's honour, I see no grounds for claiming that his teaching on this topic was influenced by Anselm.[118] It is noteworthy that Anselme Dimier, in a short paper on "Réminiscences Anselmiennes dans les écrits de Saint Bernard," makes no mention at all of the word "satisfaction."[119]

---

[114] Gillian R. Evans, *The Mind of St. Bernard of Clairvaux* (Oxford: OUP, 1983), 143, 156, 158–59.

[115] Evans, *Mind of St. Bernard of Clairvaux*, 154, 156. She also addresses whether sin offends the Son only or the whole Godhead and whether the elevation of Christ's humanity or his descent and humiliation is emphasised (157–58).

[116] Evans, *Mind of St. Bernard of Clairvaux*, 154, 156. There is an increase in confidence from her earlier "*Cur Deus Homo*: St. Bernard's Theology of the Redemption; A Contribution to the Contemporary Debate," *Studia Theologica* 36 (1982): 27–36, where the first quotation is not found and the second is introduced with a slightly more tentative "There can be little doubt that" (30). What little doubt there was is replaced by certainty.

[117] Augustine certainly taught the gravity of Adam's sin, and the irredeemability of fallen angels is a commonplace of the Christian tradition. On the perils of proving dependence by parallels, see Anthony N. S. Lane, *John Calvin: Student of the Church Fathers* (Edinburgh: T&T Clark; Grand Rapids, MI: Baker, 1999), 8–10.

[118] Linhardt, *Die Mystik des hl. Bernhard von Clairvaux*, 112, n. 10, also found nothing specifically Anselmian in Bernard's teaching on this topic.

[119] *Mélanges à la mémoire du Père Anselme Dimier*, I/2, ed. Benoît Chauvin (Arbois: Benoît Chauvin, 1987), 687–88.

What about our third question: Did Bernard *know* Anselm's *Cur Deus homo*? If, given that he does not name them, discerning Bernard's sources is hard,[120] discerning what he *read* is much harder still. It may be that the shared use of the image of painting on air indicates that he had read the *Cur Deus homo*, but there may well be other sources for such an image. Given the differences between the two on this topic and given the lack of evidence for any influence, the safest course is to remain agnostic about Bernard's knowledge of the *Cur Deus homo*.

K. The Finished Work of Christ

Bernard emphasises the completeness of the work of Christ. He regularly cites Christ's affirmation "It is accomplished" (John 19:30).[121] Christ will not die again (Rom 6:9-10;[122] Heb 6:6[123]). The lost cannot be restored—is there another Christ, or shall he be crucified again (#567)? And yet, at the same time, Christ is again suffering and persecuted in his members (#660). In a sermon on Origen's statement that Christ still grieves over our sins, Bernard defends the statement as hyperbolic and expounds his own view of the completeness of Christ's work (##468–72). In the context of Middle Eastern geopolitics, Bernard can state that Christ goes to Jerusalem to be crucified again, echoing the apocryphal *Acts of Peter* (#632).

Bernard twice cites Paul's statement in Colossians 1:24 that he is making up in his body what is lacking in the sufferings of Christ.[124]

---

[120] As argued by Leclercq at n. 103 above.

[121] *Consummatum est* (Vulg). It is quoted in #79, #112, #259, #288, and #470. The word *consummo* in #304 and #305 is best seen as an allusion to this verse. In #472 it is seen by SBOp as a citation of John 17:4, which is correct, but the use of the past participle (*consummato*) and the context of discussion of the Cross suggest an allusion also to John 19:30. The Vulgate translation helpfully brings out the aspect of completed achievement in the Greek, where the common English translation of "It is finished" can be, and has been, misinterpreted as a cry of despair.

[122] #74, #108, #307, #424, #471, and #484.

[123] #74, #108, and #455.

[124] #252 and #421 (the latter in combination with Gal 6:17). Bernard more often cites Col 1:24 for the phrase "his body, that is, the church," almost always in passages about the Cross.

Also relevant here are the passages, just cited,[125] about the satisfaction for sins that we need to offer.

L. Conclusion

The bulk of material reviewed in this chapter suggests that it is the Godward aspect of the Cross that is of prime importance for Bernard, although he devotes significant attention to the defeat of the devil and to the usward aspect.

Bernard uses a wide range of terms and images to express his teaching on the Godward aspect of Christ's work. Christ bore our sins. The Lamb of God offered himself as a sacrifice to God, shedding his blood. We are redeemed by his blood, and our sins are washed by it. Christ has paid the price for us and paid off our debt. In particular, he has borne our punishment. The Cross provides satisfaction for our sins and propitiates God. A theme that runs throughout is reconciliation. By his sacrifice, by his bearing our punishment, he has appeased the Father and reconciled us to him.

Is there a central idea that gives shape to the rest? As quoted above, Rivière claims that "the idea which has his preference is that of penal substitution."[126] While Bernard clearly does teach that Christ bore our punishment, there is no indication that this is the foundational idea. Underlying all of the language is the idea that sin has separated us from God and that Christ reconciles us to God by dealing with sin and removing the barrier between us and God. How has he done this? By offering himself as a sacrifice, by paying the price for us and paying off our debt, and by bearing our punishment.[127] These are three different ways of talking about the fact that Christ died for us and that through Christ's death the Father is appeased and our

---

[125] See section J above.

[126] Rivière, *The Doctrine of the Atonement*, 70.

[127] The brief analysis in SCh 367:45 identifies these same three basic themes: sacrifice, bearing of punishment, and redemption by payment of debt. The first is there exalted at the expense of the other two in a way that does not fit the conclusions of this chapter.

relationship with him is restored.[128] Bernard links this with sacrifice
(#428, #430), with the blood of Christ (#30), with his bearing our
punishment (#549), and with the satisfaction offered by the death
of Christ (#659).

---

[128] As pointed out above (n. 1), Linhardt, *Die Mystik des hl. Bernhard von Clairvaux*, 110, claimed that the idea of propitiation was not important for Bernard. It
is true that he does not often use this actual word, but the heart of redemption is
Christ's work in removing the barrier between ourselves and God, and "propitiation" is one of a number of words that he uses to state this.

11

OBJECTIONS
TO BERNARD'S TEACHING

Abelard protested most strongly against the idea that we need to be ransomed from Satan, but he also raised questions about the idea that the Cross pleased God and facilitated his forgiveness. These latter questions were not confined to Abelard[1] and are often raised today.[2] Bernard responds to these and similar objections both in his letter-treatise against Abelard and in his other writings. He does so by pointing to the need for the Cross, to the relation between justice/punishment and mercy/truth, to the love of the Father, to the love of Christ and the voluntary nature of his sacrifice, and to the relation between Adam and Christ.

We will begin with the specific objections raised by Abelard in his Excursus, noting how Bernard responds to them, before moving on to broader questions that have been raised. As in chapter 2, those passages quoted by Bernard are italicised.

---

[1] Bernard responds to a whole series of related questions in Tpl 11.22–24, 28.

[2] For some modern reservations in the context of Bernard, see SCh 367:42–46 and Joël Regnard, "Il nous sauve non seulement par sa mort mais aussi par sa vie," Coll 58 (1996): 141–48.

A. Abelard's Objections[3]

Apart from the first question, Bernard responds only briefly to these objections in his letter-treatise, though the brief answers often summarise what has been argued elsewhere.

1. *"Since the divine compassion could have liberated humanity from sin simply by giving the order, what was the necessity, reason, or need for the Son of God, having taken flesh, to endure so many and so great things: fasting, taunts, scourging, spitting, and finally shameful and most cruel death on the Cross, together with criminals [iniquis]?"*[4]

This question will be considered in greater detail below.[5] Bernard's short answer is that there was a threefold need: "The need was ours—and also God's and the holy angels'. We needed him to remove the yoke of our captivity; he needed to fulfil the purpose of his will; the angels needed their number to be completed." Despite this clear statement, he goes on to admit that there were many other ways open to God to save us (Abael 8.19; #609).

2. *"How does the apostle say that we are justified or reconciled to God by the death of his Son when God should have been the more angry at humanity as they offended so much more by crucifying his Son than by contravening his first command by tasting a single piece of fruit? For the more sins were multiplied by people, the more justly should God have been angered by humanity."*[6]

To this Bernard briefly responds, "As if it were not possible in one and the same act both for the iniquity of the wicked to displease

---

[3] Taken from his Excursus on Rom 3:19-26. See chap. 2C. The first of these questions can well be seen as a concluding question on the need for redemption from Satan, rounding off the conclusion on that topic. At the same time, its position and its subject matter link it with the subsequent questions about the rationale for the Cross.

[4] Excursus 7.1, quoted in #609.

[5] See section B below.

[6] Excursus 7.2, mostly quoted in #611. For the prehistory of this question, see Michael T. Clanchy, *Abelard: A Medieval Life* (Oxford: Blackwell, 1997), 86, who draws on Richard W. Southern, *Saint Anselm: A Portrait in a Landscape* (Cambridge: CUP, 1990), 379–80.

God and for the godliness of the sufferer to please him" (Abael 8.21; #611). He also rebukes Abelard for jeering at the truth.[7]

3. "*And if that sin of Adam was so great that it could be expiated only by the death of Christ, what expiation will there be for the very act of murdering Christ and for the evil deeds (so many and so great) committed against him or his people?*"[8]

To this Bernard tersely responds, "That very blood which they shed and the intercession of him whom they murdered" (Abael 8.21; #611). He returned to the issue at greater length in his sermon for Wednesday of Holy Week (4 HM) 7–10.[9]

4. "*Is it possible that the death of his innocent Son was so pleasing to God the Father that by it he was reconciled to us (who brought it about by sinning) and that it was on account of this that the innocent Lord was murdered?*"[10]

To this Bernard responds, "What pleased God was not Christ's death but his will in dying of his own accord and by that death eliminating death, effecting salvation, restoring innocence, conquering the principalities and powers, plundering the underworld [*inferos*], enriching heaven, making peace between things in heaven and on earth, and restoring all things." He goes on to note that such a death could not happen without human sin but that its effectiveness derives not from sin or sinners but from the use that God makes of the sin (Abael 8.21; #611).

5. "*Would he not have been able much more easily to pardon sin if this greatest sin had not taken place? Would he not have been able to do such a good thing for humanity if evil deeds had not been multiplied?*"[11]

This also Bernard dismisses in a brief sentence: "The blood that was shed was so great at pardoning that it also expunged that greatest sin, by which it was caused to be shed, and therefore left no doubt about the annihilation of that ancient sin, inasmuch as that was more trivial" (Abael 8.22; #612).

---

[7] On the question of Abelard's flippant approach, see Clanchy, *Abelard*, 217.

[8] Excursus 7.3, mostly quoted in #611.

[9] See chap. 6B.

[10] Excursus 7.4, quoted in #611.

[11] Excursus 7.5, mostly quoted in #611.

6. "How have we been made more righteous through the death of the Son of God than we were previously [to this greatest sin], to the extent that we should be freed from punishment?"[12]

Bernard never answers this question directly, though he does earlier argue for the retroactive effect of the Cross on those who lived before it (Abael 7.18; #608).

7. "And to whom was the price of blood paid to redeem us unless to him in whose power we were—that is, to him who handed us over to his torturer, that is, God (as we have said)? For ransoms are organised and received not by the torturers but by the lords of those held captive."[13]

As has been noted above, Bernard never states to whom the price was paid.[14]

8. "Again, in what sense did he give these captives up 'for a price' if he was himself the one that demanded or fixed the price for their release?"[15]

Abelard's question relies for its force on the premise that the ransom was paid to God, and as we have just noted, Bernard does not accept this premise. The fact that Bernard passes over this and the previous question confirms his refusal to state to whom the price was paid.

9. *"To whom does it not seem cruel and unfair that someone should demand the blood of an innocent one as payment for something or that it should be in any way pleasing to him that an innocent one is killed—let alone that God should consider the death of his Son so pleasing as by it to be reconciled to the whole world?"*[16]

Bernard responds briefly before going on to summarise Abelard's own solution to the dilemma: "God the Father did not demand the blood of the Son but nevertheless accepted it when it was offered. He thirsted not for blood but for salvation, because salvation was in the blood—salvation, clearly, and not (as Abelard understands and

[12] Excursus 7.6.
[13] Excursus 7.7.
[14] See chap. 10F.
[15] Excursus 7.8.
[16] Excursus 7.9, quoted in #612.

writes) simply a demonstration of love" (Abael 8.22; #612). The first sentence could be seen as slightly disingenuous in that while God may not have demanded the blood of the Son in particular, human sin necessitates a death. The second sentence answers the question better, the point being that what God desired was not the death of the Son itself but the salvation that would follow from it. How and why it follows, he answers at length elsewhere.[17]

B. The Necessity for the Cross

The first of these questions posed by Abelard takes us to what has been called the central issue of medieval scholasticism, the relation between faith and reason.[18] Why was it necessary for Christ to die, since God could simply forgive by a word?[19] Anselm believed that he could demonstrate rationally that no other alternative was open to God. The most commonly held view in the Middle Ages was that while *something* was needed for our salvation and the work of Christ was the most fitting response to the need, one cannot state that no other way was open to God. By the end of the Middle Ages the view had emerged that there was no inherent logic perceptible in the mode of redemption and that God opted to save us this way simply because such was his will; we must simply accept this fact in naked faith. This apparently pious fideism (reliance upon faith alone without rational argument) is in fact the reverse side of a profound scepticism, one that has abandoned all hope of discovering any rationality in the ways of God. Where does Bernard stand on this medieval spectrum, on the scale between the total optimism of Anselm and the total pessimism of some late medieval thinkers regarding the powers of reason?

---

[17] See chap. 10.

[18] "The effort to harmonize reason and faith was the motive force of medieval Christian thought" (Gordon Leff, *Medieval Thought: St. Augustine to Ockham* [Harmondsworth: Penguin, 1958], 19).

[19] On this topic, see Gillian R. Evans, *The Mind of St. Bernard of Clairvaux* (Oxford: OUP, 1983), 157–59, 162.

It is not immediately clear where Bernard stands. There are two different concerns pulling Bernard in opposite directions. On the one hand, he was concerned that faith should lead us to worship and obedience, not to curiosity and speculation. Yet on the other hand, despite the polemic against speculation, he was concerned to explain why Christ went to such pains to rescue us.[20] Unlike Anselm (and Athanasius before him), Bernard did not write in response to the charges of Jewish or Muslim critics of the incarnation and the Cross,[21] but he did want Christians to appreciate the plight from which they had been rescued in order that they might be the more grateful.

The first of these concerns emerges especially in his answer to Abelard. "We are not permitted to probe the mystery of the divine will, but we are permitted to experience the effect of its working and to feel the fruit of its usefulness" (#610). Bernard then cites a number of New Testament passages affirming our reconciliation, forgiveness, justification, redemption, and liberation through the death of Christ. But Abelard asks why God did it *this* way, since he could have done it by a word. To put it more bluntly, since God could have liberated us by a simple command, why all the blood and gore? "You ask [God]," is Bernard's reply; "I am permitted to know that it is so, not why it is so" (#610). In line with this approach, he asks, "Who denies that there were available to the Almighty many other ways to our redemption, justification, and liberation?" (#609). The simple answer to Bernard's question is of course "Anselm," who denied precisely that. It is clear from the way that he poses the question that the answer "Bernard" would be incorrect, and he proceeds to state that God *could* have saved us another way (#609).[22] About five years previously he had stated that God could have rescued us without so much hardship but chose the way of the Cross in order to cure us of our ingratitude (#7)—an answer that (so far as it goes) is not so far removed from Abelard's![23]

---

[20] For these two sides in Bernard, see Amatus van den Bosch, "L'intelligence de la foi chez saint Bernard," Cîteaux 8 (1957): 95–99.

[21] See Evans, *The Mind of St. Bernard of Clairvaux*, 158, for the pressure from Jews.

[22] Elsewhere, in a passing comment, Bernard states that God could have reconciled us any other way that he wanted (#171).

[23] Relevant here is the contrast that Bernard repeatedly draws between the ease with which God created the world by a word and the great hardship with which Christ won our salvation (#7, #21, #136, #255, #297, #355, and #448).

While Bernard's hostility to speculation leads him, in his letter-treatise against Abelard and almost exclusively there, to deny that there is any inherent need for the Cross, this is not his only or his last word on the subject. Even there, he speaks of how "we needed [God] to remove the yoke of our captivity; he needed to fulfil the purpose of his will; the angels needed their number to be completed" (#609). Although he then appears to concede to Abelard that God *could* have saved us by a mere word, elsewhere he is not willing to concede that this could have sufficed. Because of the principle of John 12:24 (the grain of wheat), it was necessary for Christ to suffer and die.[24] The seriousness of our wounds is revealed by the fact that the Lord Christ needed (*necesse est*) to be wounded to heal them. The scale of the remedy demonstrates the gravity of the danger we faced (#205). A wise physician would not use costly medicines if a cure could easily be effected without them (#206). Our redemption was costly not because he did not choose another way but because none was suitable (*oporteret*; #255). Without specifically mention-ing the Cross, Bernard states that God could find no better way in his wisdom by which the Wisdom of God could redeem us (Pent 2.3). God did not find a way in his secret plan to forgive our guilt without a fitting satisfaction (*congrua satisfactio*; #427). Defeating the devil would not have been effective without a sacrifice for sin since without that we cannot be reconciled to God (#430). Why did Christ need to become obedient to death (Phil 2:8)? To set an example for us to follow (#117). Perhaps the Cross was the best way because Christ's sufferings are a warning to us (#609). Bernard also cites Luke 24:26, 46 five times to the effect that it was necessary (*oporteo*) for the Christ to suffer and die.[25] In Luke the necessity arises from the fact that it is prophesied in the Old Testament,[26] but this is a necessity that arises only because of God's prior decision, so it is not strictly relevant to our present point, which is whether God needed to make that decision. But only two of Bernard's citations mention

[24] #13, #324, and #545. In the last of these, having applied John 12:24 to the death of Christ, he goes on to refer it to the preaching of the Word.

[25] #13, #228, #342, #346, and #462. In #346 the connection to Luke 24:46 is extremely tenuous.

[26] For an extended discussion of how Christ's saving work is prophesied in the Old Testament, see ##573–75 and #577.

the Old Testament, so in the other three he has simply used Luke's words to make a general point about the necessity of Christ's death.[27]

How can we tie all of this together? *Can* we tie all of this together?[28] Bernard seems to have been pulled in different directions by different concerns, and he does not give a clear answer to this question. But while against Abelard especially he appears to teach that the Cross was not necessary, these statements must not be abstracted from his teaching as a whole. Similarly, in his *In Praise of the New Knighthood* he states that Christ can forgive because of his omnipotence and his deity (Tpl 11.21). This could easily be taken to mean that no more was needed, but such a conclusion is clearly refuted by the argument of the eleventh chapter as a whole.

C. Punishment and Justice, Mercy and Truth

Abelard's objections, especially the first and the fifth listed above, point to a question that is often asked: If God already loves us, why could he not just forgive us? Another reason why the Cross was necessary is the fact that our sins justly merit punishment. By turning against God, we incur the punishment of death and separation from God. This punishment is required by God's truthfulness (because of the promise made in Genesis 2:17) and by his justice (Tpl 11.19). Truthfulness requires that we die, mercy that we rise again (Tpl 11.28). It is the Cross that reconciles the tension between God's mercy and his truth and justice. Christ "bore the punishment of our sin and gave us his righteousness by paying the debt of death and restoring life" (Tpl 11.22; #148). The innocent one died for the ungodly. This is mercy, not justice, but it is not contrary to justice. God is at the same time both righteous (*iustus*) and merciful (Tpl 11.23; #149).

---

[27] Elsewhere Bernard speaks of the necessity of Christ's coming without specifically mentioning the Cross—e.g., Adv 7.2.

[28] One way to do so would be to suggest that Bernard changed his mind. Here we run into the problem of trying to date his sermons. Since he continued to revise his sermons (Jean Leclercq and Henri Rochais, "La tradition des sermons liturgiques de S. Bernard," RESB 2:203–60), if he had consciously changed his mind, he could have corrected them. The same would not, however, be true of Abael.

Bernard makes the same point in his *Steps of Humility and Pride*. Sin merits eternal punishment, but God desires to spare us that. Kindness and justice are not opposed to one another, but a righteous (*iusta*) kindness is better than a lenient (*remissa*) one; indeed, kindness without justice is not even virtuous. So God is both kind and righteous or just (*iustus*) at the same time. Being righteous, he most righteously punishes offences against his goodness, yet he chose to suffer rather than let us perish (#122).

Bernard repeatedly makes this point by citing Psalm 85:10, that mercy and truth meet, righteousness and peace kiss one another. The first sermon on the annunciation is based on this text.[29] He shows how humanity, through Adam's sin, lost the four virtues of mercy, truth, righteousness, and peace (Ann 1.5–8; #264). This leads to a serious contention between these virtues, a "grand controversy" to which the rest of the sermon is devoted (Ann 1.9–14; ##265–70). Truth and righteousness demand that sinners be punished on the grounds especially of the promise made in Genesis 2:17; mercy and peace urge forgiveness (Ann 1.9–11; ##265–67). God's dilemma is that he is ruined unless Adam dies, yet he is also ruined unless Adam obtains mercy. This can be resolved by the voluntary death of an innocent one (Ann 1.12; #268). After a fruitless search for such a one (Ann 1.13; #269), Christ steps in and bears the punishment (*poena*) due to humanity. Then righteousness and peace kiss one another (Ann 1.14; #270). Here the teaching of the two treatises just expounded, *In Praise of the New Knighthood* and *Steps of Humility and Pride*, is set out in the form of an extended allegory.[30] In another sermon Bernard again mentions how God saw our misery and the claims of justice and managed to preserve justice and equity but exalt mercy above all. Because of Christ's death, the demands of Genesis 2:17 are met, and thus mercy and truth meet one another

---

[29] See chap. 6A. For an exposition of this sermon, see Jean Rivière, *Le dogme de la rédemption au début du moyen âge* (Paris: J. Vrin, 1934), 319–24. This treatment comes in a longer section (309–49) on "Le conflit des 'filles de dieu'" in medieval theology, which includes "historical conclusions" concerning the development of the tradition and Bernard's role in it (336–49).

[30] For a shorter version of the same allegory, see #519.

and righteousness kisses peace (Ps 85:10; ##427–28). Here again reconciliation is achieved by Christ's taking our punishment and offering a satisfaction that meets the claims of justice. Psalm 85:10 is also cited elsewhere.[31]

Bernard also cites, in this context, the statement of Psalm 25:10 that all the ways of the Lord are mercy and truth.[32] Not all of his citations of Psalm 25:10 and 85:10 are in the context of the Cross, but many are, and the theme is regularly applied to the Cross. Furthermore, he elsewhere refers to the tension between mercy and truth or justice, apart from the allusions to these verses.[33] Bernard also refers to mercy and justice (*iudicium*), echoing Psalm 33:5[34] or Psalm 101:1,[35] but less often with reference to the Cross specifically.

Finally, this theme recurs in a well-known hymn of William Rees (1802–83):

> Here is love vast as the ocean,
> loving kindness as the flood,
> when the Prince of life, our ransom,
> shed for us his precious blood.
> Who his love will not remember?
> Who can cease to sing his praise?
> He can never be forgotten
> throughout heaven's eternal days
>
> On the mount of crucifixion
> fountains opened deep and wide;
> through the floodgates of God's mercy
> flowed a vast and gracious tide.

---

[31] #546. #381 refers to *us* exercising righteousness and mercy. Without specific mention of the Cross: SC 6.7, 68.7; Tpl 11.28; Miss 1.1; QH 11.7–8; Sent 3.14. In #103, vv. 9 and 11 of Psalm 85 are cited, but not v. 10.

[32] #210, #395 [continuation from Ded 5.4], and #549. Without specific mention of the Cross: SC 6.7; QH 11.7; Div 87.1.

[33] In addition to #122, #149, #427 (already mentioned), see #505 and #659 (*iudicium*).

[34] ##494–95; not referring to the Cross: #384.

[35] #210 and #367; SC 6.9, 16.3, 26.13, 55.2; Adv 2.3; Ep 251. Only #367 has any direct reference to the Cross.

Grace and love, like mighty rivers,
poured incessant from above,
and heaven's peace and perfect justice
kissed a guilty world in love.

Bernard would have applauded this hymn for three reasons: for its
use of Psalm 85:10, for the doctrine of the Cross it expresses, and
for the poetic manner in which it does both.

D. The Love of the Father

Mary offered Jesus as a holy sacrifice (*hostia*), pleasing to God (*Deo placentem*), for the reconciliation of us all (#237). Christ's blood is the price of satisfaction to placate the Father (#30). He has reconciled us to God by his death, delivering us from the punishment due to us in justice (#549). On the Cross he experienced abandonment by the Father (Matt 27:46; #377). Christ was broken in body on the Cross, thus propitiating (*propitians*) the Father (#76). God may be exasperated by the horror of our villainy, but he is pacified by sorrow of the satisfaction of his Son (#659).[36]

Such language can easily convey the impression of a harsh, vengeful Father whose anger and hatred of us is only mollified by the intervention of his Son. There has always been a danger that popular accounts of the Cross will give that impression, especially if they fail to bring out the love of God the Father and the way that the work of redemption is the unified work of all three members of the Trinity. Bernard did not fall into this error.

First, Bernard emphasises the love of the Father. He repeatedly cites a number of New Testament passages that highlight the priority of God's love. It is because God loved the world that he gave his Son (John 3:16).[37] It is God who shows his love for us in Christ dying for us while we were sinners (Rom 5:8)[38] and God who effected

---

[36] On these ideas, see the previous chapter.
[37] #128, #134, and #648.
[38] #136, #288, #344, #458, #525, #541, #585, and #610; see also #542.

our reconciliation while we were still his enemies (Rom 5:10).[39] It is because God loved us that he sent his Son for us (1 John 4:10).[40] So great was his love that he didn't spare his own Son but gave him up for us all (Rom 8:32).[41] These passages teach not just the priority of the Father's love but the extent of it.

Second, the work of redemption is the unified work of all three members of the Trinity. Christ is the propitiation for our sins (1 John 2:2) offered to the Father, but Father and Son are equal in mercy and love, united in will, and one in substance (#175). It is the Father who so loved us that he gave his Son (John 3:16), the Son who gave himself up (Isa 53:12), and the Spirit who comes to us after Christ's ascension. So it is the whole Trinity that loves (#134). Again, it is the Father who did not spare his Son (Rom 8:32), the Son who most willingly gave himself up (Eph 5:2), and the Spirit that they send who intercedes for us (#354). That the Cross is not about the Son persuading a reluctant Father can be seen especially in one passage where Bernard speaks of Christ suffering in order to reconcile sinners to *himself* (rather than to the Father). On the Cross he hungered and thirsted for righteousness and exacted from himself so great a satisfaction for our sins (#186).

There is a paradox here, which was well expressed by Augustine in a famous passage from his *De trinitate*. This passage was highly influential upon subsequent discussions, and Bernard would certainly have been influenced by it, indirectly if not directly.

> But what is this *justified in his blood* (Rom 5:9)? What, I want to know, is the potency of this blood, that believers should be justified in it? Is it really the case that when God the Father was angry with us he saw the death of his Son on our behalf, and was reconciled to us? Does this mean then that his Son was already so reconciled to us that he

[39] #21, #251, #288, #450, #541, #585, and #610; without specific mention of the Cross: SC 16.2.

[40] #21, #128, #251, and #541. Also see Asspt 4.2 after #364.

[41] #16, #128, #175, #183, #288, #354, #434, #474, #541, and #585; without the mention of not sparing his Son: V Nat 1.3.

was even prepared to die for us, while the Father was still so angry with us that unless the Son died for us he would not be reconciled to us? And what about something the same teacher of the Gentiles says elsewhere: *What are we to say to all this? If God is for us, who is against us? He who did not spare his own Son but handed him over for us all, how has he not also made us a gift of all things with him* (Rom 8:[31-32])? Would the Father have not spared his own Son but handed him over for us, if he had not already been reconciled? In fact it seems, doesn't it, as if this text contradicts the former one? There the Son dies for us, and the Father is reconciled to us through his death; but here it is as if the Father were the first to love us, the Father who for our sake did not spare his Son, the Father who for our sake handed him over to death. But if it comes to that, I observe that the Father loved us not merely before the Son died for us but before he founded the world, as the apostle bears witness: *As he chose us in him before the foundation of the world* (Eph 1:4). Nor does the Father's not sparing him mean that the Son was handed over for us against his will, because of him too it is said, *Who loved me and handed himself over for me* (Gal 2:20). Thus the Father and the Son and the Spirit of them both work all things together and equally and in concord. Yet the fact remains that we have been justified in the blood of Christ and reconciled to God through the death of his Son.[42]

As with other doctrines, such as the Trinity, there is a tension here between two truths that at first sight appear to be contradictory. It is right and proper to seek to explain how they are compatible, but the danger is always that this is achieved only by undermining one or the other. As one of those who taught me patristics put it, with reference to the Trinity and the person of Christ, "If you've explained it, you're a heretic!" Bernard's objection against Abelard was precisely that he thought that the latter had explained it and so was a heretic.

---

[42] *De trinitate* 13.11.15: Augustine, *The Trinity* 1.5, trans. Edmund Hill, The Works of Saint Augustine (Brooklyn, NY: New City Press, 1990), 354–55.

E. The Voluntary Love of the Son

Talk of God not sparing but sacrificing his own Son has led some today to invoke the charge of divine child abuse.[43] Abelard similarly asks, "To whom does it not seem cruel and unfair that someone should demand the blood of an innocent one as payment for something or that it should be in any way pleasing to him that an innocent one is killed?" and questions why "God should consider the death of his Son so pleasing."[44]

In response to the second point, Bernard states that Christ's death was of value only because it was voluntary. It was not just the fact that he died but that he did so of his own accord (#611). "If he had not died voluntarily, his death would have had no merit" (#147). The voluntary nature of Christ's death is a point that Bernard frequently makes. We deserve shame and contempt, punishment and beating, but he did not. He experienced them because he chose to (#60). Christ was offered as a sacrifice because he willed it, not because he was obliged or because he was under the law. He was offered on the Cross not because he deserved it or because of Judas, but because he willed it (#237). The Latin text of Isaiah 53:7, which Bernard cites here and elsewhere, reads, "Because he willed it."[45] He also cites Isaiah 53:12 to the effect that Christ surrendered his soul to death.[46] The Good Shepherd lays down his life for the sheep (John 10:11; #53), and Christ laid down his life of his own accord (John 10:17-18).[47] "He was voluntarily incarnate, voluntarily suffered, was voluntarily crucified" (#148). One of Bernard's favourite texts when speaking of the Cross was John 15:13, that there is no greater love than to lay

---

[43] A phrase used by Joanne Carlson Brown and Rebecca Parker, "For God So Loved the World?" in *Christianity, Patriarchy, and Abuse: A Feminist Critique*, ed. Joanne Carlson Brown and Carole R. Bohn (New York: Pilgrim, 1989), 2. Apart from other considerations covered here, such language relies for its emotive force on the implication that Christ was an underage child.

[44] Excursus 7.9, quoted in #612.

[45] #60, #138, #237, #288, #324, #397, and #468.

[46] #30, #134, #175, #288, #344, and #458.

[47] #138, #202, #239, #288, #411, #461, and #468.

down one's life for one's friends.[48] We know what love is because Christ laid down his life for us (1 John 3:16).[49] His suffering was voluntary rather than necessary (#152).[50] Appropriately, he calls the Cross the Cross of Christ's love (#515).

The accusation of divine child abuse is also met by the point just argued,[51] that the work of redemption is the unified work of all three members of the Trinity, with the Son playing a fully voluntary role. The criticism of laying the punishment upon a third party effectively denies the unity of Father and Son. It is not just that the Father did not spare his Son but that the Son did not spare himself (#288); indeed, he gladly delivered himself up (#354). This is a point that Bernard makes repeatedly and in different ways. The will with which Christ submitted to the Father was the common will of the Father and the Son (#324).

In response to Abelard's first point about how cruel and wicked it is to demand the blood of an innocent person, Bernard responds that "God the Father did not demand the blood of the Son, but nevertheless he accepted it when it was offered. He thirsted not for blood but for salvation, because salvation was in the blood" (#612). As noted above,[52] this answer is not altogether satisfactory, because while God may not have demanded the blood of the Son in particular, human sin necessitates a death. Also, taken at face value, this statement does not sit happily with the idea of the Father giving, sending, and not sparing his Son, nor with Christ in the garden praying, "Not my will, but yours."

Here again there are two truths that at first sight appear to be contradictory: the Father sent the Son, who was obedient, and the Son voluntarily gave himself for us. There are two senses in which Christ's death for us was voluntary. The first is that he was voluntarily

---

[48] #23, #84, #128, #129, #133, #182, #194, #251, #253, #269, #288, #304, #370, #458, #486, #499, #501, #542, and #545. The last of these is very tenuous.

[49] #450 and #472. The first of these is very tenuous.

[50] A point that Bernard makes in many places. Apart from those mentioned elsewhere in this section, see #104, #219, and #476.

[51] Section D above.

[52] Section A.

obedient to the Father. This Bernard certainly affirms, repeatedly stating that Christ was obedient even to death on a Cross (Phil 2:8).[53] But this emphasis, on its own, remains vulnerable to the divine-child-abuse charge since it could be taken to imply a voluntary but reluctant submission to the will of the Father. Clearly, there is some element of truth in this as is seen in Jesus' subordination of his will to the Father in the Garden of Gethsemane.[54] But there is much more to it than this, and Bernard brings out the way in which Christ took the initiative. He loved me and gave himself for me (Gal 2:20);[55] he gave himself for our sins (Gal 1:4);[56] he offered himself (Heb 9:14).[57] He judged my soul more precious than his own blood (#184). Modifying 2 Corinthians 5:21, Bernard speaks of Christ as the one who made *himself* sin for us.[58] Again, on the Cross Christ hungered and thirsted for righteousness and exacted from himself so great a satisfaction for our sins (#186). Bernard says that Christ was compelled to undergo the ignominy of the Cross and death by a voluntary coercion (*coactione voluntaria*)[59]—because of his filial obedience, because of our misery, and because of the victory that would follow (#505).

F. Christ and Adam

Granted the unity of Father and Son, is it not still an external transaction where we are concerned? Not for Bernard. He assumes our unity first with Adam and then with Christ. He assumes the

---

[53] #7, #61, #117, #125, #154, #155, #159, #288, #304, #397, #475, #534, #581, #630, #657, #661, #662, and #665. See also #256, #258, #468, and #615.

[54] #140, #270, #323, #324, #410, #412, #436, #511, #519, #542, #595, and #657.

[55] #615 and #661.

[56] #100, #128, #425, and #548. "Our sins" are mentioned only in the last of these.

[57] #185, #238, #374, and #428.

[58] #38, #105, and #291.

[59] CF 55:138 very loosely translates this as "under the direction of his will." For the idea of a voluntary coercion, see also Anselm, *Cur Deus homo* 2.17, which is not to imply any direct influence.

Augustinian doctrine that it is through the sin of one man, Adam, that all people both are counted as sinners, sharing his guilt, and are actually constituted sinners because of the ensuing concupiscence or lust. We all sinned in Adam and in him received the sentence of condemnation (Adv 1.4).[60] Given that fact, how can one object to the idea that through the righteous deed of one man, Christ, we should be counted as righteous and indeed become righteous?[61] Just as we were all in Adam when he sinned and so participate in his sin, so also we are in Christ and were chosen in him before the creation of the world (Eph 1:4; Tpl 11.24). Surely we would not want to say that Adam's sin has greater efficacy than Christ's death? Bernard expounds the theme of our solidarity with both Adam and Christ in several key passages.[62]

Christ came to save those who have been polluted by an "alien" guilt following Adam's sin. But although it is alien, it is also ours; otherwise it would not pollute us. It is alien because without knowing it we all sinned in Adam; it is ours because we have all sinned, albeit in another, and God justly imputes it to us. If the effect of Adam's disobedience is the bad news, the good news is that we are rescued by Christ's obedience. If we were sold for nothing, we are also bought back for nothing (Isa 52:3). We perished without knowing it in Adam and were made alive without knowing it in Christ. We did not know it when the old Adam stretched out guilty hands to the tree, nor when Christ stretched out innocent hands on the saving tree (#231).

In his *In Praise of the New Knighthood* Bernard responds to a number of objections (#149):

---

[60] For the relation between our original sin and our personal sins, see #291.

[61] We have been imprisoned by the sin of another (Adam), and so also it is the satisfaction of another (Christ) that has prepared our return (#424).

[62] This has been recognised as a major contribution of Bernard to the doctrine of the work of Christ: Jean Rivière, *The Doctrine of the Atonement: A Historical Essay*, vol. 2 (London: Kegan Paul, Trench, Trübner and Co., 1909), 65; Laurence W. Grensted, *A Short History of the Doctrine of the Atonement* (Manchester: Manchester University Press; London: Longmans, Green and Co., 1920), 111–12; SCh 367:43–44.

- "Even if the righteous is not unjustly able to make satisfaction for the sinner, how can one do this for many? It would appear sufficient for justice for one person by dying to restore life to one person." Bernard responds to this by quoting the words of Romans 5:18-19.[63]
- "But maybe one can restore righteousness to many, but not life?" Bernard responds to this by quoting 1 Corinthians 15:21-22.[64]

He then responds to these objections with a number of rhetorical questions:

> When one sins, all are held to be guilty? Shall the innocence of the one be counted only for the one who is innocent? The sin of the one produced death for all; shall the righteousness of the one restore life to one only? Is God's justice more able to condemn than to restore? Is Adam more powerful for evil than Christ for good? Will Adam's sin be imputed to me and Christ's righteousness not pertain to me? Has the disobedience of the former ruined me, while the obedience of the latter will be of no benefit to me?"

He continues the theme in the next section, quoting Romans 5:15-16 (#150).[65]

Bernard again responds in his letter-treatise against Abelard. Just as all sinned in Adam, so all died in Christ (2 Cor 5:14). He bore the sins of all, and the satisfaction he made is imputed to all. It is not that one offended and another made satisfaction, because head and body are one Christ. It was the head that suffered for the members, Christ for his body (#605).[66]

---

[63] Bernard also cites Rom 5:18-19 in #505, #606, and #613. The first of these is rather tenuous.

[64] Bernard also cites 1 Cor 15:21-22 in #150, #231, #424, #606, and #613.

[65] Bernard also cites Rom 5:15-17 in #231, #291, #367, and #606.

[66] Many will understand this principle from their childhood, when one member of the body, not in this case the head, suffered for the misdeeds of other parts. Bernard gives medical examples of how one part of the body is treated to heal another (#220).

Our father Adam enslaved us, but our brother Christ has redeemed us. "Why not an external [*aliunde*] righteousness since the guilt was external? One made me a sinner; the other justifies me from sin— one by his seed, the other by his blood. Shall there be sin in the seed of the sinner but not righteousness in the blood of Christ?"This may seem contrary to the principle of Ezekiel 18:20, that we all live or die because of our own righteousness or guilt. But it is not fair that we should die for our father Adam's guilt yet be denied our brother Christ's righteousness. Just as death came through one, so does life (1 Cor 15:21-22). It is unreasonable to accept the former but deny the latter. Adam's sin certainly reaches us, but so does Christ's grace. "If guilt was handed down to me, why should righteousness not also be granted [*indulta*] to me?" (#606).

There is a problem with Bernard's argument in that it presupposes a full-blooded Augustinian doctrine of the Fall and original sin, a doctrine that many question today. Yet in a modified form the argument is hard to evade. Only a dogmatic Pelagian would argue that human sin is *purely* a matter of individual choice. It is hard to deny that there is in *some* sense a corporate sin of the race or to hold that our individual choice of sin has *nothing* to do with the common human condition. Grant that there is a corporate dimension to sin, and the objection to the corporate dimension of salvation is gravely weakened.

12

THE APPLICATION
OF THE DOCTRINE

A. Justification

Bernard's doctrine of the Cross led him to a doctrine of justification. Bernard often cites 1 Corinthians 1:30, "Christ is our righteousness,"[1] and it is in Christ that we become righteous (#105). We are justified by his blood (Rom 5:9)[2] and that freely (Rom 3:24-25).[3] The righteous one was unjustly killed and through justice obtains a new righteousness from the enemy. The penalty (*poena*) that he did not need to suffer he imputed to the sinful. The punishment inflicted on Christ, the innocent one, brings absolution for the guilty (#522).

Bernard expounded this doctrine at length in his twenty-second sermon on the Song of Songs.[4] Christ is our wisdom, righteousness, holiness, and redemption (1 Cor 1:30; SC 22.4-5). He brings righteousness by the forgiveness of sins and redemption by the passion that he endured for sinners (SC 22.6; #29). Christ freely justifies sinners through the righteousness that comes by faith. The blood that flowed from his side was the price of satisfaction that placated the Father (SC

---

[1] #26, #32, #33, #85, #152, #236, #247, #297, #394, and #606. He also cites it without mention of the Cross—e.g., Div 52.1.

[2] #541, #606, and #610.

[3] #606 and #610.

[4] The translation of "justification" and related words in CF 7 is very unreliable.

22.7; #30). Those who thirst for righteousness should trust in God, who justifies the ungodly so that being justified by faith alone they may have peace with God. His passion is our ultimate refuge, our unique remedy. Our righteousness and holiness are not sufficient for salvation, so our only hope is for Christ's blood to cry out for us so that we may be forgiven (SC 22.8; #31). We are righteous when the Lord does not impute our sins to us (Ps 32:2), as happened with Mary Magdalene (Luke 7:47), with the tax collector who was justified (Luke 18:14), and with Peter (Luke 22:62; SC 22.9; #32). True righteousness is found only in Christ's mercy, and they only are righteous whose sins are forgiven through his mercy (SC 22.11; #34).[5]

Similar teaching is found more briefly in the sixty-first sermon on the Song of Songs. There is refuge in the Saviour's wounds for those who are weak, for those whose conscience is uneasy. No sin is too deadly to be forgiven by the death of Christ (SC 61.3; #83). The members of Christ's body can claim as their own what belongs to their head. His wounds proclaim that God was in Christ reconciling the world to himself (2 Cor 5:19; SC 61.4; #84). My merit is the Lord's mercy. He makes Christ's righteousness mine (1 Cor 1:30), and this covers a multitude of sins (SC 61.5; #85).

Bernard contrasts Christ with Adam, the one who introduced sin into the world. Christ has paid our debt and assumed the guilt of our sins. The death of Christ has put death itself to flight, and his righteousness is imputed (*imputatur*) to us (#148). Just as the sin of Adam counts against me, the righteousness of Christ restores me (#149).

Bernard sets out the Adam-Christ contrast most clearly in his response to Abelard. We lost our righteousness in Adam but receive from Christ an alien righteousness. As Christ died for us and bore the sins of us all, so the satisfaction that he made, the head for the body, is imputed (*imputatur*) to all (#605). Through Adam's sin, which was external to us, we are counted guilty and are corrupted by original concupiscence. So also through Christ's death for us, which was external to us, we are granted Christ's righteousness and receive his spiritual grace. We are justified by his blood. Just as Adam brought

---

[5] Some of this is repeated in SC 23.15.

guilt and carnal birth, Christ brings us righteousness and spiritual rebirth (#606). Where there is reconciliation, there is the forgiveness of sins, and "what is that if not justification?" (#610).[6]

Bernard also contrasts his teaching with that of the Jews, whom he accuses of deeming themselves to be righteous on the basis of keeping the law. They are the elder brother who denies the need for the fatted calf to be slain. But through the death of the crucified Word the letter of the law that kills (2 Cor 3:6) was torn in two, like the curtain in the temple (Matt 27:51), opening the way for the church to become Christ's bride (#12).

B. Grounds for Hope

The sixty-first sermon on the Song is also one of the principle places for mining Bernard's notion of finding assurance in the wounds of Christ (SC 61, title; #82). The wounds of Christ constitute the one secure resting place for the weak. We may have sinned greatly and our conscience may be disturbed (*turbabitur*), but it is not perturbed (*perturbabitur*), because we remember the wounds of Christ, who was wounded for our transgressions (Isa 53:5;[7] SC 61.3; #83). Whatever may be lacking in our merits we can take from the heart of the Lord. His heart overflows with mercy, flowing out from the clefts, from the five wounds of Christ, which declare that God is in Christ reconciling the world to himself (2 Cor 5:19). His wounds declare God's heart, his steadfast love and mercy. There is no greater mercy than that of the one who laid down his life for those who have been judged and found guilty (SC 61.4; #84).[8] There is

---

[6] Bernard was one of the Reformers' prime witnesses to their doctrine of justification. Clearly, we have here an anticipation of the Protestant doctrine of justification, but this is only one side of Bernard's teaching, and there is more that points in a very different direction. See further Anthony N. S. Lane, *Calvin and Bernard of Clairvaux* (Princeton, NJ: Princeton Theological Seminary, 1996), 47–71; Anthony N. S. Lane, "Bernard of Clairvaux: A Forerunner of John Calvin?" in *Bernardus Magister*, ed. John R. Sommerfeldt (Kalamazoo, MI: Cistercian Publications, 1992), 533–45.

[7] Also cited in #37 and #378.

[8] See also #85–88. See chap. 10E on the wounds of Christ.

no greater cure for wounds of conscience than to meditate upon Christ's wounds (#91). His passion is a powerful argument for the forgiveness of sins, for his blood is more powerful than that of Abel (Gen 4:10; Heb 12:24).[9] His death is more powerful and effectual for good than are our sins for evil (#263).

This theme is illustrated by an interesting incident noted in the *First Life of Bernard*, written soon after his death. Bernard was at death's door, and the devil was accusing him of his sins. Bernard's reply is significant:

> I admit that I am not myself worthy; nor can I, by any merits of my own, lay claim to the Kingdom of Heaven. On the other hand, my Lord has won the kingdom by a twofold right [*duplici iure*], namely, by inheritance from his Father and by the merits of his Passion. The first he has reserved for himself, but the second he gives to me; and by that gift I assert my right and shall not be confounded.[10]

The basis for this in Bernard's own writings is found in a sermon where he refers to Christ's twofold right to rule (*ius regnandi*), in his own right as the firstborn and through the price of his sacrifice (#431).[11]

Bernard applies the Cross to those who are fearful of their salvation. What do we fear? That he will not forgive our sins? But he has fixed them to the Cross with his own hands. If we fear because we are used to soft living, he knows our weakness. If we fear the chains of bad habits, he liberates from these (#58). Finally, Bernard's pastoral skill is seen in the way in which he applies the Cross as medicine both for the overconfident and for the desperate. Those who are overconfident should remember that Christ suffered despite his

---

[9] Cited together in #263 and #559. For further allusions to Gen 4:10, see #17, #96, and #625; to Heb 12:24, see #431 and #512.

[10] *Vita prima* 1.12.57. On this, see Franz Posset, "The 'Double Right to Heaven': Saint Bernard's Impact on the Sixteenth Century," CSQ 38 (2003): 263–73, whose translation (p. 264) has been used here. See also Jean Leclercq, "The Image of St. Bernard in the Late Medieval *Exempla* Literature," *Thought* 54 (1979): 300.

[11] Posset, "The 'Double Right to Heaven,'" 265–66.

innocence and be prepared to humble themselves and share in his sufferings; those who are desperate should remember that Christ suffered for the sake of sinners like them (#553). If I have sinned greatly, I don't despair, because Christ sorrowed greatly for us. If God is provoked by the horror of my villainy, he is pacified by the sorrow of the satisfaction offered by his Son (#659). Such consolation should not, however, mislead us into sinning more securely (Ep 462.9).[12]

C. Repentance and Following Christ

Bernard taught that we are justified by faith alone and that the guilty conscience can find peace in the wounds of Christ, but the Cross is not about how to find forgiveness while leading an unchanged life. Such a doctrine of cheap grace[13] is far removed from Bernard's teaching. The Cross has radical implications for Christian living. This is a point we have to some extent covered already when considering Christ as teacher / moral influence,[14] but there are further implications. First, we are called to take up our cross and follow Christ (Matt 10:38; Luke 14:27).[15] We are to deny ourselves and take up our cross (Matt 16:24),[16] though Bernard surprisingly never quotes the Lukan injunction to do this *daily* (Luke 9:23).[17] In his first sermon on the nativity of Andrew, Bernard develops at length the theme of Andrew as one who loved the Cross and embraced death on a cross as a means to his coronation (##407–13). It is the means of defeating Satan, who will not be able to outwit with carnal delights those

[12] It should not be imagined from these few statements that Bernard held to a Protestant understanding of assurance. See further Lane, *Calvin and Bernard*, 64–68.

[13] For the idea of cheap versus costly grace, see Dietrich Bonhoeffer, *The Cost of Discipleship* (London: SCM, 1959), 35–47.

[14] See chap. 8B–C above.

[15] #406, #455, and #498.

[16] #27, #123, #230, #303, #309, #417, #426, #480, #489, #515, and #534. In #413 Bernard refers to bearing the Cross without citing any of these verses.

[17] SBOp 5:83 claims Luke 9:23 as the source for the main text of #309 and Matt 16:24 as the source for the variant text. The former citation is brief and could easily come from either Matthew or Luke. Since Bernard never elsewhere cites Luke 9:23, there is no reason to see it as the source here.

Christians whom the Cross of Christ delights (#408–9). We need to reach the point where we gladly bear Christ's Cross (#413). Again, Christians are called to crucify the flesh with its vices and lusts (Gal 5:24)[18] because the world is crucified to us and vice versa (Gal 6:14).[19] The cross that Christians are called to bear is the Cross of love (#515) in contrast to the cross of forced service carried unwillingly by Simon of Cyrene (Matt 27:32; Mark 15:21; Luke 23:26).[20] There is also the cross of penitence, as seen in the repentant thief (#515).[21] Another contrast that Bernard draws is between the Cross of Christ and the cross of the devil. The latter is a cross of torture and punishment, and it is destroyed by the Cross of Christ.[22]

Second, we are called to follow the Christ who prayed, "Not my will but yours" (Matt 26:39, 42; Mark 14:36; Luke 22:42).[23] Bernard refers to a double leprosy of the heart: following our own will (*propria voluntas*) and our own opinion (*proprium consilium*). Self-will sets itself up against God. To counter self-will we must imitate Christ, who in the garden submitted his will to God's (#323).[24] Following our own plans is even more dangerous and is seen in those who prefer their own opinion to that of the whole body (Res 3.4).[25] Christ wished to be spared the cup but surrendered his own will and opinion to that of the Father (#324). Christ was obedient to death so that we should no longer live under our own will (#662). If Christ was obedient to death, how can Christians free themselves from the yoke of obedience? (#581) Christ preferred to die rather than disobey God, and he won't put himself in the power of those who disobey (#70). In fact, he valued obedience so greatly as to prefer it to his own life (#154). Christ gave his life rather than disobey God, in contrast to

---

[18] #52, #106, #139, #230, #489, #523, #538, and #546.

[19] #178, #437, #588, and #624.

[20] #123, #261, and #515.

[21] See also #535.

[22] #523 and #532.

[23] #140, #323, #324, #412, #436, #519, #542, and #657. See also Ep 144.2 (just before #595).

[24] And who sweated blood (Luke 22:44): #292, #402, #427, #451, and #522.

[25] This comes between #323 and #324.

certain abbots who go to great lengths to avoid obedience to their bishops (#565).

Third, Bernard argues from the purpose of the Cross. The reason why Christ died for all was so that all might live for him (2 Cor 5:15).[26] Living for Christ means also living for our fellow Christians, just as neglecting those loved by Christ is incompatible with loving him (#464). He bore our sins so that we might die to sin and live to righteousness (1 Pet 2:24).[27] Christ died to be our Lord (Rom 14:9; #97).

Finally, Bernard appeals to what one might call the psychological impact of the Cross. Some are so moved by the Cross that they cannot think of it without tears. Such love is opposed to the lusts of the flesh. Those who find such sweetness in Christ's passion no longer find it in the flesh (#459). In particular, if we think rightly of the Lord's passion, we should blush at the thought of following after sensual pleasures (#322). If the Cross of Christ delights us, the enemy will not succeed in outwitting us by suggesting carnal delights (#409). We cannot glory in the Cross and put our hope in financial wealth (#132). The example of the Cross should lead us to flee luxury (#657).

For Bernard, the Cross is not simply something outside of us to inspire us and challenge us to imitate it. Underlying the Christian life is the fact that we have been baptised into Christ's death and resurrection (Rom 6:3-5).[28] We have been crucified with Christ (Rom 6:6[29]; Gal 2:20[30]) with the aim that we should no longer serve sin. "Moreover, what was the use of him educating us if he did not restore us? Surely, instructing us is useless unless the body of sin is first destroyed in us so that we may no longer serve sin?" (Rom 6:6; #613).

Bernard occasionally cites Paul's reference to bearing the stigmata of Jesus in his body (Gal 6:17). This is done by abstinence (#507)

---

[26] #59, #359, #463, #464, #564, #579, #594, and #658. Bernard's citations of this verse omit the opening words *pro omnibus mortuus est.* #515 and #517 cite the verse more briefly.

[27] #66 and #348.

[28] #105, #153, #158, #217, #300, #316, #417, #455, #504, and #614. In #629 there is the idea of a monk being buried with Christ by the baptism of the desert.

[29] #348, #417, and #515.

[30] #515, #542, and #545.

and by following Christ in other ways (#421); by contrast, bishops who dress in expensive furs do not bear the marks of Christ (#562).

D. Suffering with Christ

Today there are many who argue that Christ suffered for us in order that we should not need to suffer. Christ has done everything for us, so there is nothing that we need to do. This is not how Bernard (or the New Testament) saw it. Christ suffered for us not so that we need not suffer, but so that we can share his sufferings,[31] knowing that we will also be glorified with him.[32] To this end Bernard cites Romans 8:17.[33] Christ suffered and was obedient to death, and this is an example for us to follow.[34] Bernard repeatedly cites Revelation 14:4 (those who follow the Lamb wherever he goes) to make this point.[35] These are not mere recommendations. Those who do not imitate Christ will not share in the fruit of his passion.[36] The penitent thief (Luke 23:39-43) is given as an example of one who recognised that suffering is the path to glory.[37] Christ has not forgotten his promise and will not refuse a share in his rule to the companions of his passion (#428a).

As Christ, who is God, didn't hesitate to die, so should we be ready to suffer for obedience (#117). Christ took my injuries even to death (Phil 2:8) and suffered reproaches for me (Ps 22:6), so I consider

---

[31] #240, #247, #249, #262, #298, #316, and #317.

[32] #132, #285, #349, #376, and #417.

[33] #27, #132, #240, #317, #349, #376, #417, #456, #489, and #545. Bernard also cites 1 Pet 4:13 (#123, #175, #247, #262, #316, #405, and #553), but while all of the citations of Rom 8:17 mention glorification, none of the citations of 1 Pet 4:13 mention either glorification or rejoicing. It is just that he chose to use the latter verse to make the point that we are *communicantes Christi passionibus*, the former to teach that we also share his glory.

[34] #186, #295, (citing Phil 2:8), #117, #534, #665 (citing 1 Pet 2:21), #117, #486, and #517.

[35] #170, #348, #383, #384, #387, and #517; without reference to the Lamb: #240 and #296.

[36] ##273–74 and #295.

[37] #228, #274, #376, and #391.

the reproaches he suffers today to be my concern (#661). Suffering becomes sweet when we look back at Christ's passion (#506). Bernard spells this out in full in one of his *Sentences*. Remembering and imitating Christ's death are the waters of Siloam, in which we can bathe and be cleansed from our impurities. Christ clothed himself with our mortality and died on the Cross. We should meditate on this with affection and imitate it most devoutly, suffering with the One who suffered, being crucified with the Crucified One, dying with the one who died, if we wish to share his glory. There is no way to glory except through suffering. When we suffer something painful for Christ we should do so with joy, as though drinking from a cup that he has given us (#545).

For some, such as Andrew, bearing the Cross meant literal martyrdom (##405–8). They are those who drink the cup of Christ (Matt 20:22–23).[38] Meditation on Christ's wounds gives martyrs courage to drink this cup, by which they present to Christ a likeness of his own death (##87–88). Through the Holy Spirit, Peter was not afraid to suffer the horror of the Cross for Christ (#497).

E. Pastoral Application

In his letters Bernard exhorts his correspondents on the basis of Cross, especially the fact that this or that person is a brother for whom Christ died (Rom 14:15;[39] 1 Cor 8:11[40]). We should not deceive souls for whom Christ died (#664). Bernard accuses some people of seeking to destroy those who have been saved by the Cross.[41] We must remember that Christ's most precious possessions are the souls that he has ennobled with his image and redeemed by his blood (#618). We must remember also how precious is the soul that can be redeemed only by the Cross of Christ,[42] so the cure of souls should not be entrusted to those with no regard for

---

[38] #88, #140, #213, and #399. See also #426 for a different use of this verse.
[39] #50, #51, #78, #554, #556, and #664.
[40] #156 and #568.
[41] #555 and #557.
[42] #567 and #578.

the blood shed by Christ (#637). Pastors will be called to give account to the Lamb of God, who died for the flock.[43] Bernard also implores Humbert, by the one who was crucified for him, to fulfil his pastoral duties (#593). Those who oppose what Bernard sees as the will of God he describes as enemies of the Cross of Christ (Phil 3:18).[44] Finally, Bernard was called upon to decide the validity of an emergency baptism "in the name of God and of the holy and true Cross." He considered it valid, bearing in mind that in Acts some are baptised simply in the name of the Lord Jesus Christ (#651).

F. Preaching the Cross

So far we have looked chiefly at Bernard's theological statements about the Cross as opposed to his more allegorical use of imagery, though his first sermon on the annunciation provided an example of the latter.[45] A further example is seen in his use of the bride's statement in Song of Songs 1:5 (1:4 in Vulg) that she is black yet beautiful. Bernard develops this in various ways in his sermons on the Song of Songs (SC) 24–28.[46]

The Christian is black yet beautiful, if we contrast our former life to our converted life, our present life to that of the age to come, our bodily weakness to our inner soul (SC 25.3–6). The bride is not ashamed of her blackness, because the bridegroom has endured it before her. He became black on the Cross, enduring hardship and shame, making himself sin (2 Cor 5:21). Yet for those whom he has saved, he is beautiful, the fairest of the sons of men (Ps 44:3; SC

---

[43] #569 and #621.

[44] #142, #317, #556, #580, #592, #619, #620, #638, #641, #642, and #653.

[45] See chap. 6A.

[46] Jean Leclercq maintained that SC is a literary production, not the (revised) record of sermons actually preached. See, e.g., RESB 1:193–212; "Were the Sermons on the Song of Songs Delivered in Chapter?" in Bernard of Clairvaux, *On the Song of Songs II*, CF 7 (Kalamazoo, MI: Cistercian Publications, 1976), vii–xxx. His arguments are persuasively answered by Christopher Holdsworth, "Were the Sermons on the Song of Songs Ever Preached?" in *Medieval Monastic Preaching*, ed. Carolyn Muessig (Leiden: Brill, 1998), 295–318. The statement from Song 1:5 is quoted earlier in SC 3.2.

25.8–9; ##37–38). Christ was blackened for us all, who had been blackened by sin. His beauty was eclipsed by the darkness of the passion (Isa 53:2); he suffered the ignominy of the Cross in order to gain a beautiful bride (SC 28.2; #41). On him was laid the punishment that brings us peace (Isa 53:5), and he was burdened with our sins (Isa 53:6). He was black in the eyes of the foolish like Herod but beautiful in the minds of the faithful, such as the penitent thief and the centurion (SC 28.3; #42). With his eyes the centurion saw a deformed, blackened man, numbered with transgressors (Isa 53:12), but by faith, when he heard Christ's cry, he recognised his beauty (SC 28.4; #43). The centurion may have been uncircumcised—but not where his ear was concerned (SC 28.5; #44). It is by faith that this is discerned (SC 28.5–9). After his glorification it becomes clear (SC 28.10; #46). Unbelievers failed to see the beauty under his blackness, but this was perceived by those with faith, like the thief on the cross and the centurion,[47] who were not ashamed to be called black along with him (SC 28.11; #47).

There are other forms of blackness endured by the bride: the blackness of penance for sin, the blackness of compassion for those that suffer, and the blackness of persecution (SC 28.12; #48). Such allegory has commonly been dismissed by theologians, especially in the age of modernity. Yet Bernard was a supremely skilful communicator and knew how to get his message across. Not everyone has the ability to grasp abstract concepts, and Bernard used vivid and dynamic imagery to convey them. Such an approach is more appreciated in a postmodern age.[48]

Bernard echoes Paul's statements in 1 Corinthians 1 emphasising the importance of preaching the Cross. Those who preach the Cross of Christ as something delightful (*suavem*) are reckoned to be mad (#500). The Cross is folly and a stumbling block to those who are

---

[47] Outside of this sermon, the centurion is also mentioned in ##228–29. The penitent thief is given as an example of one who recognised Jesus (also in ##228–29).

[48] For further examples, see his exposition of the bundle of myrrh between the bride's breasts (Song 1:13; 1:12 in Vulg) in ##62–65, or of the five fountains in ##197–201, or of Christ's wounds as the clefts of the rock (Song 2:14) in ##83–88 (on this, see chap. 10E).

perishing (1 Cor 1:18, 23),[49] but it is the power of God to those who are called and believe (1 Cor 1:18, 24).[50] Bernard accuses Abelard of emptying the Cross of its power by the cleverness of his words (1 Cor 1:17; #617).[51] It is not enough just to preach Christ's passion with our lips—preachers should also feel it in their hearts (#553). This is because the purpose of preaching is not just to expound words but to inspire hearts (SC 16.1). Like preaching, the Eucharist also proclaims Christ's death.[52] It is the role of liturgy to apply the Cross to the vices of the worshipers (#650).

G. The Second Crusade

The Second Crusade was a major event in Bernard's life and ministry. Despite this, it leaves no mark on his teaching about the Cross, except in his letters.[53] There he reminds his correspondents that the Holy Land,[54] Jerusalem (#633), and the holy places,[55] have all been sanctified by the blood of Christ. Christ is suffering again in what is happening in the Holy Land, and, indeed, the very grounds of our salvation are being taken away (#663). The crusade is being conducted against the enemies of the Cross of Christ (Phil 3:18).[56] If the pope fails to take action, then, as in the apocryphal *Acts of Peter*, Christ will

---

[49] #132, #314, #419, #483, and #584. Bernard also refers repeatedly to Peter's misguided attempt to deflect Christ from the Cross (Matt 16:21; Mark 8:31: #23, #458, #460, #488, #497, #499, and #526).

[50] #314, #419, and #483; see also #364.

[51] See also #589, #607, and #653 for other allusions to this verse.

[52] #195 and #262, citing 1 Cor 11:26.

[53] Daniel L. Akin, "Bernard of Clairvaux: Evangelical of the Twelfth Century (A Critical Analysis of His Soteriology)" (PhD thesis, University of Texas at Arlington, 1989), 84, claims that "much of Bernard's thinking on the atonement is a result of two major incidents in his life," the confrontation with Abelard and his preaching of the Second Crusade. The former certainly had some effect, though does not add much to what is already found in Tpl. There is no evidence that preaching the crusade had any effect on Bernard's theology of the Cross. While Tpl was dedicated to an order of military knights, the work long predates the Second Crusade. See chap. 4, nn. 4–6.

[54] #642 and #654.

[55] #642, #654, and #663.

[56] #642 and #653.

go to Jerusalem to be crucified again (#632). Those who join the crusading army take upon themselves the saving sign of the Cross.[57] The pope has promised to all who do this and who confess their sins a full indulgence (*plena indulgentia*) for all their sins,[58] as well as complete freedom from the payment of interest on their debts (#647).

Only once does Bernard make reference to the Cross as a relic, in a letter thanking the patriarch of Jerusalem for a gift from the treasure of the ages, that is, from the Cross (*ligno*) of the Lord (#598).[59]

H. The *Amplexus Bernardi*[60]

There developed soon after Bernard's death the tradition that while he was praying before a crucifix, the risen Christ reached down and embraced him. It appeared first in the late 1170s in Herbert of Clairvaux's compilation known as the *Liber miraculorum* and then in Conrad of Eberbach's *Exordium magnum*.[61] Here we read how a monk observed Bernard at prayer. "He was prostrate before the altar, and a

---

[57] #644, #645, #653, and #655. See also #656.

[58] #645, #653, and #655.

[59] This is in contrast to the view that for Bernard the Cross was just a holy relic (see chap. 1, n. 3, above).

[60] On this theme, see Brian P. McGuire, *The Difficult Saint: Bernard of Clairvaux and His Tradition*, CS 126 (Kalamazoo, MI: Cistercian Publications, 1991), 227–49; Sheryl F. Chen, "Bernard's Prayer before the Crucifix That Embraced Him: Cistercians and Devotion to the Wounds of Christ," CSQ 29 (1994): 23–54; Franz Posset, "The Crucified Embraces Saint Bernard: The Beginnings of the *Amplexus Bernardi*," CSQ 33 (1998): 289–314; Franz Posset, "*Amplexus Bernardi*: The Dissemination of a Cistercian Motif in the Later Middle Ages," Cîteaux 54 (2003): 251–400; Antonio Montanari, "Le Crucifié embrassant saint Bernard. Une relecture de la scène," Coll 66 (2004): 59–65; James France, *Medieval Images of Saint Bernard of Clairvaux*, CS 210 (Kalamazoo, MI: Cistercian Publications, 2006), 179–203.

[61] *Liber miraculorum* 3.2.19 (PL 185:1328); *Exordium magnum* 2.7. The latter is found in PL 185:419 as part of the *Vita prima* (7.7.10), but book 7 was not added to the *Vita* until the seventeenth century (Adriaan H. Bredero, *Bernard of Clairvaux: Between Cult and History* [Edinburgh: T&T Clark, 1996], 165–67). Posset was misled by PL into claiming that this account belonged to the *Vita prima* ("The Crucified Embraces Saint Bernard," 292–93, 302, 312; "*Amplexus Bernardi*," 251, 255, 263, 270).

cross with the Crucified on it appeared on the floor in front of him. The most blessed man adored and kissed it with deepest devotion. Then it seemed as if that Majesty, detaching his arms from each side of the cross, embraced the servant of God and drew him to himself."[62]

It would be rash to declare the event historical on the basis of this account, but it does have links with Bernard's teaching. First, in his *Sentences* he refers to the Cross of Christ as not just the physical Cross but the Cross of love, on which then and now he is stretched out as if to embrace (*amplexandos*) us with his extended arms of love (#515).[63] Second, France rightly observes that the story "acknowledges Bernard's immense contribution in a developing theology centred on Christ's sacrifice on the cross."[64] In other words, it draws attention to that aspect of his teaching that is covered by this book.

Subsequent to the *Exordium magnum* there are other literary allusions to the event.[65] At the end of the fifteenth century the Cistercian abbot Nicolas Saliletus published a book of meditations that included a prayer supposedly being recited by Bernard when he received the embrace.[66] There are also similar accounts of Christ embracing other people, some of which predate Bernard.[67] As with a number of stories about Bernard such as the *Lactatio*, where Mary feeds him with her milk,[68] there are many visual images of the *Amplexus* in a variety of media, such as manuscripts, paintings, woodcuts,

---

[62] Conrad of Eberbach, *Exordium magnum cisterciense sive: Narratio de initio cisterciensis ordinis* 2.7; Conrad of Eberbach, *The Great Beginning of Cîteaux: A Narrative of the Beginning of the Cistercian Order* 2.7, trans. Benedicta Ward and Paul Savage, ed. E. Rozanne Elder, CF 72 (Collegeville, MN: Cistercian Publications, 2012), 137. Posset, "The Crucified Embraces Saint Bernard," 293, points out that *super pavimentum* implies that the crucifix was upright (as in the artistic tradition) and not lying flat on the floor.

[63] More obscure is the mystical embrace described in Hum 7.21, which is not related to the Cross.

[64] France, *Medieval Images*, 182–83.

[65] Posset, "The Crucified Embraces Saint Bernard," 293–96.

[66] McGuire, *Difficult Saint*, 238–44. Chen, "Bernard's Prayer before the Crucifix," 25–40, gives a translation of the prayer.

[67] France, *Medieval Images*, 180–85.

[68] France, *Medieval Images*, 179–80, 204–37.

and sculptures. The earliest of these dates from about 1320; the rest
are all from the fifteenth century or later. They are overwhelmingly
from the German-speaking world.[69] Finally, in 1986/87 Werner
Franzen produced a bronze sculpture of Christ reaching down from
the crucifix to embrace both Bernard and Luther. Franz Posset appropriately uses this as the frontispiece of his book on Luther and
Bernard.[70]

Ulrich Köpf sounds a note of caution here. He acknowledges that
the Cross played a central role in Bernard's personal religious experience and that he meditated upon the passion. This all took place,
however, through exposition of Scripture, prayer using the words of
Scripture, and the imitation of Christ. We never read that Bernard's
devotion to the Cross involved the use of a physical crucifix,[71] perhaps because of the early Cistercian prohibition of the use of images
in their churches, though the use of painted crosses was allowed.[72]

---

[69] Posset, "The Crucified Embraces Saint Bernard," 297–314; Posset, "*Amplexus
Bernardi,*" 256–399; France, *Medieval Images*, 186–203. There is also a CD to accompany France's book with reproductions of these images.

[70] Franz Posset, *Pater Bernhardus: Martin Luther and Bernard of Clairvaux*, CS 168
(Kalamazoo, MI: Cistercian Publications, 1999), 2.

[71] Ulrich Köpf, "Die Passion Christi in der lateinischen religiösen und theologischen Literatur des Spätmittelalters," in *Die Passion Christi in Literatur und Kunst
des Spätmittelalters*, ed. Walter Haug and Burghart Wachinger (Tübingen: Max
Niemeyer, 1993), 30–31. In a personal letter of December 12, 2010, Köpf explains
that his point is not that Bernard never used a crucifix but rather that he never
mentions a physical cross or crucifix in his exposition of the topic.

[72] France, *Medieval Images*, 190–91.

13

CONCLUSION

As we have seen, Bernard's exposition of the Cross is rich and wide ranging. Christ has redeemed us and reconciled us to God. He is the Second Adam who puts right the damage caused by the First Adam. This involves the "Great Exchange," whereby we receive his righteousness in exchange for our sin and guilt. Through his passion Christ is made merciful, at least in our perception of him. His passion demonstrates both his love and the Father's love for us. Such love evokes a response on our part and serves as an example for our behaviour. Christ brings us victory over Satan and over death, in each case by resolving the issue of our sin. The Cross is a sacrifice for sins offered to God by the Lamb of God, who shed his blood for us. He paid the debt we owed and bore the punishment that was due to us. The Cross is a satisfaction for our sins by which the Father is placated and propitiated. Through the Cross our relationship with God is restored.

Bernard's teaching on the Cross is, as we would expect, rich in imagery. It is an affective preached theology rather than a scholastic one. So, does Bernard bring his teaching into a "coherent whole" or simply leave us with a kaleidoscope of "fragmentary views and texts concerning details of the doctrine"?[1] Our study has vindicated the claim of Jean Leclercq that Bernard's theology, and his theology of the Cross in particular, is not systematic in the scholastic sense but is

---

[1] For the question, see chap. 3B above.

synthetic in the sense that all is linked closely together.[2] His teaching is scattered over many different works but is, as Gillian Evans claims, both consistent and comprehensive,[3] though not without its faults.[4] It is low on explicit critical analysis, but that does not mean that there is no such analysis. The different imagery and models cohere and are interrelated.

The claim that Bernard's theology is synthetic and consistent is vindicated by the way in which he responds to Abelard's objections, as well as the way in which he relates Christ's victory over Satan and death to his resolution of the problem of sin. At the same time, Bernard is willing to leave some questions unanswered, such as "To whom was the ransom paid?"[5] He is also willing to leave complementary truths in tension, such as that between the Father sending the Son, who was obedient, and the Son voluntarily giving himself for us.[6]

Bernard's account of the Cross is not flawless, but it has much to commend it. Unlike Anselm and Abelard, to whom so much attention is paid, he does not emphasise one model of the work of Christ to the detriment of others but rather integrates them into a whole. He is an able exponent of the historic Christian understanding of the Cross.

[2] Jean Leclercq, "General Introduction to the Works of Saint Bernard (III)," CSQ 40 (2005): 365. For a similar conclusion about Bernard's anthropology, see Richard U. Smith, "Saint Bernard's Anthropology: Traditional and Systematic," CSQ 46 (2011): 415–28.

[3] Gillian R. Evans, *The Mind of St. Bernard of Clairvaux* (Oxford: OUP, 1983), 162.

[4] In chap. 11B above, we noted some inconsistency over the issue of the need for the Cross.

[5] See chap. 11F above.

[6] See chap. 11E above.

Appendix I

INDEX OF PASSAGES ON THE CROSS WITH BIBLICAL CITATIONS

The list below gives all of the passages that have been identified where Bernard refers to the Cross. Each passage is allocated a number by which it is cited in chapters 4–14 (e.g., #27 = SC 21.2). At a late stage in the proceedings I found two new passages, which have been numbered #261a and #428a in order to avoid having to renumber over four hundred passages.

For each passage there is a list of the biblical texts cited in that passage. The texts are those that Bernard uses when writing of the Cross, even though the Cross may have nothing to do with the original context (as with Ps 69:4). Mark 16:1 is included because the reference to anointing Christ's body relates back to the previous chapter. Also included are references to the blood of Christ (such as John 6:53-55; 1 John 5:6-8) and to Jesus as the Lamb.

The tables below are heavily dependent upon the superb work of the editors of SBOp, as found in the notes to the texts and as set out in the *Index biblicus in opera omnia S. Bernardi* (SBOp 9). The ability of the editors to detect even the faintest traces of citations is truly remarkable. But the tables below omit a number of the citations recorded in SBOp and also add a smaller number not found there. Why is this?

There are a number of reasons why citations have been omitted. The most common is where the section of a verse quoted is not relevant to our theme. Thus, Hebrews 1:3 contains the statement that Christ provided purification for sins, but Bernard more often cited the earlier part of that verse to the effect that Christ is the radiance of God's glory and the representation of his being. Again, there are some verses that don't explicitly mention the Cross but which Bernard often cites in connection with it. Examples would be 1 Corinthians 1:30 and Ephesians 2:14. These are listed only where the context is Christ's work on the Cross. "Context" here is taken to include the situation where they are cited in a section that does not actually refer to the Cross but where the previous or subsequent section makes it clear that Bernard has the Cross in mind. Also, Bernard occasionally cites a verse that refers to the Cross but to a quite different end—for example, the statement that a monk was obedient to death (Ep 159.1). In some contexts this could be seen as a statement about the need to imitate Christ, but here it appears just to be a use of a biblical phrase to make a point.

A smaller number of citations not recorded by the editors of SBOp have been included. There are a number of reasons for this. First, there are places where the reference given in SBOp is faulty—Galatians 3:13 for Genesis 3:13, Psalm 21:9 for Psalm 21:19, Hebrews 3:17 for Hebrews 2:17, Romans 5:24 for Romans 4:25, Miss 1.9 for Miss 1.8, and so forth. Second, there are places where a biblical passage is being expounded over a number of sections even if it is not quoted in every section. The exposition of Psalm 85:10–11 in Ann 1.9–14 is a good example. Again, there are places where Bernard can refer clearly to a passage without using its wording, and SBOp does not always list such citations. For example, Bernard states that Christ prayed for those who crucified him, a clear allusion to Luke 23:34 (#3). The same applies to the thief on the cross (#42 and #229). Also, I have occasionally been more generous than SBOp in acknowledging citations where the wording has changed. Thus, Bernard often cites the reference in Philippians 3:18 to enemies of the Cross of Christ (*inimicos crucis Christi*), but I have also seen a reference to that verse where Bernard refers to *crucis adversarii* (#642) or *hostes crucis Christi* (#653). Very occasionally, there are clear verbal allusions that have been missed by the editors, often because the allusion is a blend of two passages, only one of which has been spotted (e.g., #474). Where I have for any reason listed an allusion not found in SBOp, it is listed in italics in appendix 2.

I have given chapter and verse numbers as they appear in modern English Bibles, which is sometimes different from the Vulgate. Thus, as is well known, Psalm 85:10, for example, appears as 84:11 in the Vulgate, and, as is less well known, John 6:53-63 appears as John 6:54-64 and Galatians 2:20 as Galatians 2:19-20. Also, where in the index a whole passage is given (e.g., Luke 23:39-43), places where Bernard cites any part of that passage (e.g., Luke 23:40 only) are listed. Where the same material is found in more than one gospel, all the passages are placed together in the index.

No.	Source	SBOp	Texts
1	SC 2.3	1:10	Eph 2:14; Col 1:20
2	SC 2.8	1:13	Rom 4:25; 2 Cor 5:19
3	SC 6.3	1:27	Luke 23:34
4	SC 8.1	1:36	
5	SC 10.3	1:49–50	
6	SC 11.3	1:56	
7	SC 11.7	1:58–59	Phil 2:8
8	SC 12.6	1:64	Mark 16:1
9	SC 12.7	1:65	Heb 2:9
10	SC 12.10	1:67	
11	SC 13.5	1:71	
12	SC 14.4	1:78	Matt 27:51
13	SC 15.3	1:84	Luke 24:46; John 12:24
14	SC 15.4	1:85	Ps 22:14
15	SC 15.6	1:86	1 Cor 2:2
16	SC 16:4	1:92	Rom 8:32
17	SC 16:5	1:92	Gen 4:10
18	SC 16.12	1:96	
19	SC 16.14	1:97	Matt 12:29
20	SC 19.3	1:109	

No.	Source	SBOp	Texts
21	SC 20.2	1:115	Rom 5:10; 1 John 4:10
22	SC 20.3	1:115–16	Ps 49:8
23	SC 20.5	1:117–18	Mark 8:31; John 15:13
24	SC 20.6	1:118	
25	SC 20.7	1:119	John 6:63; 2 Cor 5:16
26	SC 20.8	1:120	1 Cor 1:30
27	SC 21.2	1:122–23	Matt 16:24; Rom 8:17
28	SC 21.7	1:126	John 12:32
29	SC 22.6	1:132–33	
30	SC 22.7	1:133	Isa 53:12; Rom 3:24; Col 1:13
31	SC 22.8	1:133–35	Isa 5:4; Luke 23:34, 40-43; John 12:32
32	SC 22.9	1:135–36	1 Cor 1:30
33	SC 22.10	1:136–37	1 Cor 1:30
34	SC 22.11	1:137	
35	SC 23.4	1:141	Eph 2:14; Col 1:20
36	SC 24.3	1:153	
37	SC 25.8	1:168	Isa 53:2-5; Gal 6:14
38	SC 25.9	1:168–69	Ps 22:6; Isa 53:2; 2 Cor 5:21
39	SC 26.11	1:179	Luke 23:46
40	SC 27.9	1:188	
41	SC 28.2	1:193–94	Isa 53:2-3, 9; John 11:50; 1 Pet 2:22
42	SC 28.3	1:194	Isa 53:5-6; Mark 15:39; Luke 23:40-43; John 6:63; Heb 2:17
43	SC 28.4	1:194–95	Isa 53:12; Mark 15:39
44	SC 28.5	1:195	Matt 27:54
45	SC 28.9	1:198	
46	SC 28.10	1:199	

No.	Source	SBOp	Texts
47	SC 28.11	1:199–200	Matt 27:42, 54; Luke 23:40-43; John 1:29; 1 Cor 2:8
48	SC 28.12	1:201	1 Pet 2:24
49	SC 29.1	1:202	
50	SC 29.4	1:206	Rom 14:15
51	SC 29.5	1:206	Rom 14:15
52	SC 30.10	1:216	Gal 5:24
53	SC 31.10	1:225–26	John 6:55, 10:11
54	SC 32.8	1:231	John 20:25
55	SC 32.9	1:232	John 20:27
56	SC 33.5	1:236–37	1 Cor 2:8
57	SC 33.6	1:237	2 Cor 5:16
58	SC 38.2	2:15	Col 2:14
59	SC 41.6	2:32	2 Cor 5:15
60	SC 42.7	2:37	Isa 53:7
61	SC 42.8	2:38	Phil 2:8
62	SC 43.1	2:41–42	Eph 2:13
63	SC 43.2	2:42	
64	SC 43.3	2:42–43	Matt 27:48; John 19:39
65	SC 43.4	2:43	1 Cor 2:2
66	SC 44.1	2:44–45	Matt 27:34; Rom 4:25; 1 Pet 2:24
67	SC 45.3	2:51	1 Cor 2:2
68	SC 45.4	2:52	
69	SC 45.6	2:53	Isa 53:2
70	SC 46.5	2:59	
71	SC 47.5	2:64	Ps 22:7; Heb 13:12-13
72	SC 47.6	2:65	
73	SC 54.1	2:103	Matt 20:28; John 6:55

No.	Source	SBOp	Texts
74	SC 54.3	2:104	Rom 6:9; 1 Cor 2:8; Heb 6:6
75	SC 56.1	2:114–15	Isa 53:4; Heb 2:17, 5:8
76	SC 56.2	2:115	1 John 5:6
77	SC 58.6	2:130	
78	SC 58.7	2:131	Matt 27:42; John 19:15; Rom 14:15
79	SC 60.4	2:144	John 19:30
80	SC 60.5	2:144	
81	SC 60.8	2:146	
82	SC 61 cap	2:148	
83	SC 61.3	2:149–50	Isa 53:5; John 12:32
84	SC 61.4	2:150–51	Ps 22:16; John 15:13, 19:34; 2 Cor 5:19
85	SC 61.5	2:151	1 Cor 1:30; Heb 9:12
86	SC 61.6	2:152	
87	SC 61.7	2:152–53	Isa 53:5
88	SC 61.8	2:153	Matt 20:22
89	SC 62.1	2:154–55	
90	SC 62.6	2:159	1 Cor 2:2
91	SC 62.7	2:159	Ps 22:16
92	SC 65.1	2:172	
93	SC 65.4	2:174	
94	SC 65.8	2:177	
95	SC 66.8	2:183	
96	SC 66.9	2:184	Gen 4:10
97	SC 66.10	2:185	Rom 14:9
98	SC 66.11	2:185	John 11:49–51
99	SC 67.5	2:191	Isa 53:12
100	SC 68.3	2:198	Gal 1:4
101	SC 68.4	2:198–99	Acts 20:28

No.	Source	SBOp	Texts
102	SC 68.5	2:199	Col 1:13
103	SC 70.6	2:211	Ps 85:11; Isa 53:7; Acts 8:32
104	SC 70.7	2:212	
105	SC 71.11	2:222	Rom 3:24, 6:5-6; 2 Cor 5:21; 1 Pet 2:22
106	SC 72.9	2:231	Gal 5:24
107	SC 75.2	2:248	John 6:55; 2 Cor 5:16
108	SC 75.5	2:250	Rom 6:9-10; Eph 1:10; Heb 6:6; 1 Pet 3:19
109	SC 75.6	2:250	
110	SC 75.7	2:251	
111	SC 75.8	2:251–52	Luke 23:56; 2 Cor 5:16
112	SC 76.1	2:254–55	Matt 27:42; John 12:32, 19:30
113	SC 76.8	2:259	
114	SC 78.4	2:268–69	Rom 8:3; Gal 3:13
115	SC 79.2	2:273	
116	Hum 3.6	3:21	Heb 2:17-18, 5:8
117	Hum 3.7	3:21–22	Phil 2:8; Heb 2:17, 5:8; 1 Pet 2:21
118	Hum 3.8	3:22	Heb 2:17-18
119	Hum 3.9	3:23	Isa 53:3-4; Heb 2:18
120	Hum 3.12	3:25–26	Heb 2:17
121	Hum 6.19	3:30	John 19:37
122	Hum 10.33	3:42	
123	Apo 1.2	3:82	Matt 16:24; Luke 23:26; 1 Pet 4:13
124	Apo 3.5	3:85–86	Isa 53:7; John 1:29; Acts 8:32; 1 Pet 2:22
125	Apo 3.6	3:86	John 19:23; Phil 2:8
126	Apo 6.12	3:92	

No.	Source	SBOp	Texts
127	Apo 9.19	3:97	
128	Dil 1.1	3:120	John 3:16, 15:13; Rom 5:10, 8:32; Gal 1:4; 1 John 4:10
129	Dil 3.7	3:124–25	John 15:13, 19:17, 34; 1 Cor 2:2, 8
130	Dil 3.8	3:125–26	
131	Dil 3.9	3:126	Rom 4:25
132	Dil 4.11	3:128	John 6:54; Rom 8:17; 1 Cor 1:18; Gal 6:14
133	Dil 4.12	3:129	John 15:13; Gal 6:14
134	Dil 4.13	3:130	Isa 53:12; John 3:16
135	Dil 5.14	3:130	Heb 9:12
136	Dil 5.15	3:131–32	Rom 5:8
137	Dil 7.22	3:137	
138	Gra 3.8	3:172	Isa 53:7; John 10:18; 1 Pet 2:22
139	Gra 4.12	3:174	Gal 5:24
140	Gra 6:17	3:178	Matt 20:22, 26:39; Mark 14:36; Luke 22:42
141	Gra 14.48	3:201	
142	Tpl 1.1	3:214	Phil 3:18
143	Tpl 6.12	3:225	John 6:63; 1 Cor 2:2; 2 Cor 5:16
144	Tpl 7.13	3:226	John 1:29, 19:1; 1 Cor 2:8; 1 Pet 2:22, 24
145	Tpl 10.17	3:229	John 19:17; Heb 1:3; Rev 1:5
146	Tpl 11.18	3:229–30	
147	Tpl 11.20	3:231	
148	Tpl 11.22	3:231–32	
149	Tpl 11.23	2:232–33	2 Macc 1:24; Rom 5:6, 18–19; 1 Cor 15:21-22
150	Tpl 11.25	3:234	Rom 5:12, 15–17; 1 Cor 15:22

No.	Source	SBOp	Texts
151	Tpl 11.26	3:234	
152	Tpl 11.27	3:235	Ps 69:4; John 19:28; 1 Cor 1:30; 2 Cor 8:9
153	Tpl 11.29	3:236	Rom 6:4–5
154	Tpl 13.31	3:239	Phil 2:8
155	Pre 6.12	3:262	Phil 2:8
156	Pre 9.20	3:268	Luke 23:34; 1 Cor 2:8, 8:11
157	Pre 10.24	3:270	Isa 53:12; 1 John 2:1–2
158	Pre 17.54	3:289	Rom 6:5; Col 1:13
159	V Mal 12.25	3:335	Phil 2:8
160	V Mal 29.65	3:369	
161	V Mal 30.67	3:372	
162	Csi 1:4.5	3:398	1 Cor 7:23
163	Csi 2.6.11	3:419	Gal 6:14
164	Csi 2.6.12	3:419	
165	Csi 2.8.15	3:424	
166	Csi 4.4.12	3:458	
167	OfVict	3:505–6	
168	OfVict	3:506	
169	Miss 1.2	4:15	Luke 11:21–22
170	Miss 1.8	4:20	Isa 53:7; Acts 8:32; Rev 14:4
171	Miss 2.13	4:30–31	2 Cor 5:18–19
172	Miss 3.8	4:42	
173	Miss 3.10	4:43	Matt 1:21
174	Miss 3.11	4:43	Matt 1:21
175	Miss 3.14	4:45–46	Isa 53:12; Rom 8:32; Gal 2:21; 1 Pet 4:13; 1 John 2:2; Rev 1:5
176	Miss 4.2	4:47	John 19:15
177	Miss 4.8	4:53	

No.	Source	SBOp	Texts
178	Miss 4.10	4:56	Gal 6:14
179	Conv 8.15	4:89	
180	Conv 19.32	4:109	Luke 23:34
181	Conv 21.37	4:113	Matt 26:28; Luke 22:20
182	Adv 2.1	4:171	John 15:13
183	Adv 2.4	4:174	Rom 8:32
184	Adv 3.6	4:179	
185	Adv 4.4	4:184–85	Heb 9:14
186	Adv 4.7	4:187	Isa 53:7; Luke 23:34; Acts 8:32; 1 Pet 2:22; Rev 7:14
187	Adv 5.1	4:188	John 19:37; Rom 3:24
188	Adv 6.1	4:191	John 1:29
189	V Nat 2.7	4:210	Acts 20:28; 1 Pet 1:19
190	V Nat 3.9	4:218	
191	V Nat 3.10	4:219	
192	V Nat 4.3	4:222	Isa 53:4
193	V Nat 4.5	4:223	Lev 9:3; John 1:29
194	V Nat 4.7	4:224–25	John 15:13; 1 Cor 2:2; Gal 6:14
195	V Nat 6.6	4:239	1 Cor 11:26
196	V Nat 6.11	4:243–44	John 12:32
197	Nat 1.4	4:247	Matt 12:29
198	Nat 1.5	4:247	Rev 1:5
199	Nat 1.6	4:249	
200	Nat 1.7	4:249	
201	Nat 1.8	4:250–51	Ps 22:16, 49:8; John 19:30, 34
202	Nat 2.5	4:255–56	Ps 22:16; John 10:17–18
203	Nat 3 cap	4:257	
204	Nat 3.3	4:260	
205	Nat 3.4	4:260–61	

No.	Source	SBOp	Texts
206	Nat 3.5	4:261	
207	Nat 3.6	4:262	
208	Nat 5.1	4:266	Rom 5:10
209	Nat 5.2	4:267	
210	Nat 5.3	4:267	Ps 25:10
211	Nat 5.4	4:268	John 1:29
212	Nat 5.5	4:269	Matt 1:21
213	Innoc 1	4:271	Matt 20:23
214	Circ 1.3	4:275	Matt 1:21; Luke 22:20; Rom 4:25; 1 Cor 15:3
215	Circ 1.5	4:276	Luke 11:21; Rom 3:25, 5:10
216	Circ 2.1	4:278	Lev 9:3; Ps 69:4; Isa 53:7, 12; Luke 22:37; Acts 8:32; Heb 1:3; 1 Pet 2:22
217	Circ 2.3	4:280	Rom 6:5
218	Circ 3.1	4:282	Heb 9:22
219	Circ 3.2	4:283	Rom 5:6; Gal 6:14
220	Circ 3.3	4:284	Heb 1:3
221	Circ 3.4	4:284–85	John 1:29; 1 Pet 2:22; Rev 7:14
222	Epi 1.2	4:292–93	
223	Epi 1.3	4:294	Matt 1:21
224	Epi 1.4	4:295	
225	Epi 1.6	4:297–98	Lev 9:3; John 1:29; Heb 1:3
226	Epi 1.7	4:298	
227	Epi 2.1	4:301	
228	Epi 2.3	4:302–3	Matt 27:54; Luke 23:42, 24:26; John 19:5
229	Epi 2.4	4:303	Matt 27:54; Luke 23:40–43
230	Epi 3.6	4:307	Matt 16:24; Gal 5:24
231	P Epi 1.3	4:316	Isa 52:3; John 19:34; Rom 5:12, 14–15; 1 Cor 15:22; Heb 1:3

No.	Source	SBOp	Texts
232	P Epi 1.4	4:317	
233	P Epi 2.1	4:319–20	Lev 9:3; John 6:63; 1 Cor 2:2; 2 Cor 5:16
234	P Epi 2.3	4:321	
235	Pl 2	4:328	Ps 49:8; Col 2:14; Heb 9:12
236	Pur 1.3	4:336–37	1 Cor 1:30; Col 1:20
237	Pur 3.2	4:342–43	Isa 53:7; Heb 9:12
238	Pur 3.3	4:343–44	Heb 9:14
239	Sept 2.1	4:350	John 10:18
240	Quad 1.1	4:353–54	Rom 8:17; Rev 14:4
241	Quad 1.2	4:354	Isa 53:4
242	Quad 2.6	4:363	John 19:23-24
243	Quad 6 cap	4:377	
244	Quad 6.3	4:378–79	Gal 6:14
245	QH Pref.1	4:383	
246	QH 3.2	4:394	John 19:15
247	QH 3.3	4:394	John 6:53; 1 Cor 1:30; 1 Pet 4:13
248	QH 5.1	4:401–2	
249	QH 6.2	4:405	
250	QH 7.15	4:424	John 19:34
251	QH 9.3	4:437–38	John 15:13; Rom 5:6, 10; Heb 2:9; 1 Pet 2:22; 1 John 4:10
252	QH 9.4	4:438	Col 1:24
253	QH 9.6	4:440	John 15:13
254	QH 12.5	4:460	
255	QH 14.3	4:470	
256	QH 14.4	4:471	Phil 2:8
257	QH 14.5	4:472	Heb 9:12
258	QH 14.8	4:474	Phil 2:8

No.	Source	SBOp	Texts
259	QH 16.2	4:482	John 19:30; Heb 12:2
260	Ben 3	5:2	
261	Ben 6	5:5	Matt 27:32; Luke 23:26
261a	Ben 11	5:11	
262	Ben 12	5:11–12	John 6:53-54; 1 Cor 11:26; 1 Pet 4:13
263	Ann 1.4	5:15	Gen 4:10; Rom 4:25; Heb 12:24
264	Ann 1.7	5:19	John 19:23-24
265	Ann 1.9	5:22–23	Ps 85:10
266	Ann 1.10	5:23–25	Ps 85:10
267	Ann 1.11	5:25–26	Ps 85:10
268	Ann 1.12	5:26–27	Ps 85:10; Matt 12:29; Luke 11:21; Rom 5:7 (v.l.); Eph 2:14
269	Ann 1.13	5:27	Ps 85:10; John 15:13
270	Ann 1.14	5:28–29	Ps 85:10; Matt 26:42
271	Ann 2:3	5:32	
272	Palm 1 cap	5:42	
273	Palm 1.1	5:42–43	Isa 53:12; 1 Pet 2:22
274	Palm 1.2	5:43–44	Luke 23:40-43
275	Palm 2 cap	5:46	
276	Palm 2.1	5:46	
277	Palm 2.3	5:48	Isa 53:7; Luke 23:34; Acts 8:32; 1 Pet 2:23
278	Palm 2.4	5:48	Ps 22:18; Matt 27:35; John 19:15
279	Palm 3 cap	5:51	
280	Palm 3.1	5:51–52	
281	Palm 3.3	5:53–54	Matt 27:38
282	Palm 3.4	5:54–55	John 6:55

No.	Source	SBOp	Texts
283	Palm 3.5	5:55	Luke 23:27
284	4 HM cap	5:56	
285	4 HM 1	5:56–57	Matt 27:51
286	4 HM 2	5:57	Ps 22:16-17, 69:4; Acts 8:32; 2 Cor 5:19
287	4 HM 3	5:58	Ps 22:6; Isa 53:2-4, 12; Acts 8:33
288	4 HM 4	5:58–59	Isa 53:7, 12; John 10:18, 15:13, 19:30; Rom 3:24, 4:25, 5:7-8, 10, 8:32; 1 Cor 15:3; Phil 2:8
289	4 HM 5	5:59–60	John 1:29; Rev 5:12
290	4 HM 6	5:60–61	
291	4 HM 7	5:61	Rom 5:15-16, 8:3; 2 Cor 5:21; 1 Pet 2:24
292	4 HM 8	5:61–62	Isa 53:12; Matt 27:29; Mark 15:15; Luke 22:44, 23:34
293	4 HM 9	5:62–63	Luke 23:21, 23:34
294	4 HM 10	5:63–64	1 Cor 2:8; Heb 9:28
295	4 HM 11	5:64	Isa 53:3-4; Heb 10:29
296	4 HM 12	5:65	Rev 14:4
297	4 HM 13	5:65–66	1 Cor 1:30
298	4 HM 14	5:66–67	
299	5 HM 1	5:67	Matt 27:51
300	5 HM 2	5:68–69	Rom 6:5
301	5 HM 3	5:70	1 Cor 11:27; Col 2:14
302	Res 1.1	5:73–74	Matt 12:29, 27:39, 42, 44 (v.l.); Mark 15:29, 32; Luke 11:21; John 11:50; Heb 2:14
303	Res 1.2	5:74–76	Matt 16:24 (v.l.) 27:40, 42; John 19:19-22

No.	Source	SBOp	Texts
304	Res 1.3	5:76–78	Num 21:8-9; Ps 22:6 (v.l.); Matt 27:42; John 12:32, 15:13, 19:30; Eph 5:2 (v.l.); Phil 2:8
305	Res 1.4	5:79–80	Matt 27:42; John 19:30
306	Res 1.5	5:80–81	Matt 27:42; John 19:34-35; Rev 7:14
307	Res 1.6	5:81–82	Matt 27:42; Rom 6:9-10
308	Res 1.7	5:82–83	
309	Res 1.8	5:83–84	Matt 16:24
310	Res 1.9	5:84–85	John 19:15; Rev 5:12
311	Res 1.10	5:85–87	Rev 5:6, 9, 12
312	Res 1.11	5:87–88	Luke 22:37, 23:33
313	Res 1.12	5:89–90	Rom 6:9; 1 Cor 2:8; Rev 5:12
314	Res 1.13	5:90	Matt 27:42; 1 Cor 1:18, 23, 5:7; Gal 6:14
315	Res 1.14	5:90–92	Rom 4:25 (v.l.), 6:4, 10
316	Res 1.15	5:92	Rom 6:5; 1 Pet 4:13
317	Res 1.16	5:92–93	Rom 4:25, 8:17; Phil 3:18
318	Res 1.17	5:93–94	John 6:53
319	Res 2.3	5:96	Mark 16:1
320	Res 2.4	5:97	Luke 23:27-28; John 19:17
321	Res 3.1	5:103	2 Cor 8:9
322	Res 3.2	5:104–5	Isa 53:7; Ps 22:6; Acts 8:32; 1 Pet 2:23
323	Res 3.3	5:106	Luke 22:42
324	Res 3.5	5:108	Isa 53:7; Matt 26:39; John 12:24-25
325	Res 3.6	5:109	
326	Res 4.1	5:110	
327	O Pasc 1.2	5:113	Luke 11:21

No.	Source	SBOp	Texts
328	O Pasc 1.4	5:114	1 John 5:6
329	O Pasc 1.5	5:114–15	John 11:51-52, 19:34; 1 Pet 1:18; 1 John 5:6; Rev 7:14
330	O Pasc 1.6	5:115–16	John 6:63; 1 John 5:6-8
331	O Pasc 1.7	5:116	Heb 9:22
332	O Pasc 1.8	5:117	1 John 5:7-8
333	O Pasc 2.1	5:118	1 John 5:7-8
334	O Pasc 2.4	5:120	John 19:34; 1 Cor 11:27; Heb 9:12; 1 John 5:8
335	O Pasc 2.5	5:120–21	1 John 5:8
336	Asc 2.1	5:127	Col 2:14-15
337	Asc 2.2	5:127	John 19:23
338	Asc 2.3	5:128	John 19:23
339	Asc 2.4	5:128	
340	Asc 2.6	5:130	
341	Asc 3.2	5:132	
342	Asc 3.3	5:133	Luke 24:26, 46
343	Asc 4.2	5:138–39	
344	Asc 4.6	5:142	Ps 22:17, 69:4; Isa 53:12; John 20:25; Rom 5:8
345	Asc 4.9	5:145	Isa 53:2
346	Asc 4.12	5:147	Luke 24:46; John 12:32
347	Asc 4.13	5:148	John 12:32; Gal 6:14; Col 1:20
348	Asc 6.3	5:151–52	Rom 6:4, 6, 14:9; 1 Pet 2:24; Rev 14:4
349	Asc 6.4	5:152	Rom 6:4, 8:17
350	Asc 6.10	5:156	
351	Asc 6.11	5:156	John 1:29
352	Pent 1.6	5:164	
353	Pent 2.5	5:168	

No.	Source	SBOp	Texts
354	Pent 2:7	5:170	Isa 53:7; Acts 8:32; Rom 8:32; Eph 5:2
355	Pent 2.8	5:170	Isa 5:4; 1 Pet 1:18-19
356	JB 11	5:183	John 1:29; Heb 9:19
357	JB 12	5:184	Heb 1:3
358	PP 1.1	5:188	Col 1:20; 1 Pet 2:22
359	PP 3.5	5:199–200	2 Cor 5:15; 1 John 2:1
360	Asspt 2.1	5:232	Matt 12:29; Luke 11:21-22
361	Asspt 2.2	5:232	Luke 11:22
362	Asspt 2.4	5:234	Matt 12:29; Luke 11:22
363	Asspt 3.5	5:241	Isa 53:3
364	Asspt 4.1	5:245	1 Cor 1:18; 2 Cor 8:9; Gal 6:14; 1 John 4:10
365	Asspt 5.10	5:257	John 11:53
366	Asspt 5.12	5:259	
367	O Asspt 1	5:262	Rom 5:15; Heb 2:17, 5:8
368	O Asspt 11	5:271	
369	O Asspt 14	5:273	Matt 27:50; John 19:34
370	O Asspt 15	5:273–74	John 15:13
371	Nat BVM 6	5:278	
372	Nat BVM 11	5:282	John 20:25, 27
373	Mich 1.2	5:295	Matt 20:28
374	Mich 1.3	5:295	Heb 9:14
375	1 Nov 1.1	5: 304	Ps 22:17; Isa 53:2, 4
376	1 Nov 1.2	5:305	Isa 53:4; Luke 23:40-43; John 3:14; Rom 8:17; 1 Cor 2:2
377	1 Nov 5.3	5:319	Matt 27:46; 1 Cor 2:2
378	1 Nov 5.4	5:320	Isa 53:2-5
379	1 Nov 5.11	5:325	1 Cor 2:8
380	OS 1.6	5:331	Luke 23:40-43

No.	Source	SBOp	Texts
381	OS 1.14	5:340	Ps 85:10; Rom 5:10; Col 1:20
382	OS 1.15	5:341	
383	OS 3.2	5:350–51	Rev 14:4
384	OS 3.3	5:351	Rev 14:4
385	OS 3.4	5:353	Rev 1:5
386	OS 4.1	5:354–55	Col 2:14
387	OS 4.4	5:358	Rev 14:4
388	OS 5.2	5:362	Rev 7:14
389	OS 5.8	5:367	
390	OS 5.9	5:367–68	Isa 53:2; Mark 15:17–20; 1 Cor 11:26
391	OS 5.11	5:369	Luke 23:40-43
392	Ded 1.4	5:373	John 19:34
393	Ded 1.5	5:373	
394	Ded 3.1	5:379	1 Cor 1:30
395	Ded 5.5	5:391	Ps 25:10; Heb 9:15–18
396	Mart 4	5:402	Eph 2:14; Col 1:20, 2:13-15
397	Mart 8	5:405	Isa 53:7; Phil 2:8
398	Mart 10	5:406	2 Cor 5:16
399	Clem 3	5:414	Matt 20:22; 1 Cor 6:20; Rev 5:9
400	Clem 4	5:415	John 19:34–35; 1 John 5:6; Rev 19:9
401	Clem 5	5:415–16	1 John 5:8
402	Clem 6	5:416	Luke 22:44; John 19:34
403	Mal 3	5:419	
404	Mal 4	5:419–20	Col 2:14
405	V And 3	5:425–26	1 Pet 4:13
406	V And 4	5:426	Luke 14:27
407	And 1.1	5:427	Luke 23:28; John 19:17

No.	Source	SBOp	Texts
408	And 1.2	5:428	
409	And 1.3	5:428–29	
410	And 1.5	5:430	Matt 26:39
411	And 1.6	5:431	John 10:18
412	And 1.7	5:431	Matt 26:39; Mark 14:36
413	And 1.8	5:432	Eph 2:14
414	And 2 cap	5:434	
415	And 2.3	5:435–36	
416	And 2.4	5:436–37	
417	And 2.5	5:437	Matt 16:24; Rom 6:5-6, 8:17
418	And 2.6	5:437–38	
419	And 2.7	5:438–39	Mark 15:26; 1 Cor 1:18
420	And 2.8	5:439–40	Gal 6:14
421	Humb 5	5:444	Gal 6:17; Col 1:24
422	Humb 6	5:446	Luke 23:28
423	Adv var 1	6/1:9	
424	Adv var 2	6/1:10	Rom 6:9; 1 Cor 15:22
425	Adv var 3	6/1:12	Gal 1:4
426	Adv var 4	6/1:13–14	Matt 16:24, 20:22
427	Epi var 4	6/1:24	Matt 26:38; Luke 22:44; Eph 2:14
428	Epi var 5	6/1:24–25	Ps 85:10; Col 2:14; Heb 9:14
428a	Vict 2.3	6/1:35	
429	Vict 2.4	6/1:36	
430	Doni 1	6/1:44–46	Luke 11:21; Col 2:14
431	Doni 2	6/1:46	Heb 12:24
432	Doni 5	6/1:49	Isa 53:7; Acts 8:32
433	S Mal 1	6/1:51	1 Cor 6:20; 1 Pet 1:18-19
434	Div 1.5	6/1:76	Rom 8:32

No.	Source	SBOp	Texts
435	Div 3.5	6/1:90	Col 2:14
436	Div 3.9	6/1:93	Mark 14:36
437	Div 4.4	6/1:96	Gal 6:14
438	Div 5.1	6/1:98	John 6:63
439	Div 6.3	6/1:107	Isa 53:5; John 19:34, 36
440	Div 8.5	6/1:114	Matt 12:29; Luke 11:21; 1 John 5:6
441	Div 11.1	6/1:124	Col 1:13
442	Div 11.2	6/1:125	Matt 12:29; Luke 11:21–22; Heb 2:14
443	Div 13:1	6/1:131–32	
444	Div 13:2	6/1:132	Matt 27:51
445	Div 16:6	6/1:148	
446	Div 17:5	6/1:153	Matt 27:29; John 19:34, 20:25
447	Div 18:2	6/1:158	1 Cor 2:2; 2 Cor 5:16
448	Div 19.5	6/1:163–64	Isa 5:4
449	Div 22.3	6/1:172	Luke 11:22
450	Div 22.5	6/1:173–74	Rom 5:7, 10; 1 Pet 3:18; 1 John 3:16
451	Div 22.6	6/1:174–75	Luke 22:44
452	Div 22.7	6/1:175–76	
453	Div 25.1	6/1:188	
454	Div 28.1	6/1:204	Lev 9:3; 1 Pet 2:22
455	Div 28.2	6/1:205	Luke 14:27; John 19:36; Rom 6:5; Heb 6:6
456	Div 28.3	6/1:206	Rom 8:17
457	Div 29.2	6/1:211	
458	Div 29.3	6/1:212	Ps 69:4; Isa 5:4, 53:12; Matt 16:21; John 15:13; Rom 5:8
459	Div 29.4	6/1:212–13	

No.	Source	SBOp	Texts
460	Div 29.5	6/1:213	Matt 16:21
461	Div 33.3	6/1:224	John 10:18; 1 Pet 2:22
462	Div 33.4	6/1:224	Luke 24:26, 46
463	Div 33.5	6/1:225	2 Cor 5:15
464	Div 33.6	6/1:226	2 Cor 5:15
465	Div 33.7	6/1:226	John 12:32
466	Div 33.8	6/1:227	John 12:32; Eph 1:10
467	Div 33.9	6/1:228	John 12:32
468	Div 34.2	6/1:229	Isa 53:7; John 10:17; Phil 2:8
469	Div 34.3	6/1:230	Ps 69:4
470	Div 34.4	6/1:231	Matt 26:38; John 19:30; 1 Pet 2:22
471	Div 34.5	6/1:232	Rom 6:9
472	Div 34.6	6/1:232	John 19:30; 1 John 3:16
473	Div 40.2	6/1:235–36	Luke 23:40-43
474	Div 40.5	6/1:239	Isa 5:4; Rom 5:6, 8:32; 1 Pet 3:18
475	Div 41.1	6/1:244	Phil 2:8; Heb 5:8
476	Div 41.10	6/1:251–52	Luke 23:39-43
477	Div 42.1	6/1:255–56	Ps 49:8
478	Div 49	6/1:270	
479	Div 50.1	6/1:271	Mark 15:17
480	Div 51	6/1:273–74	Matt 16:24
481	Div 53.1	6/1:277	
482	Div 54	6/1:280	
483	Div 57.1	6/1:287	1 Cor 1:23-24
484	Div 57.2	6/1:287	Rom 6:9
485	Div 58.1	6/1:288	Mark 16:1
486	Div 60.2	6/1:291–92	Isa 5:4; John 15:13; Gal 6:14; 1 Pet 2:21

No.	Source	SBOp	Texts
487	Div 61.2	6/1:294	
488	Div 62	6/1:295	Matt 16:21
489	Div 63	6/1:296	Matt 16:24; Rom 8:17; Gal 5:24
490	Div 66.3	6/1:301	
491	Div 67	6/1:302	Ps 69:4
492	Div 75	6/1:314	Luke 23:39–43
493	Div 87.6	6/1:333	Mark 16:1
494	Div 90.1	6/1:337	
495	Div 90.2	6/1:338	Isa 53:3; Heb 2:17
496	Div 90.5	6/1:340–41	Mark 16:1
497	Div 96.6	6/1:360	Mark 8:31
498	Div 97.2	6/1:362	Matt 10:38; Luke 14:27
499	Div 101	6/1:368	Matt 16:21; John 15:13; 2 Cor 5:16
500	Div 111.3	6/1:387	
501	Div 119	6/1:397	John 15:13
502	Div 123.1	6/1:400–401	Isa 53:2; 1 Cor 2:2; Heb 2:9
503	Sent 1.1	6/2:7	1 John 5:7-8
504	Sent 1.41	6/2:20–21	Rom 6:3-4, 6; 1 John 5:8
505	Sent 2.4	6/2:24	Rom 5:19
506	Sent 2.16	6/2:28	
507	Sent 2.18	6/2:29	Gal 6:17; Rev 7:14
508	Sent 2.24	6/2:31	Luke 23:34; Acts 8:32
509	Sent 2.31	6/2:32	
510	Sent 2.36	6/2:33	
511	Sent 2.80	6/2:40	Matt 26:39, 42; Mark 14:36; Luke 22:42
512	Sent 2.124	6/2:48	John 19:34; Heb 12:24
513	Sent 2.131	6/2:49	Matt 27:34

No.	Source	SBOp	Texts
514	Sent 2.169	6/2:56	Mark 16:1
515	Sent 3.1	6/2:59–60	Matt 16:24, 27:50; Mark 15:21; Luke 23:40-43, 46; John 19:28,30; Rom 6:6; 2 Cor 5:15; Gal 2:20
516	Sent 3.11	6/2:71	
517	Sent 3.17	6/2:75	2 Cor 5:15; 1 Pet 2:21; Rev 14:4
518	Sent 3.20	6/2:76	Matt 12:29
519	Sent 3.23	6/2:80–82	Ps 85:10-11; Matt 26:39, 42
520	Sent 3.53	6/2:94–96	
521	Sent 3.67	6/2:100–101	
522	Sent 3.70	6/2:103–106	Isa 53:3; Matt 12:29; Luke 22:44; 1 Cor 2:8
523	Sent 3.74	6/2:112–15	Gal 5:24, 6:14
524	Sent 3.79	6/2:118	John 6:54
525	Sent 3.82	6/2:119–20	Rom 5:8
526	Sent 3.83	6/2:120–21	Matt 16:21
527	Sent 3.84	6/2:121	
528	Sent 3.85	6/2:123	
529	Sent 3.87	6/2:126–29	Gal 3:13; Col 1:20
530	Sent 3.88	6/2:131–35	Isa 53:7; Matt 1:21, 27:38; Luke 23:40-43
531	Sent 3.89	6/2:136–39	Matt 12:29; Luke 11:21-22; Gal 6:14
532	Sent 3.90	6/2:139	Gal 6:14
533	Sent 3.92	6/2:148–49	1 John 3:16
534	Sent 3.94	6/2:152	Matt 16:24; Phil 2:8
535	Sent 3.97	6/2:157	
536	Sent 3.98	6/2:163	Luke 11:21-22
537	Sent 3.106	6/2:171	

No.	Source	SBOp	Texts
538	Sent 3.109	6/2:182–84	Gal 2:20, 5:24
539	Sent 3:110	6/2:188	
540	Sent 3.112	6/2:193	
541	Sent 3.113	6/2:199–201	Rom 5:8-10, 8:32; 1 John 4:10
542	Sent 3.114	6/2:205–6	Matt 26:38-39, 27:29; John 15:13; Rom 5:6-8; Gal 2:20; Eph 1:10
543	Sent 3.115	6/2:209	John 1:29
544	Sent 3.116	6/2:209–10	John 19:34; Rev 5:9
545	Sent 3.119	6/2:215–18	Zech 12:10; John 12:24-25, 15:13, 18:11; Rom 8:17; Gal 2:20; Rev 1:7, 19:9
546	Sent 3.120	6/2:219–24	Ps 85:10-11; Luke 23:40-43; Gal 5:24, 6:14
547	Sent 3.122	6/2:230–33	John 19:5, 23; 1 Pet 1:19; Rev 7:14
548	Sent 3.126:5	6/2:244	Gal 1:4
549	Sent 3.127	6/2:250	Ps 25:10; Matt 12:29
550	Par 4.1	6/2:277	
551	Par 4.5	6/2:280	John 19:23; 1 Pet 1:19
552	Par 4.6	6/2:281	Rev 7:14
553	Par 6	6/2:289–94	Isa 53:7; John 1:29; Acts 8:32; 1 Pet 2:22, 4:13 (x2)
554	Ep 1.6	7:5	Rom 14:15
555	Ep 2.4	7:15	Rev 5:9
556	Ep 2.6	7:17	Rom 14:15; Phil 3:18
557	Ep 4.1	7:25	
558	Ep 7.7	7:36	Heb 9:12
559	Ep 7.11	7:39–40	Gen 4:10; Matt 27:46; John 11:51-52; Col 1:20; Heb 12:24
560	Ep 8.2	7:48	Luke 23:40-43
561	Ep 32.1	7:86	Isa 53:4

No.	Source	SBOp	Texts
562	Mor 2.4	7:104	Gal 6:17
563	Mor 2.7	7:106	1 Pet 1:18-19
564	Mor 3:11	7:109	2 Cor 5:15
565	Mor 9.33	7:127–28	
566	Ep 51	7:143	2 Cor 5:19; Col 1:20
567	Ep 54	7:146	
568	Ep 61	7:154	1 Cor 8:11
569	Ep 62	7:155	
570	Ep 69.2	7:170	
571	Ep 69.3	7:171	
572	Bapt 2.7	7:189	Luke 23:40-43
573	Bapt 3.10	7:192	
574	Bapt 3.11	7:193	
575	Bapt 3.15	7:196	
576	Bapt 4.17	7:197	Luke 23:34; 1 Cor 2:8
577	Bapt 5.19	7:199	
578	Ep 79.1	7:211	
579	Ep 82.1	7:215	2 Cor 5:15
580	Ep 82.2	7:215	Phil 3:18
581	Ep 87.2	7:226	Phil 2:8
582	Ep 92	7:241	
583	Ep 98.4	7:251	
584	Ep 98.5	7:251	1 Cor 1:23
585	Ep 107.8	7:273	Rom 5:8, 10, 8:32; 1 Cor 2:2
586	Ep 107.9	7:273–74	John 6:63
587	Ep 107.13	7:276	Matt 20:28
588	Ep 108.2	7:278	1 Cor 2:2; Gal 6:14
589	Ep 109.1	7:280–81	John 11:52; 1 Cor 1:17, 2:8
590	Ep 126.5	7:312	Gal 6:14

No.	Source	SBOp	Texts
591	Ep 126.6	7:313–14	John 19:34, 37; 1 Cor 2:8; 2 Cor 5:16
592	Ep 126.7	7:314	Phil 3:18
593	Ep 141.2	7:339	
594	Ep 143.3	7:343	2 Cor 5:15
595	Ep 144.3	7:345	
596	Ep 158.2	7:366	
597	Ep 174.8	7:392	Heb 1:3
598	Ep 175	7:393	
599	Ep 188.1	8:10	1 John 5:6
600	Abael 4.9	8:25	
601	Abael 5.11	8:26–27	
602	Abael 5.12	8:27	
603	Abael 5.13	8:27–28	John 11:51-52
604	Abael 5.14	8:28–29	Matt 12:29; Luke 11:21; Col 1:13
605	Abael 6.15	8:29–30	2 Cor 5:14; Col 2:13-15
606	Abael 6.16	8:30–31	Isa 52:3; Rom 3:24, 5:9, 15-16, 18-19; 1 Cor 1:30, 15:21-22; Col 1:13
607	Abael 7.17	8:31–32	1 Cor 1:17, 2:8
608	Abael 7.18	8:32–33	
609	Abael 8.19	8:33–34	
610	Abael 8.20	8:34	Matt 26:28; Luke 22:20; Rom 3:24, 5:8-10; Eph 1:7
611	Abael 8.21	8:35	Rom 5:10, 8:3; Eph 1:10; Col 1:20, 2:15
612	Abael 8.22	8:35–36	
613	Abael 9.23	8:36–37	Rom 5:18, 6:6; 1 Cor 15:22
614	Abael 9.24	8:37	Rom 6:5; Gal 6:14

No.	Source	SBOp	Texts
615	Abael 9.25	8:37–38	John 6:53, 55; 1 Cor 5:7; Gal 2:20; Phil 2:8
616	Abael capit	8:39–40	
617	Ep 193	8:45	1 Cor 1:17
618	Ep 195.1	8:49	
619	Ep 195.2	8:50	Phil 3:18
620	Ep 198.1	8:54	Phil 3:18
621	Ep 203	8:62	1 Pet 1:18–19
622	Ep 219.2	8:81	Matt 27:35; John 19:23-24, 34
623	Ep 230	8:101	John 11:52
624	Ep 237.1	8:113	Gal 6:14
625	Ep 239	8:121–22	Gen 4:10; 1 Cor 6:20; 1 Pet 1:18–19
626	Ep 241.1	8:126	
627	Ep 241.2	8:126	
628	Ep 244.2	8:135	
629	Ep 250.2	8:146	Rom 6:4
630	Ep 254.4	8:159	Phil 2:8
631	Ep 256.1	8:163	
632	Ep 256.2	8:164	
633	Ep 288.1	8:203	
634	Ep 289.2	8:206	1 Cor 2:2
635	Ep 322.1	8:257	Num 21:8-9
636	Ep 322.2	8:257	
637	Ep 328	8:264	Ps 49:8
638	Ep 331	8:269–70	Phil 3:18
639	Ep 334	8:273	Matt 27:35; John 19:23
640	Ep 338.1	8:278	Luke 23:40-43
641	Ep 348.2	8:292	Phil 3:18
642	Ep 363.1	8:312	Phil 3:18; Heb 9:18; 1 Pet 1:19
643	Ep 363.2	8:313	

No.	Source	SBOp	Texts
644	Ep 363.4	8:314	
645	Ep 363.5	8:315	
646	Ep 363.6	8:316	
647	Ep 363.7	8:317	
648	Ep 393.1	8:364	Luke 23:46; John 3:16, 12:32
649	Ep 393.2	8:366	1 John 5:6; Rev 7:14
650	Ep 398.2	8:378	
651	Ep 403:1	8:383–84	Gal 6:14
652	Ep 449	8:427	
653	Ep 457	8:433	1 Cor 1:17-18; Phil 3:18
654	Ep 458.3	8:435	Heb 9:18; 1 Pet 1:19
655	Ep 458.4	8:436	
656	Ep 459	8:437	
657	Ep 462.2	8:439–40	Luke 22:42; Rom 8:3; Phil 2:8
658	Ep 462.4	8:441	1 Cor 6:20; 2 Cor 5:15; 1 Pet 1:19
659	Ep 462.8	8:444–45	Rom 4:25; 1 Cor 15:3
660	Ep 501	8:458	
661	Ep 510	8:468	Ps 22:6; Gal 2:20; Phil 2:8
662	Ep 515	8:474	Phil 2:8
663	Ep 521	8:483	
664	Ep 540	8:507	Rom 14:15
665	Ep 541	8:508	Phil 2:8
666	Ep 544	8:511–12	
667	Ben var 4[1]	526:184–85	Matt 26:38

[1] This sermon is not found in SBOp but was published by Gaetano Raciti: "Un nouveau sermon de S. Bernard—*Verba lectionis huiu*—pour la fête de saint Benoît," Coll 60 (1998): 60–107. On pp. 60–68 and 100–105 is Raciti's explanation of why he considers it to be authentic. The sermon is found in SCh 526, where an introduction is provided on pp. 161–72.

Appendix II

INDEX OF BIBLICAL TEXTS CITED[1]

Biblical Text	Passage Number	Biblical Text	Passage Number
Gen 4:10	17, 96, 263, 559, 625		474, 486
		Isa 52:3	231, 606
Lev 9:3	*193, 216,* 225, *233, 454*	Isa 53:2-33	7–38, 41, 69, 119, 287, 295, 345, 363, 375, 378, 390, 495, 502, 522
Num 21:8-9	304, 635		
Ps 22:6-7	38, 71, 287, 304, 322, 661		
Ps 22:14	14	Isa 53:4-6	37, 42, 75, 83, 87, 119, 192, 241, 287, 295, 375–76, 378, 439, 561
Ps 22:16	84, 91, 201–2, 286		
Ps 22:17	286, 344, 375		
Ps 22:18	*278*		
Ps 25:10	210, 395, 549		
Ps 49:8	22, 201, 235, *477,* 637	Isa 53:7-9	*41,* 60, 103, 124, 138, 170, *186,* 216, 237, 277, 288, *322,* 324, 354, 397, 432, 468, 530, 553
Ps 69:4	152, 216, 286, 344, 458, 469, 491		
Ps 85:10-11	103, 265, *266, 267, 268–69,* 270, *381,* 428, 519, 546		
		Isa 53:12	30, 43, 99, 134, 157, 175, 216, 273, 287–88, 292, 344, 458
Isa 5:4	31, 355, 448, 458,		

[1] Where I have for any reason listed an allusion not found in SBOp, the passage number is listed in italics.

263

Biblical Text	Passage Number	Biblical Text	Passage Number
Zech 12:10	545		511, 522, 657
2 Macc 1:24	149	Matt 27:29	292, 446, 542
Matt 1:21	173–74, 212, 214,	= Mark 15:17-20	390, 479
	223, 530	= John 19:5	228, 547
Matt 10:38	498	Matt 27:32	261
= Luke 14:27	406, 455, 498	= Mark 15:21	515
Matt 12:29	19, 197, 268, 302,	= Luke 23:26	123, 261
	360, 362, 440,	Matt 27:34	66, 513
	442, 518, 522,	Matt 27:35	278, 622, 639
	531, 549, 604	= John 19:23-24	125, 242, 264,
= Luke 11:21-22	169, 215, 268,		337–38, 547,
	302, 327,		551, 622, 639
	360–62, 430,	Matt 27:38-44	47, 78, 112, 281,
	440, 442, 449,		302–5, *306*,
	531, 536, 604		307, 314, 530
Matt 16:21[2]	*458, 460, 488,*	= Mark 15:29, 32	302
	499, 526	Matt 27:46	377, 559
= Mark 8:31	23, *497*	Matt 27:48	64
Matt 16:24	27, 123, 230, 303,	Matt 27:50	369, 515
	309, 417, 426,	Matt 27:51	12, 285, 299, 444
	480, 489, 515,	Matt 27:54	44, 47, 228, *229*
	534	= Mark 15:39	42–43
Matt 20:22-23	88, 140, 213, 399,	Mark 8:31	*See under* Matt
	426		16:21
Matt 20:28	73, 373, 587	Mark 14:36	*See under* Matt
Matt 26:28	181, 610		26:39, 42
= Luke 22:20	181, 214, 610	Mark 15:15	292
Matt 26:38	427, 470, 542, 667	= John 19:1	144
Matt 26:39, 42	140, 270, 324,	Mark 15:17-20	*See under* Matt
	410, 412, 511,		27:29
	519, 542	Mark 15:21	*See under* Matt
= Mark 14:36	140, 412, 436, 511		27:32
= Luke 22:42, 44	140, 292, 323,	Mark 15:26	419
	402, 427, 451,	= John 19:19-22	303

---

[2] These are all listed by SBOp as allusions to Matt 16:22 but are included here because in each of these cases there is a clear reference back to Christ's mention of the passion in 16:21.

Biblical Text	Passage Number	Biblical Text	Passage Number
Mark 15:29, 32	*See under* Matt 27:38-44		225, 289, 351, 356, 543, 553
Mark 15:39	*See under* Matt 27:54	John 3:14	376
Mark 16:1	8, 319, 485, 493, 496, *514*	John 3:16	128, 134, 648
		John 6:53-55	53, 73, 107, 132, 247, *262*, 282, 318, *524*, 615
Luke 11:21-22	*See under* Matt 12:29	John 6:63	25, 42, 143, 233, 330, 438, 586
Luke 14:27	*See under* Matt 10:38	John 10:11	53
Luke 22:20	*See under* Matt 26:27-28	John 10:17-18	138, 202, 239, 288, 411, 461, 468
Luke 22:37	216, 312	John 11:49-53	41, 98, 302, 329, 365, 559, 589, 603, 623
Luke 22:42, 44	*See under* Matt 26:39, 42		
Luke 23:21	293	John 12:24-25	13, 324, 545
= John 19:15	78, 176, 246, 278, 310	John 12:32	28, 31, 83, 112, 196, 304, 346–47, 465–67, 648
Luke 23:26	*See under* Matt 27:32		
Luke 23:27-28	283, 320, 407, 422	John 15:13	23, 84, 128–29, 133, 182, 194, 251, 253, 269, 288, 304, 370, 458, 486, 499, 501, 542, 545
Luke 23:33	312		
Luke 23:34	*3*, 31, 156, 180, 186, 277, 292–93, 508, 576		
Luke 23:39-43	31, *42*, 47, 228, *229*, 274, 376, 380, 391, 473, 476, 492, 515, 530, 546, 560, 572, 640	John 18:11	545
		John 19:1	*See under* Mark 15:15
		John 19:5	*See under* Matt 27:29
Luke 23:46	39, 515, 648	John 19:15	*See under* Luke 23:21
Luke 23:56	111	John 19:17	129, 145, 320, 407
Luke 24:26	228, 342, 462	John 19:21-22	*See under* Mark 15:26
Luke 24:46	13, 342, 346, 462		
John 1:29	47, 124, *144*, 188, 193, 211, 221,	John 19:23-24	*See under* Matt 27:35

Biblical Text	Passage Number	Biblical Text	Passage Number
John 19:28	152, 515	Rom 5:15-19	149–50, 231, 291, 367, 505, 606, 613
John 19:30	79, 112, 201, 259, 288, 304, *305*, 470, *472*, 515	Rom 6:3-4	153, 315, 348–49, 504, 629
John 19:34-35	84, 129, 201, 231, 250, 306, 329, 334, 369, 392, 400, 402, 439, 446, 512, 544, 591, 622	Rom 6:5	105, 153, 158, 217, 300, 316, 417, 455, 614
		Rom 6:6	105, 348, 417, 504, 515, 613
John 19:36	439, 455	Rom 6:9-10	74, 108, 307, 313, 315, 424, 471, 484
John 19:37	121, 187, 591		
John 19:39	64		
John 20:25, 27	54–55, 344, 372, 446	Rom 8:3	114, 291, 611, 657
Acts 8:32-33	*103, 124, 170,* 186, *216*, 277, *286*, 287, 322, 354, 432, *508, 553*	Rom 8:17	27, 132, 240, 317, 349, 376, 417, 456, 489, 545
		Rom 8:32	16, 128, 175, 183, 288, 354, 434, 474, 541, 585
Acts 20:28	101, 189		
Rom 3:24-25	30, 105, 187, 215, 288, 606, 610	Rom 14:9	97, 348
		Rom 14:15	50, *51*, 78, 554, 556, 664
Rom 4:25	2, 66, 131, 214, 263, 288, 315, 317, *659*	1 Cor 1:17	589, 607, 617, 653
		1 Cor 1:18	132, 314, 364, 419, 653
Rom 5:6-8	136, 149, 219, 251, 268, 288, 344, 450, 458, 474, 525, 541– 42, 585, 610	1 Cor 1:23	314, 483, *584*
		1 Cor 1:24	483
		1 Cor 1:30	26, *32*, 33, 85, 152, 236, 247, 297, 394, 606
Rom 5:9	541, 606, 610		
Rom 5:10	21, 128, 208, 215, 251, 288, 381, *450*, 541, 585, 610–11	1 Cor 2:2	15, 65, 67, 90, 129, 143, 194, 233, 376–77, 447, 502, 585, 588, 634
Rom 5:12	150, 231		

Biblical Text	Passage Number	Biblical Text	Passage Number
1 Cor 2:8	47, 56, 74, 129, 144, 156, 294, 313, 379, 522, 576, 589, 591, 607		486, 523, 531, 532, 546, 588, 590, 614, 624, 651
1 Cor 5:7	314, *615*	Gal 6:17	421, *507*, 562
1 Cor 6:20	399, 433, 625, 658	Eph 1:7	610
1 Cor 7:23	162	Eph 1:10	108, 466, 542, 611
1 Cor 8:11	156, 568	Eph 2:13-14	1, 35, 62, 268, 396, 413, 427
1 Cor 11:26	195, 262, 390	Eph 5:2	304; 354
1 Cor 11:27	301, 334	Phil 2:8	7, *61*, 117, 125,
1 Cor 15:3	*2, 66, 131, 214, 288, 315,* 659		154–55, 159, 256, 258, 288, 304, 397, *468*,
1 Cor 15:21-22	149, 150, 231, 424, 606, 613		475, 534, 581, 615, 630, 657,
2 Cor 5:14-15	59, 359, 463, *464*, 515, 517, 564, 579, 594, 605, 658		661, 662, 665
		Phil 3:18	142, 317, 556, 580, 592, 619– 20, 638, 641, *642, 653*
2 Cor 5:16	25, 57, 107, 111, 143, 233, 398, 447, 499, 591	Col 1:13	30, 102, 158, 441, 604, 606
2 Cor 5:18-19	2, 84, 171, 286, 566	Col 1:20	1, 35, 236, 347, 358, 381, 396,
2 Cor 5:21	38, 105, 291		529, 559, 566,
2 Cor 8:9	152, 321, 364		611
Gal 1:4	100, 128, 425, 548	Col 1:24	252, 421
Gal 2:20	515, 538, *542, 545*, 615, 661	Col 2:13-15	58, 235, 301, 336, 386, 396, 404,
Gal 2:21	175		428, 430, 435,
Gal 3:13	114, 529		605, 611
Gal 5:24	52, 106, 139, 230, 489, 523, 538, 546	Heb 1:3	145, 216, 220, 225, 231, 357, 597
Gal 6:14	37, 132–33, 163, 178, 194, 219, 244, 314, 347, *364, 420*, 437,	Heb 2:9	9, 251, 502
		Heb 2:14	302, 442
		Heb 2:17-18	42, 75, 116–20, 367, *495*

Biblical Text	Passage Number	Biblical Text	Passage Number
Heb 5:8	75, 116, *117*, 367, 475	1 Pet 3:18	450, *474*
		1 Pet 3:19	108
Heb 6:6	74, 108, 455	1 Pet 4:13	123, 175, 247, 262, 316, 405, 553
Heb 9:12	85, 135, 235, 237, 257, 334, 558		
Heb 9:14	185, 238, 374, *428*	1 John 2:1-2	157, 175, 359
Heb 9:15-19	356, 395, 642, 654	1 John 3:16	450, 472, 533
Heb 9:22	218, 331	1 John 4:10	21, *128*, 251, 364, 541
Heb 9:28	294		
Heb 10:29	*295*	1 John 5:6-8	76, 328–30, 332–35, 400–401, 440, 503–4, 599, 649
Heb 12:2	259		
Heb 12:24	263, 431, 512, 559		
Heb 13:12-13	71		
1 Pet 1:18-19	*189*, 329, 355, 433, 547, *551*, 563, 621, 625, 642, 654, *658*	Rev 1:5	145, 175, 198, 385
		Rev 1:7	545
		Rev 5:6	311
1 Pet 2:21	117, 486, 517	Rev 5:9	311, 399, 544, 555
1 Pet 2:22-23	41, 105, 124, 138, *144*, 186, 216, 221, 251, 273, 277, 322, 358, 454, 461, 470, 553	Rev 5:12	289, 310–11, 313
		Rev 7:14	186, 221, 306, 329, 388, 507, 547, 552, 649
		Rev 14:4	170, 240, 296, 348, 383, *384*, 387, 517
1 Pet 2:24	48, 66, *144*, *291*, 348	Rev 19:9	400, 545

BIBLIOGRAPHY

Primary

Abailard, Peter. Sic et non: *A Critical Edition*, vol. 1. Edited by Blanche B. Boyer and Richard McKeon. Chicago and London: University of Chicago Press, 1976.

Anselm of Canterbury. *The Major Works*. Oxford: OUP, 1998.

Augustine. *The Trinity*. Translated by Edmund Hill. The Works of Saint Augustine 1:5. Brooklyn, NY: New City Press, 1990.

Bernard of Clairvaux. *Sermons for the Seasons of the Year*. Translated by William B. Flower. London: John Masters, 1861.

———. *St. Bernard's Sermons for the Seasons and Principal Festivals of the Year*. 3 vols. Translated by Ailbe J. Luddy. Dublin: Browne and Nolan, 1921–25.

———. *Treatises III: On Grace and Free Choice, In Praise of the New Knighthood*. Translated by Daniel O'Donovan. CF 19. Kalamazoo, MI: Cistercian Publications, 1977.

———. *The Steps of Humility*. Edited by George B. Burch. Notre Dame: University of Notre Dame Press, 1963.

Bono, Donato. "Il *Servo Sofferente* (Is 53) nelle opere di san Bernardo." *Rivista cistercense* 28 (2011): 49–86.

Burnett, Charles S. F. "Peter Abelard, *Confessio fidei 'universis'*: A Critical Edition of Abelard's Reply to Accusations of Heresy." *Medieval Studies* 48 (1986): 111–38.

Carra de Vaux Saint-Cyr, M.-B. "Disputatio catholicorum patrum adversus dogmata Petri Abaelardi." *Revue des sciences philosophiques et théologiques* 47 (1963): 205–20.

CETEDOC. *Thesaurus Sancti Bernardi Claraevallensis: Index formarum singulorum operum; Concordantia formarum*. Turnhout: Brepols, 1987.

Fairweather, Eugene R., ed. *A Scholastic Miscellany: Anselm to Ockham*, Library of Christian Classics, vol. 10. London: SCM, 1956.

Hardy, Edward R., with Cyril C. Richardson, eds. *Christology of the Later Fathers*, Library of Christian Classics, vol. 3. London: SCM, 1954.

Leclercq, Jean, Henri M. Rochais, and Charles H. Talbot, eds. *Sancti Bernardi Opera*. 8 vols. Rome: Storia e Letteratura, 1962–92.

Minnis, Alastair J., and Alexander B. Scott, eds. *Medieval Literary Theory and Criticism c. 1100–c. 1375: The Commentary-Tradition.* Revised ed. Oxford: OUP, 1991.

Raciti, Gaetano. "Un nouveau sermon de S. Bernard—*Verba lectionis huius*—pour la fête de saint Benoît." Coll 60 (1998): 60–107.

Secondary

Akin, Daniel L. "Bernard of Clairvaux: Evangelical of the 12th Century (An Analysis of His Soteriology)." *Criswell Theological Review* 4 (1990): 327–50.

———. "Bernard of Clairvaux: Evangelical of the Twelfth Century (A Critical Analysis of His Soteriology)." PhD thesis, University of Texas at Arlington, 1989.

———. "Bernard of Clairvaux and the Atonement." In *The Church at the Dawn of the 21st Century: Essays in Honor of Dr. W. A. Criswell,* edited by P. Patterson, J. Pretlove, and L. Pantoja, 103–28. Dallas: Criswell Publications, 1989.

Altermatt, Alberich. "Christus pro nobis: Die Christologie Bernhards von Clairvaux in den 'Sermonum per annum.'" AC 33 (1977): 3–176.

Anderson, John D. "Paul in Book 5 of the *De consideratione* of Bernard of Clairvaux." CSQ 42 (2007): 137–50.

Aulén, Gustaf. *Christus Victor: An Historical Study of the Three Main Types of the Idea of the Atonement.* 2nd ed. London: SPCK, 1970.

Billy, Dennis J. "Redemption and the Order of Love in Bernard of Clairvaux's *Sermon 20 on 'The Canticle of Canticles.'*" *Downside Review* 112 (1994): 88–102.

Bond, H. Lawrence. "Another Look at Abelard's Commentary on Romans 3:26." http://www.vanderbilt.edu/AnS/religious_studies/SBL2004/larrybond.pdf.

Bouton, Jean de la Croix. *Bibliographie bernardine 1891–1957.* Paris: P. Lethielleux, 1958.

Bredero, Adriaan H. *Bernard of Clairvaux: Between Cult and History.* Edinburgh: T&T Clark, 1996.

Brésard, Luc. *Bernard et Origène, commentent le Cantique.* Forges: Abbaye Notre-Dame de Scourmont, 1983.

———. "Bernard et Origène: Le symbolisme nuptial dans leurs oeuvres sur le Cantique." Cîteaux 36 (1985): 129–51.

Brigitte, Sr. "Jésus et Jésus crucifié chez saint Bernard." Coll 57 (1995): 219–37.

Burns, J. Patout. "The Concept of Satisfaction in Medieval Redemption Theory." *Theological Studies* 36 (1975): 285–304.

Buytaert, Eligius M. "The Anonymous *Capitula Haeresum Petri Abaelardi* and the Synod of Sens, 1140." *Antonianum* 43 (1968): 419–60.

Carlson, David. "The Practical Theology of Saint Bernard and the Date of the *De laude novae militiae*." In *Erudition at God's Service*, edited by John R. Sommerfeldt, 133–47. CS 98. Kalamazoo, MI: Cistercian Publications, 1987.

Cave, Sydney. *The Doctrine of the Work of Christ*. London: University of London Press and Hodder and Stoughton, 1937.

Châtillon, Jean. "L'influence de S. Bernard sur la pensée scolastique au XIIᵉ et au XIIIᵉ siècle." In *Saint Bernard théologien*. ASOC 9, no. 3-4 (July–December 1953): 268–88.

Chauvin, Benoît, ed. *Mélanges à la mémoire du Père Anselme Dimier* I/2. Arbois: Benoît Chauvin, 1987.

Chen, Sheryl F. "Bernard's Prayer before the Crucifix That Embraced Him: Cistercians and Devotion to the Wounds of Christ." CSQ 29 (1994): 23–54.

Clanchy, Michael T. *Abelard: A Medieval Life*. Oxford: Blackwell, 1997.

Colish, Marcia. "Systematic Theology and Theological Renewal in the Twelfth Century." *Journal of Medieval and Renaissance Studies* 18 (1988): 135–56.

Daniélou, Jean. "Saint Bernard et les pères grecs." In *Saint Bernard théologien*, ASOC 9, no. 3-4 (July–December 1953): 46–51.

Déchanet, Jean-Marie. "La christologie de S. Bernard." In *Saint Bernard théologien*, ASOC 9, no. 3-4 (July–December 1953): 78–91.

———. *William of St. Thierry: The Man and His Work*. CS 10. Spencer, MA: Cistercian Publications, 1972.

Dietz, Elias. "Saint Bernard's Sermon 42 *De diversis*: Taking a Closer Look." CSQ 39 (2004): 103–26.

Doyle, Matthew A. *Bernard of Clairvaux and the Schools*. Spoleto: Fondazione Centro Italiano di Studi sull'alto Medioevo, 2005.

Dumontier, Pierre. *Saint Bernard et la Bible*. Paris: Desclée de Brouwer, 1953.

Eastman, Patrick W. H. "The Christology in Bernard's *De Diligendo Deo*." CSQ 23 (1988): 119–27.

Elder, E. Rozanne. "The Christology of William of Saint Thierry." RTAM 58 (1991): 79–112.

Evans, Gillian R. *Anselm*. London: Continuum, 2005, reprint of 1989.

———. *Anselm and Talking about God*. Oxford: OUP, 1978.

———. "*Cur Deus Homo*: St. Bernard's Theology of the Redemption; A Contribution to the Contemporary Debate." *Studia Theologica* 36 (1982): 27–36.

————. *The Mind of St. Bernard of Clairvaux*. Oxford: OUP, 1983.

Figuet, Jean. "La Bible de Bernard: Données et ouvertures." SCh 380:237–69.

————. "Des jeux de mots de saint Bernard . . . à saint Bernard." Coll 52 (1990): 66–83.

France, James. *Medieval Images of Saint Bernard of Clairvaux*. CS 210. Kalamazoo, MI: Cistercian Publications, 2006.

Franks, Robert S. *A History of the Doctrine of the Work of Christ in Its Ecclesiastical Development*, vol. 1. London: Hodder and Stoughton, 1919.

Frischmuth, Gertrud. *Die paulinische Konzeption in der Frömmigkeit Bernhards von Clairvaux*. Gütersloh: C. Bertelsmann, 1933.

Gilson, Étienne. *The Mystical Theology of Saint Bernard*. London: Sheed and Ward, 1940.

Gössman, Elisabeth. "Dialektische und rhetorische Implikationen der Auseinandersetzung zwischen Abaelard und Bernhard von Clairvaux um die Gotteserkenntnis." In *Sprache und Erkenntnis im Mittelalter*, vol. 2, edited by Jan P. Beckmann and others, 890–902. Berlin and New York: Walter de Gruyter, 1981.

————. "Zur Auseinandersetzung zwischen Abaelard und Bernhard von Clairvaux um die Gotteserkenntnis im Glauben." In *Petrus Abaelardus (1079–1142)*, edited by Rudolf Thomas, 233–42. Trier: Paulinus-Verlag, 1980.

Gottschick, Johannes. "Studien zur Versöhnungslehre des Mittelalters." ZKG 22 (1901): 378–438.

Green, Joel B., and Mark D. Baker. *Recovering the Scandal of the Cross: Atonement in New Testament and Contemporary Contexts*. Downers Grove, IL: IVP, 2000.

Grensted, Laurence W. *A Short History of the Doctrine of the Atonement*. Manchester: Manchester University Press; and London: Longmans, Green and Co., 1920.

Grill, Leopold. "Die neunzehn 'Capitula' Bernhards von Clairvaux gegen Abälard." *Historisches Jahrbuch* 80 (1961): 230–39.

Grosse, Sven. "Der Messias als Geist und sein Schatten: Leiblichkeit Christi und Mystik in der Alten Kirche und bei Bernhard von Clairvaux." AC 58 (2008): 170–222.

————. "*Spiritus ante faciem nostram Christus Dominus*: Zur Christozentrik der Mystik Bernhards von Clairvaux." *Theologie und Philosophie* 76 (2001): 185–205.

Hagenbach, Karl R. *A History of Christian Doctrines*, vol. 2, translation of 5th German edition of 1867. Edinburgh: T&T Clark, 1880.

Hänsler, Basilius. "Christi Blut und das Heilige Land, sowie Christi Blut und die Ordensleute nach dem Hl. Bernhard." *Cistercienser Chronik* 37 (1925): 59–61.

———. "Christi Blut und die Irrlehre bzw: Das Schisma nach dem Hl. Bernhard." *Cistercienser Chronik* 35 (1923): 133–36.

———. "Vom Blut Christi in St. Bernhards Kapitelreden." *Cistercienser Chronik* 40 (1928): 110–14.

Häring, Nikolaus M. "Abelard Yesterday and Today." In *Pierre Abélard: Pierre le Vénérable*, 341–403. Paris: Éditions du centre national de la recherche scientifique, 1975.

———. "Die Vierzehn *Capitula Haeresum Petri Abaelardi*." Cîteaux 31 (1980): 35–52.

Harnack, Adolf. *History of Dogma*, vol. 6. New York: Russell and Russell, 1958.

———. *Lehrbuch der Dogmengeschichte*, vol. 3, 4th ed. Tübingen: J. C. B. Mohr (Paul Siebeck), 1910.

Hendrix, Guido. *Conspectus bibliographicus sancti Bernardi ultimi patrum 1989–1993*. RTAM Supplementa 2, 2nd ed. Leuven: Peeters, 1995.

———, ed. *Index biblicus in opera omnia S. Bernardi.* Turnhout: Brepols, 1998 = SBOp 9.

Hesbert, René-Jean. "Saint Bernard et l'eucharistie." In *Mélanges saint Bernard*, 156–76. Dijon: Association des amis de saint Bernard, 1954.

Hogg, David S. *Anselm of Canterbury: The Beauty of Theology*. Aldershot, Hants, and Burlington, VT: Ashgate, 2004.

Holdsworth, Christopher. "Were the Sermons on the Song of Songs Ever Preached?" In *Medieval Monastic Preaching*, edited by Carolyn Muessig, 295–318. Leiden: Brill, 1998.

Hopkins, Jasper. *A Companion to the Study of St Anselm*. Minneapolis: University of Minnesota Press, 1972.

Janauschek, Leopold. *Bibliographia Bernardina qua sancti Bernardi primi abbatis Claravallensis operum cum omnium tum singulorum editiones ac versiones vitas et tractatus de eo scriptos.* Vienna: Alfred Hölder, 1891.

Jolivet, Jean. *Arts du langage et théologie chez Abélard*, 2nd ed. Paris: J. Vrin, 1982.

———. "Sur quelques critiques de la théologie d'Abélard." *Archives d'histoire doctrinale et littéraire du moyen âge* 38 (1963): 7–51.

Kelly, John N. D. *Early Christian Doctrines*, 5th ed. London: Adam and Charles Black, 1977.

Kleineidam, Erich. "Wissen, Wissenschaft, Theologie bei Bernhard von Clairvaux." In *Bernhard von Clairvaux: Mönch und Mystiker*, edited by Joseph Lortz, 128–67. Wiesbaden: F. Steiner, 1955.

Klibansky, Raymond. "Peter Abailard and Bernard of Clairvaux: A Letter by Abailard." *Mediaeval and Renaissance Studies* 5 (1961): 1–27.

Knoch, Wendelin. "Der Streit zwischen Bernhard von Clairvaux und Petrus Abaelard—ein exemplarisches Ringen um verantworteten Glauben." *Freiburger Zeitschrift für Philosophie und Theologie* 38 (1991): 299–315.

Knotzinger, Kurt. "Kreuzweg nach St. Bernhard von Clairvaux." *Cistercienser Chronik* 74 (1967): 105–10.

Knowles, David. "The Middle Ages 604–1350." In *A History of Christian Doctrine*, edited by Hubert Cunliffe-Jones, 227–86. Edinburgh: T&T Clark, 1978.

Köpf, Ulrich. "Kreuz IV: Mittelalter." In *Theologische Realenzyklopädie*, vol. 9, 732–61. Berlin and New York: Walter de Gruyter, 1990.

————. "Monastische und scholastische Theologie." In *Bernhard von Clairvaux und der Beginn der Moderne*, edited by Dieter R. Bauer and Gotthard Fuchs, 96–135. Innsbruck and Vienna: Tyrolia, 1996.

————. "Die Passion Christi in der lateinischen religiösen und theologischen Literatur des Spätmittelalters." In *Die Passion Christi in Literatur und Kunst des Spätmittelalters*, edited by Walter Haug and Burghart Wachinger, 21–41. Tübingen: Max Niemeyer, 1993.

————. "Schriftauslegung als Ort der Kreuzestheologie Bernhards von Clairvaux." In *Bernhard von Clairvaux und der Beginn der Moderne*, edited by Dieter R. Bauer and Gotthard Fuchs, 194–213. Innsbruck and Vienna: Tyrolia, 1996.

————. "Zentrale Gedanken der monastischen Theologie Bernhards von Clairvaux." *Cistercienser Chronik* 111 (2004): 49–64.

Landgraf, Artur M. *Dogmengeschichte der Frühscholastik* 2/2. Regensburg: F. Pustet, 1954.

————. "Der heilige Bernhard in seinem Verhältnis zur Theologie des zwölften Jahrhunderts." In *Bernhard von Clairvaux: Mönch und Mystiker*, edited by Joseph Lortz, 44–62. Wiesbaden: Franz Steiner, 1955.

————. "Probleme um den Hl. Bernhard von Clairvaux." *Cistercienser Chronik* 61 (1954): 1–16.

Lane, Anthony N. S. "Bernard of Clairvaux: A Forerunner of John Calvin?" In *Bernardus Magister*, edited by John R. Sommerfeldt, 533–45. CS 135. Kalamazoo, MI: Cistercian Publications, 1992.

————. "Bernard of Clairvaux:Theologian of the Cross." In *The Atonement Debate*, edited by D.Tidball, D. Hilborn, and J.Thacker, 249–66. Grand Rapids, MI: Zondervan, 2008.

————. *Calvin and Bernard of Clairvaux*. Princeton, NJ: Princeton Theological Seminary, 1996.

Leclercq, Jean. "Aux sources des sermons sur les Cantiques." RESB 1:275–98 = R Ben 69 (1959): 237–57.

————. *Bernard of Clairvaux and the Cistercian Spirit*. CS 16. Kalamazoo, MI: Cistercian Publications, 1976.

————, and Jean Figuet. "La Bible dans les homélies de S. Bernard sur 'Missus est.'" RESB 3:213–48 = *Studi medievali* 5 (1964): 613–48.

————. "Le cheminement biblique de la pensée de S. Bernard." RESB 4:11–33 = *Studi medievali* 8 (1967): 1–22.

————. "La concordance de S. Bernard." RESB 4:401–7 = Cîteaux 32 (1981): 357–62.

————. "La dévotion médiévale envers le crucifié." *La maison dieu* 75 (1963): 119–32.

————. "Un document sur les débuts des Templiers." RESB 2:87–99 = *Revue d'histoire ecclésiastique* 52 (1957): 81–91.

————. "Les écrits de Geoffroy d'Auxerre." RESB 1:27–46 = R Ben 62 (1952): 274–91.

————. "*Errata corrigenda* dans l'édition de S. Bernard." RESB 4:409–18.

————. "Études sur le vocabulaire monastique du moyen âge." *Studia Anselmiana* 48 (1961).

————. "Études sur saint Bernard et le texte de ses écrits." ASOC 9 (1953).

————. "Les formes successives de la lettre-traité de saint Bernard contre Abélard." RESB 4:265–83 = R Ben 78 (1968): 87–105.

————. "General Introduction to the Works of Saint Bernard (III)." CSQ 40 (2005): 378–92.

————. "The Image of St. Bernard in the Late Medieval *Exempla* Literature." *Thought* 54 (1979): 291–302.

————. "Introduction to Saint Bernard's *Sermones varii*." CSQ 43 (2008): 147–60.

————. "Introduction to the *Sentences* of Bernard of Clairvaux." CSQ 46 (2011): 277–304.

————. "The Joy of Dying according to St Bernard." CSQ 25 (1990): 163–74.

————. "Les lettres de Guillaume de Saint-Thierry à saint Bernard." RESB 4:349–70 = R Ben 79 (1969): 375–91.

————. *The Love of Learning and the Desire for God: A Study of Monastic Culture.* New York: Fordham University Press, 1961.

————. *Memoirs: From Grace to Grace.* Petersham, MA: St. Bede's, 2000.

————. "Le mystère de l'ascension dans les sermons de saint Bernard." RESB 5:117–24 = Coll 15 (1953): 81–88.

————. "The Mystery of the Ascension in the Sermons of Saint Bernard." CSQ 25 (1990): 9–16.

————. "Naming the Theologies of the Early Twelfth Century." *Mediaeval Studies* 53 (1991): 327–36.

————. "De quelques procédés du style biblique de S. Bernard." RESB 3:249–66 = Cîteaux 5 (1964): 330–46.

————. *Recueil d'études sur saint Bernard et ses écrits.* 5 vols. Rome: Storia e Letteratura, 1962–92.

————. "The Renewal of Theology." In *Renaissance and Renewal in the Twelfth Century,* edited by Robert L. Benson and Giles Constable, 68–87. Cambridge, MA: Harvard University Press, 1982.

————. "Le saint Bernard de Gilson: Une théologie de la vie monastique." *Doctor communis* 38 (1985): 227–33.

————. "Saint Bernard docteur." RESB 2:387–90 = Coll 16 (1954): 284–86.

————. "Saint Bernard et Origène d'après un manuscrit de Madrid." RESB 2:373–85 = R Ben 59 (1949): 183–95.

————. "S. Bernard et la théologie monastique du XIIᵉ siècle." In *Saint Bernard théologien,* ASOC 9, no. 3-4 (July–December 1953): 7–23.

————. "S. Bernard et la tradition biblique d'après les Sermons sur les Cantiques." RESB 1:298–319 = *Sacris erudiri* 11 (1960): 225–48.

————. "S. Bernard prêcheur." RESB 4:81–93 = *Mélanges offerts à M.-D. Chenu,* 345–62. Paris, 1967.

————. "Sur le caractère littéraire des sermons de S. Bernard." RESB 3:163–210 = *Studi medievali* 7 (1966): 701–44.

————, and Henri Rochais. "La tradition des sermons liturgiques de S. Bernard." RESB 2:203–60 = *Scriptorium* 15 (1961): 240–84.

————. "Were the Sermons on the Song of Songs Delivered in Chapter?" In Bernard of Clairvaux, *On the Song of Songs II,* vii–xxx. CF 39. Kalamazoo, MI: Cistercian Publications, 1976.

Leff, Gordon. *Medieval Thought: St Augustine to Ockham.* Harmondsworth: Penguin, 1958.

Linhardt, Robert. *Die Mystik des Hl. Bernhard von Clairvaux.* Munich: Natur und Kultur, 1923.

Little, Edward. "Bernard and Abelard at the Council of Sens, 1140." In *Bernard of Clairvaux: Studies Presented to Dom Jean Leclercq*, 55–71. Washington, DC: Cistercian Publications, 1973.

Little, Edward F. "The Source of the *Capitula* of Sens of 1140." In *Studies in Medieval Cistercian History II*, edited by John R. Sommerfeldt, 87–91. CS 24. Kalamazoo, MI: Cistercian Publications, 1976.

Loofs, Friedrich. *Leitfaden zum Studium der Dogmengeschichte*, 4th ed. Halle: Max Niemeyer, 1906.

Lubac, Henri de. *Medieval Exegesis*, vol. 1. Grand Rapids, MI: Eerdmans; and Edinburgh: T&T Clark, 1998.

Luscombe, David E. "Berengar, Defender of Peter Abelard." RTAM 33 (1966): 319–37.

———. *The School of Peter Abelard*. Cambridge: CUP, 1969.

McDonnell, Kilian. "Spirit and Experience in Bernard of Clairvaux." *Theological Studies* 58 (1997): 3–18.

McGinn, Bernard. *The Growth of Mysticism*, vol. 2 of *The Presence of God: A History of Western Medieval Mysticism*. London: SCM, 1995.

McGrath, Alister. "The Moral Theory of the Atonement: An Historical and Theological Critique." *Scottish Journal of Theology* 38 (1985): 205–20.

McGuire, Brian P. *The Difficult Saint: Bernard of Clairvaux and His Tradition*. CS 126. Kalamazoo, MI: Cistercian Publications, 1991.

McIntyre, John. *St Anselm and His Critics. A Re-Interpretation of the* Cur Deus Homo. Edinburgh and London: Oliver and Boyd, 1954.

Manning, Eugène. *Bibliographie bernardine (1957–1970)*, Documentation cistercienne 6. Rochefort: 1972.

Marenbon, John. *The Philosophy of Peter Abelard*. Cambridge: CUP, 1997.

Merton, Thomas. *The Last of the Fathers*. London: Hollis and Carter, 1954.

Mews, Constant J. "The Council of Sens (1141): Abelard, Bernard and the Fear of Social Upheaval." *Speculum* 77 (2002): 342–82.

———. "The List of Heresies Imputed to Peter Abelard." R Ben 95 (1985): 73–110.

———. "The *Sententiae* of Peter Abelard." RTAM 53 (1986): 130–84.

Mohrmann, Christine. "Observations sur la langue et le style de saint Bernard." SBOp 2:ix–xxxiii.

Montanari, Antonio. "Le Crucifié embrassant saint Bernard: Une relecture de la scène." Coll 66 (2004): 59–65.

Murray, A. Victor. *Abelard and St Bernard: A Study in Twelfth Century 'Modernism.'* Manchester: Manchester University Press, 1967.

Olmedo, M. José. "Devoción de san Bernardo a la pasión." *Cistercium* 26 (1953): 41–44.

Orr, James. *The Progress of Dogma*. London: Hodder and Stoughton, 1901.

Paul, Robert S. *The Atonement and the Sacraments*. London: Hodder and Stoughton, 1961.

Pelikan, Jaroslav. *The Growth of Medieval Theology (600–1300)*. Chicago: University of Chicago Press, 1978.

Peppermüller, Rolf. *Abaelards Auslegung des Römerbriefes*. Münster: Aschendorff, 1972.

Posset, Franz. "*Amplexus Bernardi*: The Dissemination of a Cistercian Motif in the Later Middle Ages." Cîteaux 54 (2003): 251–400.

———. "The Crucified Embraces Saint Bernard: The Beginnings of the *Amplexus Bernardi*." CSQ 33 (1998): 289–314.

———. "The 'Double Right to Heaven': Saint Bernard's Impact on the Sixteenth Century." CSQ 38 (2003): 263–73.

———. *Pater Bernhardus: Martin Luther and Bernard of Clairvaux*. CS 168. Kalamazoo, MI: Cistercian Publications, 1999.

Quinn, Philip L. "Abelard on Atonement: 'Nothing Unintelligible, Arbitrary, Illogical, or Immoral about It.'" In *Reasoned Faith: Essays in Philosophical Theology in Honor of Norman Kretzmann*, edited by Eleanore Stump, 281–300. Ithaca, NY, and London: Cornell University Press, 1993.

Rashdall, Hastings. *The Idea of Atonement in Christian Theology*. London: Macmillan, 1919.

Regnard, Joël. "Il nous sauve non seulement par sa mort mais aussi par sa vie: La rédemption chez saint Bernard." Coll 58 (1996): 141–48.

Renna, Thomas J. "Bernard vs. Abelard: An Ecclesiological Conflict." In *Simplicity and Ordinariness*, edited by John R. Sommerfeldt, 94–138. CS 61. Kalamazoo, MI: Cistercian Publications, 1980.

Ritschl, Albrecht. *Die christliche Lehre von der Rechtfertigung und Versöhnung*, vol. 1. Bonn: Adolph Marcus, 1870.

———. *A Critical History of the Christian Doctrine of Justification and Reconciliation*. Edinburgh: Edmonston and Douglas, 1872.

Rivière, Jean. "Le conflit des 'filles de dieu' dans la théologie médiévale." RSR 13 (1933): 553–90.

———. *The Doctrine of the Atonement: A Historical Essay*, 2 vols. London: Kegan Paul, Trench, Trübner and Co., 1909.

———. *Le dogme de la rédemption: Essai d'étude historique*. Paris: Lecoffre, 1905.

————. *Le dogme de la rédemption: Études, critiques et documents.* Louvain: Bureaux de la Revue [d'Histoire Ecclésiastique], 1931.

————. *Le dogme de la rédemption au début du moyen-âge.* Paris: J.Vrin, 1934.

————. "Le dogme de la rédemption au début du moyen-âge III—rôle de saint Bernard." RSR 13 (1933): 186–208.

————. "Rédemption." In DThC 13:1912–2004.

Rochais, Henri, and Jean Figuet. "Le jeu biblique de Bernard." Coll 47 (1985): 119–28.

Rousseau, Olivier. "S. Bernard, 'Le dernier des pères.'" In *Saint Bernard théologien,* ASOC 9, no. 3-4 (July–December 1953): 300–308.

Rydstrøm-Poulsen, Aage. *The Gracious God: Gratia in Augustine and the Twelfth Century.* Copenhagen: Akademisk, 2002.

Sabersky-Bascho, Dorette. *Studien zur Paranomasie bei Bernhard von Clairvaux.* Freiburg (CH): Universitätsverlag, 1979.

Schönbeck, Oluf. "Saint Bernard, Peter Damian, and the Wounds of Christ." CSQ 30 (1995): 275–84.

Schwane, Joseph. *Dogmengeschichte der mittleren Zeit (787–1517).* Freiburg: Herder, 1882.

Seeberg, Reinhold. *Lehrbuch der Dogmengeschichte,* vol. 3, 2nd/3rd ed. Leipzig: A. Deichert, 1913.

————. "Die Versöhnungslehre des Abälard und die Bekämpfung derselben durch den heiligen Bernhard." *Mittheilungen und Nachrichten für die evangelische Kirche in Rußland* 44 (1888): 121–53.

Smith, David. *The Atonement in the Light of History and the Modern Spirit.* London: Hodder and Stoughton, 1918.

Smith, Richard U. "Saint Bernard's Anthropology: Traditional and Systematic." CSQ 46 (2011): 415–28.

Sommerfeldt, John R. "Abelard and Bernard of Clairvaux." *Papers of the Michigan Academy of Science, Art and Letters* 46 (1961): 493–501.

————. "Bernard of Clairvaux and Scholasticism." *Papers of the Michigan Academy of Science, Art and Letters* 48 (1963): 265–77.

————. *Bernard of Clairvaux on the Life of the Mind.* New York and Mahwah, NJ: Newman Press, 2004.

————. "Bernard of Clairvaux on the Truth Accessible through Faith." In *The Joy of Learning and the Love of God,* edited by E. Rozanne Elder, 239–51. CS 160. Kalamazoo, MI, and Spencer, MA: Cistercian Publications, 1995.

Southern, Richard W. *Saint Anselm: A Portrait in a Landscape.* Cambridge: CUP, 1990.

Thomas, Robert. "La dévotion à Notre-Seigneur et à sa passion dans l'ordre de Cîteaux." In *Autour de la spiritualité cistercienne (Pain de Cîteaux* 16), 117–206. Chambarand: 1962.

Turner, Henry E. W. *The Patristic Doctrine of Redemption*. London: Mowbray, 1952.

Vacandard, Elphège. "Bernard (saint), abbé de Clairvaux." In DThC 2:746–85.

———. *Vie de saint Bernard, abbé de Clairvaux*. Paris: Victor Lecoffre, 1895.

Van den Bosch, Amatus. "L'intelligence de la foi chez saint Bernard." Cîteaux 8 (1957): 85–108.

Van Kirk, Natalie B. "Finding One's Way through the Maze of Language: Rhetorical Usages That Add Meaning in Saint Bernard's Style(s)." CSQ 42 (2007): 11–35.

Verger, Jacques. "Le cloître et les écoles." In *Bernard de Clairvaux: Histoire, mentalités, spiritualité* (SCh 380), 459–73.

———. "Saint Bernard et les scolastiques." In *Vies et légendes de saint Bernard de Clairvaux*, 201–10. Cîteaux: Commentarii Cistercienses, 1993.

———. "Saint Bernard vu par Abélard et quelques autres maîtres des écoles urbaines." In *Histoire de Clairvaux*, 161–75. Bar-sur-Aube: Némont, 1991.

Walters, Gwenfair M. "The Atonement in Medieval Theology." In *The Glory of the Atonement: Biblical, Historical and Practical Perspectives*, edited by C. E. Hill and F. A. James, 239–62. Downers Grove, IL: IVP, 2004.

Ward, Benedicta, ed. *The Prayers and Meditations of Anselm*. Harmondsworth: Penguin, 1973.

Weingart, Richard E. *The Logic of Divine Love: A Critical Analysis of the Soteriology of Peter Abailard*. Oxford: OUP, 1970.

Williams, Thomas. "Sin, Grace and Redemption." In *The Cambridge Companion to Abelard*, edited by Jeffery E. Brower and Kevin Guilfoy, 258–78. Cambridge: CUP, 2004.

Wilmart, André. "L'ancienne bibliothèque de Clairvaux." Coll 11 (1949): 101–27, 301–19.

Zerbi, Piero. "Guillaume de Saint-Thierry et son differend avec Abélard." In *Saint-Thierry: Une abbaye du VIe au XXe siècle*, edited by Michel Bur, 395–412. Saint-Thierry: Association des Amis de l'Abbaye de Saint-Thierry, 1979.

———. "William of Saint Thierry and His Dispute with Abelard." In *William, Abbot of St. Thierry*, 181–203. CS 94. Kalamazoo, MI: Cistercian Publications, 1987.